Adobe Acrobat Ninja

A productivity guide with tips and proven techniques for
business professionals using Adobe Acrobat

Urszula Witherell

BIRMINGHAM—MUMBAI

Adobe Acrobat Ninja

Copyright © 2023 Packt Publishing

Associate Group Product Manager: Alok Dhuri

Publishing Product Manager: Harshal Gundetty

Content Development Editor: Rosal Colaco

Technical Editor: Pradeep Sahu

Copy Editor: Safis Editing

Project Coordinator: Deeksha Thakkar

Proofreader: Safis Editing

Indexer: Rekha Nair

Production Designer: Alishon Mendonca

Business Development Executive: Uzma Sheerin

Developer Relations Marketing Executive: Rayyan Khan and Deepak Kumar

First published: February 2023

Production reference: 1200223

Published by Packt Publishing Ltd.
Livery Place
35 Livery Street
Birmingham
B3 2PB, UK.

ISBN 978-1-80324-817-2

www.packtpub.com

I would like to dedicate this book to my husband Mike, my partner and friend who has so steadfastly supported me through life and shared his thoughts, experience, and perspective through this project.

Also, to our beloved daughters Natalia, Kelly, and Isabella, whose love, honesty, creativity, and dreams continue to keep us both inspired and young.

– Urszula Witherell

Contributors

About the author

Urszula Witherell is a graphic designer, publisher, and expert in the publishing industry. She lives and works in the United States as a software consultant and instructor on Adobe InDesign, FrameMaker, Acrobat Pro, and all related services. She has taught thousands of people about topics that range from an introduction to a document layout to the automation of the publishing process. She has worked with different US government agencies on projects involving long statistical publications, interactive PDF forms, and dynamic, XML-based forms developed in Adobe LiveCycle Designer. She has published articles on authoring documents for a successful export to WCAG and ADA-compliant, accessible PDF publications. As new software tools became available, Urszula designed curriculum and reference materials that demonstrated how to properly construct documents in the relevant authoring software, such as Adobe InDesign, FrameMaker, and MS Word.

My sincere thanks go to my husband, daughters, and friends who inspire and patiently support me every day, but especially did so during writing this book.

Words of deep appreciation also go to the team at Packt, the editors, and the technical reviewers for their guidance, constructive feedback, and support while working on this project.

About the reviewers

Lukas Engqvist is an Adobe Certified Instructor and an Adobe Education Leader. He has taught Adobe applications and print-related subjects in higher vocational education at Brobygrafiska in Sunne, Sweden for the past 10 years. He also is involved in contract training and professional development of teachers as Adobe Education Leader. Before going into teaching, he worked as a prepress manager for 10 years, moving the workflow from analog to digital techniques.

Sarah Nitschmann started her career as a media designer at a product communication agency in Munich. She focused on the technical side of graphic design and artwork creation for print production. With a bachelor's degree in print and media technology from the BHT, Berlin, she gained in-depth experience in color management, prepress, and printing technology. Today, Sarah is a senior product manager at callas software, a leading software provider of PDF automation technology for quality assurance and improvement. Her main areas of application are document exchange, print production, and archiving.

Table of Contents

6

Using Acrobat in a Document Review Process   125

7

Creating and Modifying PDF Forms   155

8

Adding Digital Signatures and Security Settings   191

9

Designing Multimedia Presentations   213

10

Integration with Adobe InDesign   231

Preface

There are many technology books on the market. Some are called guides, bibles, references, and so on.

It is 2023. Do people still read books? Of course they do. Some read more than ever. This book was written just after the lockdowns, fear, and isolation of COVID-19. It is meant to flow like a classroom presentation transcript, with an instructor and students interacting directly in person. I want it to have soul, some quirky humor, and a way of explaining a function that may strike you as different. Got an urge to argue? Have I made you scrunch your face? Either's okay.

No book can replace the wonderful exchanges with other human beings – the banter, the eye rolls, the smiles, and the pleasantries. My assumption is that you are experienced enough to understand the many details of Adobe Acrobat Pro, and my intention is to share what I have learned over the years and encourage you to learn new skills and methods or expand on what you already know. The dry, impossibly correct, and scholastic phrasing of help manuals that often do not explain much is banished here, although realistically that cannot be avoided entirely.

I took a much lighter approach and assumed that you are already familiar with some basics of the software. Instead of covering every detail and combination of functions available in the application, I presented possibilities using tools and methods that work for me. Diagrams are a lot like flipchart presentations and are meant to be simple and convey a general idea, rather than explain every detail.

This is an acknowledgment that the tools and options presented here were chosen and used arbitrarily, and many features, especially those that are still evolving, had to be left out. Acrobat is forever changing, and every `.pdf` file is forever different. Software, workflows, and methods are updated faster than ever, and by choosing a certain method of doing things and teaching that, I hope to have conveyed enough information so that you, the reader, have a solid foundation to expand your knowledge and get the latest data using other means, most likely online. The most stable sources for this information are referenced in the concluding chapter.

I hope you will find the book informative and supportive in your quest to learn Adobe Acrobat Pro. I certainly enjoyed writing it.

Office document tools have changed enormously since the first release of Adobe Acrobat in 1993. From what began as an essentially static image of a printed page, PDF files have evolved into a complex, interactive format, fulfilling most office communication needs. The application is now a mature software that is designed to replace the handling of physical paper documents in practically any situation, from office memos to legally binding contracts.

PDF is an abbreviation that stands for **Portable Document Format**.

The most recent updates to Adobe Acrobat Pro depart from the desktop-only application model. Most functions depend now on a subscription model for software usage and connection to Adobe Document Cloud. It is our goal in this book to bridge application features with Document Cloud functions, focusing on Adobe Acrobat Pro, a full-featured desktop software with a complete set of options available directly on a user's computer hard drive.

Due to the popularity of mobile devices and on-the-go collaboration, some features of Acrobat Mobile apps will be also discussed.

Who this book is for

This book is intended for professionals that could be described as knowledge workers, including but not limited to skilled professionals, including analysts, administrators, architects, doctors, engineers, journalists, lawyers, pharmacists, and scientists.

It is also for professionals that could be described as communications workers, including but not limited to communications art workers, graphic designers, researchers, technical writers, web designers, and accessibility workers.

You need to be familiar with the basic functions of Adobe Acrobat Pro and its workspace. Understanding the process of creating a PDF as an output format from authoring software and experience using other Adobe applications will be helpful, but it is not necessary.

What this book covers

Chapter 1, Understanding Different Adobe Acrobat Versions and Services, looks at the many versions of Acrobat and Adobe web-based services that are now available to work with PDF documents. We will sort out the differences in options based on the version of Acrobat.

Chapter 2, Creating and Enhancing PDF Files from Scans, discusses the process of converting to PDF, and enhancing and optimizing scans of paper pages and images from tablets or smartphones.

Chapter 3, Converting Microsoft Office Files to Adobe PDF Using PDFMaker, explores how PDFMaker allows us to create interactive and accessible PDF files. We will explain how different choices made during this process affect code and, therefore, features of the final PDF.

Chapter 4, Modifying and Editing PDF Files, delves into the many instances when changes or improvements need to be made to the final PDF. We will learn how to adjust the order and content of pages, work with bookmarks, links, headers, and footers, edit text and images, and take a first look at accessibility tags.

Chapter 5, Remediation for Accessibility in PDF Publications, discusses what accessibility legal guidelines are, how to include features when authoring a publication so that the resulting PDF document complies with these guidelines, and how to test and remediate it if needed.

Chapter 6, Using Acrobat in a Document Review Cycle, explores the purpose of different commenting and markup tools, how to customize them, and how to use them in editorial responses. Different PDF-based review workflows will be explored.

Chapter 7, Creating and Modifying PDF Forms, examines the process of creating a form page background, then adding interactive fields, and setting their properties, and it will explore methods for submitting and gathering form data.

Chapter 8, Adding Digital Signatures and Security Settings, explores the options available in Acrobat Pro to protect different publications. Books, journals, and magazines may require copyright protection through passwords, contracts, and agreements, and forms may need to be certified for content integrity before being signed.

Chapter 9, Designing Multimedia Presentations, delves into the tools available in Acrobat for adding, editing, and viewing multimedia. PDF documents designed as presentations can include audio, video, interactive, and 3D elements.

Chapter 10, Integration with InDesign, focuses on two areas of InDesign and Acrobat integration – accessibility and PDF-based editorial review. We will learn how to create a fully accessible `.pdf` in InDesign and how Acrobat can be used in a collaborative review by editors working on any device.

Chapter 11, Using Acrobat in Professional Publishing, explores some of the tools that Acrobat offers to identify, control, and compensate for potential issues when a document is printed on paper by a commercial printing press.

Chapter 12, Privacy, Bates Numbering and Other Specialized Features for A Law Office, looks at how to depersonalize a document by removing private information, redacting sensitive content, removing hidden data, and applying Bates numbering to ensure that `.pdf` documents comply with legal standards.

Chapter 13, Acrobat Pro Tools, Shortcuts, References, and Mac Notes, contains a special section for creating `.pdf` files in MS Office for macOS. You will also find here lists showing all Acrobat tools, the most commonly used keyboard shortcuts, and accessibility tags with an explanation of their meaning. References to links to online sources for Acrobat user support are also included.

To get the most out of this book

This book explores features that are often overlooked by users who likely already work with Acrobat. The best way to use this book is to plan a little and think about what you already do while working with your `.pdf` documents. Do you comment using Acrobat? Or remediate files for accessibility? Jump to those chapters in the book to learn more detail or consider a different approach to get the best results.

Adobe Acrobat family software

Adobe Acrobat is a large family of applications. Adobe helps to support our multi-device users by offering an app for any device on the market. Users, however, often get lost in the choices available. The following table will guide you to what software version you need based on the device(s) that you use. Some decisions in this area need to be made at a time when a subscription is purchased.

Adobe Acrobat includes desktop products, free mobile apps, and online services available through Adobe Document Cloud. The following table gives an overview of platforms for Acrobat:

Software/hardware covered in the book	Operating system requirements
Adobe Acrobat Pro and Reader	Desktop/laptop Windows or macOS
Adobe Acrobat Standard	Desktop/laptop Windows only
Adobe Acrobat online	Web browser on any operating system
Adobe online services and mobile apps	Mobile devices

Acrobat technical requirements

These are the **Windows** system requirements:

- **Processor**: Intel® or AMD processor – a 1.5GHz or faster processor
- **Operating system**: Windows 11 (64-bit), Windows 10 (32-bit and 64-bit) version 1809 or later, Windows 8 or 8.1 (32-bit and 64-bit), Windows 7 SP1 (32-bit and 64-bit), or Windows Server – 2008 R2 (64-bit), 2012 (64-bit), 2012 R2 (64-bit), 2016 (64-bit), or 2019 (64-bit)
- **RAM**: 2 GB of RAM
- **Hard disk space**: 4.5 GB of available hard-disk space
- **Monitor resolution**: 1024x768 screen resolution
- **Graphics card**: Video hardware acceleration is optional

Here are the **macOS** system requirements:

- **Processor**: Intel processor – M1 Apple Silicon processor
- **Operating system**: macOS v10.15, macOS v11, or macOS v12
- **RAM**: 2 GB of RAM
- **Hard disk space**: 2.75 GB of available hard-disk space
- **Monitor resolution**: 1024x768 screen resolution

To follow the step-by-step instructions in the book, you will need desktop versions of Adobe Acrobat Pro and MS Office installed. For chapters covering online services, you will need internet access and an Adobe account to sign in.

The **Acrobat** tab in MS Office applications needs to be available to access PDFMaker. If you don't see it, visit this link with instructions on how to fix it: `https://support.microsoft.com/en-us/topic/get-the-adobe-acrobat-tab-to-appear-b83cbba3-7bc1-4c75-b8dc-511e07a283f0`.

Additionally, review the *Changing the default application to open PDF* section in *Chapter 1*, *Understanding Different Adobe Acrobat Versions and Services*, to see if you need to change any operating system preferences to open `.pdf` files in Adobe Acrobat Pro by double-clicking in a file browser. The default may be set to launch Adobe Reader.

Chapter 6 and *Chapter 8* may require a friend to swap `.pdf` files with while testing reviewing and signature functions. You will have more fun too.

Chapter 10, *Integration with Adobe InDesign*, requires Adobe InDesign and Bridge installed.

You can follow the author on GitHub (`https://github.com/Uwitherell`) or make a connection with her on LinkedIn (`https://www.linkedin.com/in/urszula-witherell-925a1020/`).

Download the color images

We also provide a PDF file that has color images of the screenshots and diagrams used in this book. You can download it here: `https://packt.link/NZpvI`.

Conventions used

There are a number of text conventions used throughout this book.

`Code in text`: Indicates code words in text, database table names, folder names, filenames, file extensions, pathnames, dummy URLs, and user input. Here is an example: "Browser-based use of Acrobat features is a new approach to working with `.pdf` files."

Bold: Indicates a new term, an important word, or words that you see onscreen. For instance, words in menus or dialog boxes appear in **bold**. Here is an example: "Select the **File | Create | PDF from scanner** options."

> **Tips or important notes**
> Appear like this.

Get in touch

Feedback from our readers is always welcome.

General feedback: If you have questions about any aspect of this book, email us at `customercare@ packtpub.com` and mention the book title in the subject of your message.

Errata: Although we have taken every care to ensure the accuracy of our content, mistakes do happen. If you have found a mistake in this book, we would be grateful if you would report this to us. Please visit `www.packtpub.com/support/errata` and fill in the form. Any errata related to this book can be found at `https://github.com/PacktPublishing/Adobe-Acrobat-Ninja`.

Piracy: If you come across any illegal copies of our works in any form on the internet, we would be grateful if you would provide us with the location address or website name. Please contact us at `copyright@packt.com` with a link to the material.

If you are interested in becoming an author: If there is a topic that you have expertise in and you are interested in either writing or contributing to a book, please visit `authors.packtpub.com`.

Share Your Thoughts

Once you've read *Adobe Acrobat Ninja*, we'd love to hear your thoughts! Scan the QR code below to go straight to the Amazon review page for this book and share your feedback.

`https://packt.link/r/1-803-24817-3`

Your review is important to us and the tech community and will help us make sure we're delivering excellent quality content.

Download a free PDF copy of this book

Thanks for purchasing this book!

Do you like to read on the go but are unable to carry your print books everywhere?

Is your eBook purchase not compatible with the device of your choice?

Don't worry, now with every Packt book you get a DRM-free PDF version of that book at no cost.

Read anywhere, any place, on any device. Search, copy, and paste code from your favorite technical books directly into your application.

The perks don't stop there, you can get exclusive access to discounts, newsletters, and great free content in your inbox daily

Follow these simple steps to get the benefits:

1. Scan the QR code or visit the link below

https://packt.link/free-ebook/9781803248172

2. Submit your proof of purchase
3. That's it! We'll send your free PDF and other benefits to your email directly

1

Understanding Different Adobe Acrobat Versions and Services

Office tools have changed enormously since the first release of **Adobe Acrobat** in 1993. From what were essentially static images of publication pages, PDF documents are now complex and interactive, filling most office communication needs and near-enough ready to replace paper. To address changing demands, Adobe has gradually introduced many features and services that support working with PDF as a truly portable format. Users are now able to work with the same `.pdf` file on a desktop computer, a tablet, or a smartphone.

PDF documents are meant to be very portable. As the reasons for using the format expanded, so did the ways of interacting with the files. We do so much more than read `.pdf` publications. We edit text and images, add accessibility, fill out and submit forms, prepare files for commercial printing, and much more. Some functions are only available when a file is saved on a desktop or a laptop computer hard drive, while some, such as reviewing or signing, can be done entirely online using any device, including a mobile.

Portability, collaboration, management, and access to files on the go are now the main issues addressed by Adobe online services and storage. Motivated by a vision to streamline and automate the administrative aspect of working with PDFs, Adobe introduced **Acrobat** and **Document Cloud** subscription-based services so that all the steps and time that everyone must take to save and locate files are simplified by background web-server automation. This helps us to focus on business and information content rather than the logistics of sending, receiving, attaching, collating responses, gathering form field information, and other time-consuming steps.

This book focuses mainly on Adobe Acrobat Pro, a full-featured desktop software with a complete set of tools and options, available directly on a user's system, where an internet connection is optional. Due to the popularity of mobile devices, some features of Acrobat mobile apps will also be mentioned.

In this chapter, we will attempt to sort out the differences in options available to users based on the version of Acrobat they use. As Adobe has added many web-based services that support working with PDF documents, we will discuss which tasks are performed entirely on a user system versus those that require a document to be processed using web-based services. This information will help you assess the need for internet access and security issues while working with `.pdf` files.

In this chapter, we'll cover the following topics:

- Adobe Acrobat Pro subscription
- Adobe Acrobat Standard subscription (not available on macOS)
- Adobe Acrobat Reader (free version)
- Adobe Document Cloud
- Adobe Acrobat online services
- Adobe Acrobat Sign
- The mobile PDF experience – Adobe mobile apps

Adobe Acrobat Pro subscription

Acrobat Pro is Adobe's **Portable Document Format** (**PDF**) fully featured editing software. It's the most flexible, productive, and collaborative PDF solution Adobe offers. Adobe is transitioning to a subscription-only support model; standalone licenses of Acrobat are gradually being phased out. **Acrobat Pro** subscription includes the following:

- Acrobat Pro desktop software
- **Acrobat Reader**, enabled with features for use on mobile devices
- **Premium Adobe Document Cloud**: Document Cloud is a web-based storage service, allowing users to work connected to the internet and access many online services with any device they use

As a subscriber to Acrobat Pro, not only can you work on `.pdf` documents with your installed desktop application, but you can also continue editing the same `.pdf` document using a tablet or smartphone device. The ultimate goal of this approach is to allow you to edit, export, share, or sign a `.pdf` document. You start working on one document, create more, organize them, collaborate with others, and then complete tasks having access to a full set of features, regardless of what device, browser, or computer you use. We are not quite there yet when it comes to uniformity of tools or interfaces, but that is the destination envisioned by Adobe teams.

Adobe Acrobat Pro desktop software running on Windows or macOS contains the most complete set of tools in the Acrobat family. Here are some functions that it allows you to do:

- **Editing PDF text and images**: PDF documents installed on your laptop or desktop computer can be updated by changing most of the properties of text, such as font, size, and color. Images can be moved, resized, replaced, or edited through a link in the original application that created them, such as Adobe Photoshop or Illustrator. Editing, though somewhat limited, can be also done on an iPad or Android tablet.

- **Editing scanned documents**: The desktop application can be configured with a scanner, allowing a continuous scan and conversion of documents to PDF in one step. Similarly, saved images of documents taken with a camera or a fax can be converted to a PDF. **Optical Character Recognition (OCR)** tools allow you to convert image-only text to editable, live text. As a result, the text of the document will flow if it is read on a very small screen, such as an iPhone.

- **Creating protected PDFs**: Files that need to be protected for privacy and integrity can be set up to restrict opening or having their passwords changed. Selective restrictions can be applied to copying, editing, or printing sensitive information.

- **Exporting PDFs to MS Office formats**: The latest updates to Acrobat give great results when PDF files need to be converted to MS Word, Excel, or PowerPoint. Exported content preserves the formatting of fonts, text layouts, such as headers, footers, and columns, and the positioning of images.

- **Validating PDF documents** according to ISO standards, such as PDF/A and PDF/X.

- **Preflighting** and preparing files for high-end printing.

- Ensuring **accessibility** and verifying PDF files' compliance with established standards.

- **Working with Dropbox, Box, Google Drive, OneDrive, and SharePoint**: Access, edit, share, and store files in most online file storage accounts while working in Acrobat by linking your file storage accounts to Adobe's Document Cloud.

- **Signing anything from anywhere**: Fill, sign, and send forms from anywhere with smart autofill.

- **Deleting sensitive information**: Find and redact text, images, or even metadata, removing it permanently.

- **Storing up to 100 GB**: You can store up to 100 GB of cloud-based documents and files for either Acrobat Pro or Standard.

> **Important note**
>
> The **Acrobat Pro or Standard 2020** desktop software version is available as a one-time purchase. It does not include quarterly Acrobat feature enhancements or access to premium Adobe Document Cloud services, such as Acrobat Sign, via your web browser and mobile devices.

Adobe Acrobat Standard subscription

Adobe Acrobat Standard is Windows-only; it is not available on macOS. It is the next tier down from the Pro version. It has fewer features than the Pro version. Here is a list of functions that are *not* included:

- The ability to compare two versions of a PDF to review differences.

- The ability to turn basic scanned-image PDFs into text-editable and text-searchable PDFs.

- Redaction tools for removing/blocking information.
- PDF validation to ISO and accessibility standards.
- Measuring tools.
- Actions, which are scripts that perform several steps on a PDF file. You cannot add JavaScript to expand interactivity.
- A Bates numbering feature for legal documents.
- High-end print production preflight tools.
- The ability to add audio, video, and interactive objects to PDF files.
- The ability to optimize PDFs to reduce file size.

What does that leave in Acrobat Standard? Here is a list of available features:

- You can view, interact, and comment on PDFs on a desktop, mobile device, or web browser
- You have file storage in the Document Cloud
- You can track the activity of viewing, reviewing, and signing PDFs
- You can connect to other online storage systems
- You can create and combine PDFs, including converting web pages into PDFs
- You can insert, delete, split, extract, rotate, and organize pages
- You can add bookmarks, headers, page numbering, and watermarks
- You can add security to PDFs
- You can edit PDF text and images and export them to **Microsoft Office** apps
- You can make fillable forms, with most of the sharing, commenting, and signing features being the same as Acrobat Pro

> **Important note**
>
> The **DC** (short for **Document Cloud**) suffix is no longer used in product names. Previously part of the Acrobat family product names, it was dropped in versions released in 2022.

Adobe Acrobat Reader (free version)

The simplest form of Acrobat is the free Acrobat Reader software. Unlike Adobe Acrobat Standard, Acrobat Reader is available both on Windows, macOS, and all mobile devices. The reader is mainly meant to allow you to view a PDF document, but you can also comment/annotate, share, sign, print, collect signatures, and fill out, and save forms.

Here are the limitations of Acrobat Reader, both in desktop and mobile versions:

- It does not allow you to edit the text and images in a PDF.
- You cannot scan or convert a PDF into **Word**, **PowerPoint**, or **Excel**.
- It allows only a limited amount of signing, tracking, and sending of PDFs.
- You cannot redact content or add password protection.
- The compare files feature is not included.
- Accessibility features are built-in to help users with visual and/or hearing impairments. The application can read out loud, for example, but it does not have the tools to test or make a PDF meet **PDF/Universal Accessibility (PDF/UA)**, **Web Content Accessibility Guidelines (WCAG)**, or **Americans with Disabilities Act (ADA)** accessibility requirements. For that, you must have Acrobat Pro.

To use Adobe Acrobat Reader, you must have a free Adobe Document Cloud account. This requires setting up an email address and a password. The free Acrobat Reader account gets 2 GB of free cloud-based file and document storage, rather than the 100 GB that comes with Acrobat Pro.

As tools are constantly shifting, depending on what version of Acrobat is currently available, you can check the Adobe website for the most recent list of features offered in each version, also referred to as a *plan*. Here is the link: `https://www.adobe.com/acrobat/pricing.html`.

Recognizing an active Acrobat application

Many users open PDFs by double-clicking a file in a file browser or Finder on macOS. It often becomes an irritation if you are reading and commenting on a `.pdf` file in a desktop Acrobat Reader, only to realize that you must reopen the file in Acrobat Pro, often going through a lengthy process of saving, closing, and reopening the same file, looking for it somewhere in a folder.

Both Acrobat Reader and Acrobat Pro (or Standard) can be installed on the same system. To control the environment, you can set up one application as a default to open PDFs. Here is what you can do.

If a file is opened using Adobe Acrobat Pro, then you'll notice the following indicators:

- The title bar at the top of the application is labeled as **Adobe Acrobat Pro**.

- The menu gives you access to a full set of navigation panes on the left side of the screen:

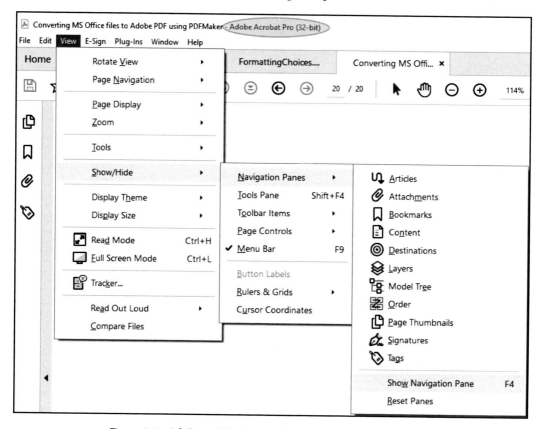

Figure 1.1 – A full set of Navigation Panes available in Acrobat Pro

If you're using Adobe Reader, then you'll notice these things:

- The title bar at the top of the application is labeled as **Adobe Acrobat Reader**.

- The menu gives access to some navigation panes on the left side of the screen:

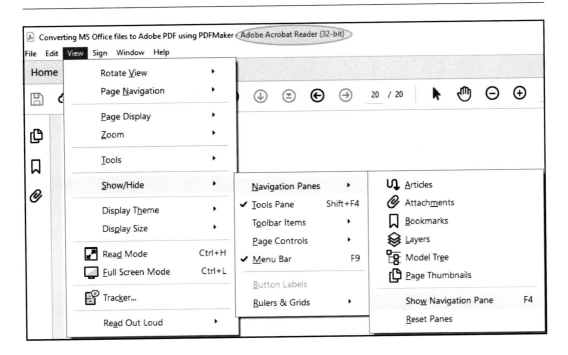

Figure 1.2 – A limited set of navigation panes in Acrobat Reader

Double-clicking on a file in a file browser launches a default application associated with the file format/extension. You can control which software or software version will launch. This applies to all file formats, not only PDFs, both on Windows and macOS systems. Here are the steps to change the defaults for opening files.

Changing the default application to open a PDF on a Windows PC

If you frequently run into the preceding situation, change the default setting for launching an application to open a PDF. Here are the steps:

1. Open a file browser and locate a PDF file with which you will work. You will only need to do this one time.

2. Right-click on the filename and hover your cursor over the **Open with | Choose another app** options.

3. Select the Acrobat version that you want to become a default, then check the box to select **Always use this app to open .pdf files**, and click **OK**:

Figure 1.3 – Options for changing a default application to open a file format in Windows

Changing the default application to open a PDF on a Mac computer

The following steps are for changing the default application to open a PDF on macOS:

1. Locate a PDF file in File Finder.
2. Select **Get Info** and go to the **Open With:** dropdown.
3. Select **Adobe Acrobat**.
4. Select **Change All...** to make the application the default:

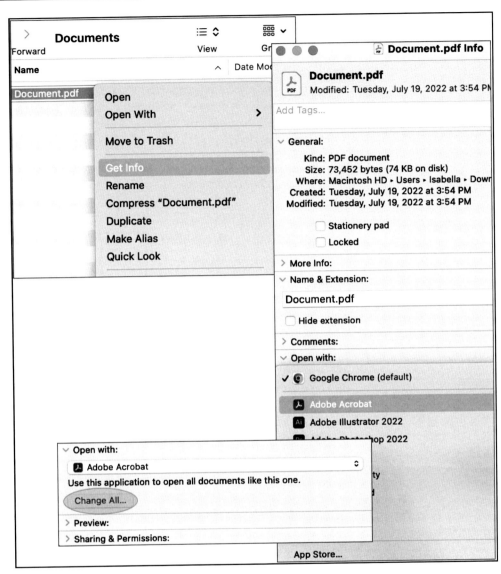

Figure 1.4 – Options for changing a default application to open a file format in macOS

We have become familiar with three Acrobat desktop applications published by Adobe Inc., learned what to expect from each one, and how to set a default app to open a .pdf file when double-clicking it in a browser.

Continuing our exploration of Acrobat environments, we will next take a look at a brief overview of Adobe Document Cloud, a subscription-based online service that focuses on the concept of portability when working with .pdf documents provided by Adobe Inc.

Adobe Document Cloud

Adobe Document Cloud refers to a range of storage solutions and tools integrated across desktop, mobile, and web designed specifically to work with .pdf. If you work with other applications from Adobe, such as InDesign, Photoshop, or Illustrator, be aware that the 100 GB of Document Cloud storage you get with an Acrobat Pro subscription is not the same storage you get with a **Creative Cloud** subscription, even if you use both. This can cause issues related to the synchronization of projects that need to be addressed when .pdf files are edited by users of Creative Cloud-based authoring tools.

When working with .pdf publications, Document Cloud enables automation by allowing the creation of workflows, where digital documents can be stored and accessed regardless of the device or physical location of the user:

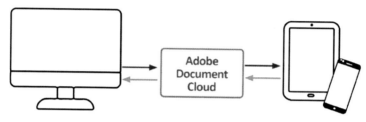

Figure 1.5 – Desktop software, mobile apps, and Adobe Document Cloud collaboration flow

Services and tools are offered to streamline collecting form data and accommodate workflows where multiple signatures are required.

Services that depend on Document Cloud are **Acrobat Sign**, some functions in Adobe Acrobat Pro such as **Fill & Sign** and **Send for Comments**, and other apps and services that work standalone or integrate with your existing systems. Online storage is located at https://documentcloud. adobe.com. Files can also be accessed from **OneDrive**, **Dropbox**, or other cloud storage options designated on your mobile phone or tablet.

We will refer to Adobe Document Cloud throughout the chapters in this book when considering an editorial review and collecting .pdf form data.

In the next section, we will learn about Adobe Acrobat online services that depend on Adobe Document Cloud.

Adobe Acrobat online services

Browser-based use of Acrobat features is a new approach to working with .pdf files on any device. Users do not have to install Acrobat at all on any device that they use; functions are available in a browser window with Acrobat-like tools and a workspace. The interface is in the process of being fully developed, but the service is already available for **PDF shared review** collaboration, mostly used by editors for commenting and feedback on a publication. Working with tools feels similar to Acrobat on desktop.

Since interaction with a `.pdf` document happens entirely in a browser session, reliable and continuous internet access is necessary. While working with tools, you will also experience a bit of lag in responses. Here is a screenshot of tools for reviewing:

Figure 1.6 – Acrobat online, a browser-based reviewing tool

Likely, this is where we can expect the most updates to occur in the future. More details on currently available options and limitations are discussed in *Chapter 6, Using Acrobat in a Document Review Cycle*, under the *Shared group review process using the Adobe Cloud* section.

Adobe Acrobat Sign

Acrobat Sign (formerly known as **EchoSign**) is a cloud-based service that helps businesses transform paper processes, making digital workflows a reality with trusted and legal e-signatures. It does not come with any Acrobat subscriptions, nor is a perpetual license available. It is a separate subscription-based service from Adobe. With Acrobat Sign, workers and organizations can get signatures quickly. Users may request signatures from others and sign documents. Documents then can be tracked and managed electronically throughout the entire process, using only a web browser or a mobile app. A link to sign documents is provided, and those who sign can do it at any location, time, or on any device.

There is no need to sign up or download any documents. Everything is done online through a browser. Acrobat Sign provides security and legal compliance. Here is an overview of the types of signatures and methods used to confirm the signer's identity during the Acrobat Sign cycle.

Digital signatures overview

Users and organizations can set up several different types of electronic signatures. A **basic signature** is the simplest form of an electronic signature, where the signer is primarily identified via an e-mail address. This may also include a **One-Time Password** (**OTP**) sent to a mobile phone.

A **verified signature** is an electronic signature that is created after the signer's identity is verified or confirmed by a trusted third party during the signing process. Here are some basic features of electronic signatures and certificates of authenticity:

- **A digital signature** is a secure electronic stamp that verifies the authenticity of the document and validates the identity of the signer by a third-party public entity. When confirmed, the recipient of a signed document can have very high confidence that the document was not altered, and that the person signing is in fact a known signer.

- **A cloud signature** is a digital signature, with the certificate verifying its authenticity stored in the cloud. Adobe Acrobat Sign incorporates several **Trust Service Providers** (**TSPs**), depending on the level of security and geographical location. Cloud signatures eliminate the need for smartcard readers or USB keys.

- **An electronic seal** is somewhat like a digital signature. It confirms that a document was issued by a specific legal entity at a specific time. Any changes following the application of a seal are traceable, and if a document is modified, the seal becomes invalid. An electronic seal is created by a legal person or entity, unlike a digital signature that is created by a natural/real person. Seals can be applied as part of an automated process; signatures require the action of a real person. The European Union term **Qualified Electronic Seal** (**QES**) refers to seals compliant with EU regulations.

> **Important note**
>
> **Acrobat Standard** and **Acrobat Pro** e-signatures do not offer the same level of security and legal compliance as **Acrobat Sign solutions**.

Business activity is no longer confined to a computer system in an office. Editing files, signing documents, and collecting data can be done anywhere with internet access. Adobe Acrobat supports this kind of environment through mobile apps, which we will review next.

The mobile PDF experience – Adobe mobile apps

Coffee shops and cars have become our office spaces, and this became possible because smartphones and tablets are now the communication and work centers for those on the go. Adobe mobile apps make it possible to continue the workflow, regardless of where a user is located.

The following sections provide an overview of how PDFs are read on small screens, how collaboration is implemented, and how signatures or forms can be completed in a mobile workflow.

PDFs on smartphones, tablets, and Chromebooks

Adobe Acrobat free mobile apps – **Adobe Acrobat Reader, Adobe Scan**, and **Fill & Sign** – help you get your work done from anywhere by making a PDF available on your tablet, smartphone, or Chromebook. They must be installed on your device. Some features are available only in the Premium version, which requires a subscription. Adobe Document Cloud allows you to sync files on all devices that are used, both desktop and mobile (see *Figure 1.5*).

> **Important note**
>
> All documents edited in mobile apps are external to a device, so an internet connection is necessary. Edited files can be downloaded and saved locally.
>
> It is also important to understand that **Acrobat Pro and Standard are desktop applications and work only on Windows or macOS**. Mobile apps work in a unique mobile device OS.

Reading .pdf documents on small screens of smartphones and tablets creates a challenge, since a .pdf is essentially a representation of a printed page, commonly sized 8.5" by 11". To address this, the Acrobat Reader mobile app has **Liquid Mode** for reading – no pinching and zooming are needed for legible text size. Font size, character spacing, and line spacing can be adjusted in user settings.

Documents edited by the Acrobat family of applications were meant from the start to be shared. Initially, commenting and markup tools were available on desktop systems only. As mobile devices became commonplace and many business functions moved online, Adobe released mobile apps with limited features compared to desktop tools.

This book covers collaboration as it falls into two groups – desktop-based, discussed in detail in *Part 2, PDF in Office Communication and Collaboration*, and mobile, for which only a brief overview is given in the next section.

Collaboration in mobile apps

Collaboration implies that several users need to access a file for the purpose of reviewing, filling out a form, or signing. Mobile functions focus mostly on the end user, meaning the person who fills out a form, not the one who creates it, or someone who signs a document, not the one who builds it from the ground up. Many features for mobile devices are still being added and tested at the time of writing.

Reviewing

Using mobile apps, you can share PDFs and collect feedback from smartphones or tablets used by reviewers.

The mobile-enabled collaboration process begins when a file is saved and the owner sends emails with a link to the `.pdf` location. An email subject and personal message are usually added. A deadline for replies can also be set. Once **Send** is clicked, the `.pdf` document is in transit to reviewers, shared as a cloud service.

They can open the file in **Acrobat mobile** and provide feedback using some commenting tools, such as the following:

- Highlighter
- Strikethrough, underline text, and add text
- Freeform (pencil) markup with options to change the color or weight of the line
- Sticky notes

The choice of markup tools is limited. It is a much shorter list than a desktop version of the **Comment** toolbar. Here is an example of tools available on an iPad:

Figure 1.7 – An example of iPad reviewing tools

Comments are visible in the **Comments** panel. More reviewers can be added. When the list of comments is very long, they can be filtered. Anyone with the link to the `.pdf` document will see the reviews.

The moment a shared PDF is opened, downloaded, or shared, the initial document sender is notified of the progress of the review process.

Signatures

Signatures are used in many types of documents. The reason for providing a signature by a signer will dictate how a process is constructed. A letter or a memo with a signature may provide evidence of approval. A contract may need relatively few form fields, such as name, address, email, and signature. Fillable forms are built to collect user data validated through a signature and often include field functions, such as data validation, calculation, or other actions defined in a script associated with a specific field.

The process of signing can take place in the following electronic environments:

- **Adobe Sign**, a subscription-based service, automates the entire signing process, including security issues. It provides an extensive set of distribution and security controls, including third-party identity and signature verification.

- **Desktop Acrobat Pro** provides a full set of tools to create interactive, fillable forms. Different tools, including Signature, allow a document author to define a specific area where a document needs to be signed. A signer clicks on the field and places a signature by providing a password confirming their identity. This process does not require an internet connection and has been in use for many years by corporations and agencies. Details of this approach are discussed in *Chapter 8, Adding Digital Signatures and Security Settings*.

- **Acrobat mobile** uses the **Fill & Sign** tool that simplifies the signing process by allowing mobile app users to quickly create their signature, either hand-drawn or with a saved image of their real signature. Once signed, the file cannot be changed. This is not a legally binding signature but sufficient for many business needs.

Signing .pdf documents on a mobile device is highly interconnected. It may begin with an email app attachment, Acrobat mobile, or the Fill & Sign app. In each case, you will see instructions on what to do next when you receive a .pdf file that needs to be signed.

Actual signature placement happens using the Adobe Fill & Sign app, which must be installed on a device and is dependent on Document Cloud. Here is the process:

1. Open the **Fill & Sign** app:

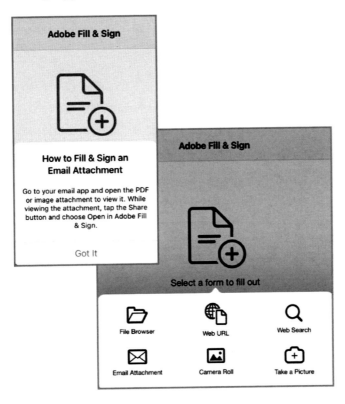

Figure 1.8 – Adobe Fill & Sign opens .pdf options

2. Make a selection from one of the sources listed in the preceding screenshot.

    When a PDF is open, an alert is displayed – **Preparing file… It may take several minutes to prepare your files depending on the number selected and your network connection**. This means that a new copy of the original is created. If a document is a fillable form, all interactive fields are preserved, except for any signature fields; those are removed.

3. Tap on the signature symbol in the toolbar and choose one option, as shown in the following screenshot:

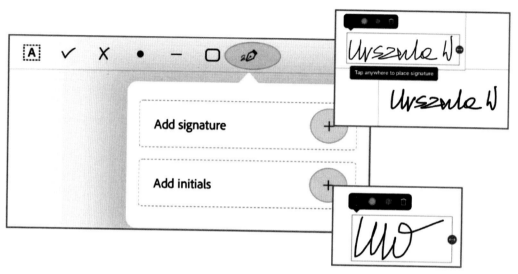

Figure 1.9 – Adding a signature and initials in the Fill & Sign mobile app

4. Both signature and initials need to be set up by the mobile device owner the first time they are used. Either option can be changed at any time.

5. A **Tap anywhere to place signature** alert appears and the signature is placed in the document, but it is still editable and the color can be changed. Tapping outside the live area places the signature.

6. Clicking on **Done** completes the signing process, and the file can no longer be changed.

> **Important note**
>
> Authors of documents that are signed by users of mobile apps need to keep in mind the limitations of those applications. Advanced interactive forms already in use on desktops can include signature fields, scripts, actions, and so on. Those functions will not work on mobile apps. Structured forms created in **LiveCycle Designer** cannot be opened or edited in Acrobat mobile.

Reviewing and signing are what can be referred to as *document markup*. On the other hand, often, there is a need to change the actual content of a PDF file. The next section will give you an overview of what can be done in a mobile app environment.

Editing and converting PDF

The free **Acrobat Reader** mobile app limits usage to markup functions, such as commenting, filling out existing fields, and signing only. **Acrobat Premium** mobile or **Adobe Acrobat Pro** subscriptions give users tools to change the content of a file using a mobile device. Users can do the following:

- Add edit text and images
- Organize, insert, extract, and rotate pages
- Export a PDF to MS Office formats – `.jpeg` or `.png`
- Combine multiple files into one PDF
- Compress files
- Set password for document protection

PDF editing tasks that require a rich set of tools in Acrobat Pro are primarily performed in a desktop office environment; they will be discussed in more detail in *Chapter 4, Modifying and Editing PDF Files*.

Using a mobile device as a scanner

Adobe Scan is a free mobile app, and it expands options to modify PDFs even if you do not have paid subscription. OCR automatically detects text and converts image text to real text. Limits on OCR scans are 25 pages for general users and up to 100 pages with a paid subscription. Scans can be edited using a variety of functions. You can add photos to existing scans, reorder, crop, delete and rotate pages, apply filters, clean up an image, and add markups. Premium features such as exporting or combining PDFs, setting a password, or compressing a file are only available to Acrobat Pro subscribers.

Adobe Scan uses a device camera to take a photo, a step equivalent to a traditional desktop scanner function. It recognizes five types of images:

- Whiteboard
- Book
- Document
- ID card
- Business card

Based on the selection, document edges are automatically detected. They can be refined by cropping an image manually. If text characters are detected, OCR converts them to live, editable text. A Quick action allows the resulting OCR text to be copied to the clipboard and pasted as editable text in another app, such as email. Be prepared to do quite a bit of cleanup, though, as OCR is not perfect.

Scan filters allow documents to be converted to grayscale or a full-color photo. The cleanup tool gives us a nice option to replace the color in areas where the image may need to be obscured or presented as a white paper page.

Scans can be saved as .pdf or .jpeg, and the default file names can be changed.

You can see the available tools in the following screenshot:

Figure 1.10 – Adobe Scan editing tools

Adobe Scan works together with **Fill & Sign** and **Adobe Reader**, giving users options to add text as a form field, place a checkbox, add geometric markup, and place a signature. Scans can be printed. **Add to Siri** is a feature meant to address .pdf accessibility requirements for impaired users.

This chapter aimed to give an overview of different Acrobat versions and related Adobe services. We learned that there are desktop full-featured applications, and mobile apps configured to work either independently or together as part of a workflow. In any previous situation where a paper document was used, it is now possible to work strictly with a .pdf document. It is truly a portable format.

Summary

It is my hope that this chapter explained the options available to you to interact with digital paper documents such as .pdf.

We learned in this chapter that Windows or macOS-based Adobe Acrobat Pro is a desktop application with a rich set of features that allow us to read, edit, mark up, and sign a document. All these tasks can be accomplished on a desktop system without a document ever leaving a local or network drive.

Adobe Sign, **Adobe Fill & Sign**, **Request E-signatures**, **Share**, and **Send for Comments** are some of the services available. While they are accessed from the Acrobat Tools page, they require a document to be saved and processed in Adobe Document Cloud. Services such as these allow us to create a workflow where users can fully collaborate and communicate, regardless of their physical location.

Adobe mobile apps such as **Acrobat Reader**, **Adobe Scan**, and **Fill & Sign** are available to users as free tools installed on their devices, allowing them to be included in the Document Cloud-based workflow. These applications always depend on an internet connection to access files and perform tasks.

In the next chapter, we will expand the discussion on creating PDF files from scanned images or photos, using functions available in the desktop Acrobat Pro application.

2

Creating and Enhancing
PDF Files from Scans

Many publications produced on paper are being moved to an electronic format. Old contracts, books that were written long before computers existed, and typed letters are being scanned and made available online. This process has been taking place for quite some time. Reading archives from a library in a small town in Eastern Europe, for example, can lead to a great discovery. Likely, the chosen format for posting this information is PDF. The process of transferring these documents to the internet begins with scanning.

Scanning is also at the heart of communicating by fax. Faxes depend on bitmap images to transfer document pages. The most common graphic file format utilized by faxes is `.tiff`, which is a bitmap. This method of communication, though, is no longer sufficient. Readers need to search text, make corrections, and extract text and images for other projects. Therefore, enhancing scans is an important feature of **Acrobat Pro**.

This chapter will detail the process of scanning paper pages and converting them to PDF. We will also discuss how images from tablets or smartphones are converted to PDF and enhanced and optimized in Acrobat.

We'll cover the following topics in this chapter:

- Creating a PDF by using a scanner
- Enhancing a scanned image through OCR
- Optimizing a scanned document

Creating a PDF by using a scanner

All photos and scans are pixel-based images. File formats vary depending on the editing software or the selection of output by the user. The most common application-independent formats are the following:

- **JPEG** (or **JPG**), short for **Joint Photographic Experts Group**

- **PNG**, short for **Portable Network Graphics**

- **GIF**, short for **Graphics Interchange Format**

- **TIFF**, short for **Tagged Image File Format**

Bitmap or **raster image** (as opposed to vector) means that it is built by tiny squares arranged in columns and rows. Each square contains color information. You do not see pixels; you only see the content until the view is magnified very closely on the screen. Here are some examples of pixel-based images:

Example a   Example b

Figure 2.1 – Examples of text and photo in pixel-based images

The limitation of pixel-based images is that they are flat, meaning text is not editable. Therefore, scanned pages of publications need to be enhanced so that the text can be searched, copied, and possibly reused if the process does not infringe on copyrights.

The following discussion will take you through two separate though similar paths in creating PDFs from scans:

- Using a scanner connected to a desktop system with Acrobat Pro

- Using an image captured from a camera, and saved and opened in Acrobat Pro

For more information on the Adobe Scan mobile application, see the *Using a mobile device as a scanner* section in *Chapter 1, Understanding Different Adobe Acrobat Versions and Services*.

Scanning document pages

Scanners, as opposed to cameras, provide an optimal environment for converting paper pages to a digital format, especially pages with a lot of text. It is much easier to align paper edges and the content is more accurately represented in the scan, as opposed to photos, which need quite a bit of alignment adjustment.

Scanners come with their own application, but you can also work directly from Acrobat by selecting a connected scanner device (**TWAIN** scanner drivers and **Windows Image Acquisition** (**WIA**) drivers are supported). This allows you to also use the scanner interface and buttons.

 On macOS, Acrobat supports TWAIN and **Image Capture** (**ICA**). Configuration options appear after you choose a scanner and click **Next**.

> **Important note**
>
> The options and specific steps are different in Microsoft Windows and macOS. I will do my best to at least acknowledge the differences and when possible include information for Mac users; however, our examples will focus on Windows and Microsoft Office for a Windows environment.

We will now learn how to scan a paper document. Here are the steps in **Windows**:

1. Select the **File | Create | PDF from scanner** options. If you prefer using the **Tools** panel, select the **Create PDF | Scanner** options.

2. The **Scan & OCR** options page opens with multiple choices to refine the output of the scanned pages. They will vary slightly based on the selected scanning device, which may include a smartphone if it is connected to your system. If you select a scanner, the following warning may appear: **WIA Scanner Driver might face problems using "Hide Scanner's Native Interface" mode. Switching to "Show Scanner's Native Interface" mode.**

The following are the steps on **macOS**:

1. Select the **File | Create | PDF from scanner** options. This will open a window with options. If you prefer using the **Tools** panel, select the **Create PDF | Scanner | Next** options to open the available settings.

2. The **Scan & OCR** options page opens with multiple choices to refine the output of the scanned pages. The settings will vary based on the scanning device connected to your system.

   The following options are consistent in both the Mac and Windows OSs, though the specific location of each setting may vary. You can probably figure this one out. We are going to base our examples on Windows. We will go through the choices for optimizing scan quality.

3.   You can select the option to append to an existing file in a specified location. This will allow you to create a multipage scan saved in a specific location.

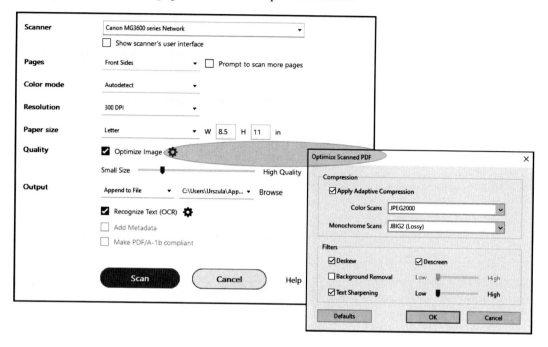

Figure 2.2 – Scanner options (availability of options depends on the selected scanner)

4.   Selecting the **Scan | Default Settings** options will open a dialog box, as shown in *Figure 2.2*, with options based on the selected scanner type. Here are some settings that you can define if you are using a **Canon MG3600 series** scanner:

  • Whether the front or both sides of the page are to be scanned.

  • The color model. The **Black and White** option is the best choice for black text on white pages, typically for office memos, forms, contracts, and more.

  • The resolution of the scan, where the higher the resolution, the larger the file size. The recommended scanning resolutions are 300 dpi for grayscale and RGB input, or 600 dpi for black-and-white input for pages with a very small font size, 9 points or lower.

Important note

OCR stands for **optical character recognition**. It is a process where software analyzes an image of the text created by bitmaps/pixels and converts it into font-based editable type. Since fonts are mapped to international text character standards, enhancing a scanned image of text with OCR adds a dimension to a `.pdf` file. It makes its text content accessible, searchable, and editable, allowing it to expand document features to include other interactive enhancements.

Selecting the proper resolution setting for scanning sets a good balance between page image quality that affects OCR accuracy and file size. For black-and-white, mostly text pages, 300 dpi is optimal. Lower settings, such as 150 dpi or lower, produce a higher rate of font-recognition errors. On the other hand, 400 dpi or higher resolution slows down the scanning process and produces much larger file sizes.

For pages with very small font sizes, you may need to increase the resolution value to prevent OCR **unrecognized word** errors. To scan text-rich pages, the **Black and White** setting works best.

- The **Deskew** option rotates any page that is not square with the sides of the scanner bed, to make the PDF page align vertically. Choose a checked or unchecked box.

- **Background Removal** should be applied to pages with photos. What you see as white paper color is not pure white when interpreted by a scanner. To increase the contrast, this function whitens almost all white areas of grayscale and color to produce a white background. This is not needed in black-and-white input.

- The **Descreen** setting allows you to remove halftone dots. Photos printed on paper are built with tiny dots of ink: **Cyan**, **Magenta**, **Yellow**, and **Black** (**CMYK**) arranged in a very precise pattern to create a wide range of colors. When pages containing photos are scanned, a new pattern is created and it often disrupts the original pattern of dots, which degrades the quality of images. In the print industry, it is called a **moire pattern**. If text is part of a photo, the moire pattern also makes it difficult to recognize it by OCR. Toggling this setting on applies a filter that improves legibility for the OCR. If pages have no photos, the setting should be turned off.

- **Text Sharpening** sharpens the text of the scanned `.pdf` file. The default value is set to **Low** but works for most documents. Increase it if the quality of the printed document is low and the text is unclear.

- **Paper size** provides many standards listed as options or fields where you can type a custom page size.

- The **Optimize Image** options let you choose the format for color photo output, such as `.jpeg`, `.jpeg2000`, or monochrome (black and white) images:

  - The `.jpeg` format refers to a standard for images established by the *Joint Photographic Experts Group* designed to balance image quality and file size in digital photography. The format is lossy, meaning the process of compression deletes pixel data. It was created in 1992 and since then has been widely adopted by all browsers on the World Wide Web and social media.

  - `.jpeg2000` was created in the year 2000 by the same group with the intent to address the limitations of the original format caused by loss of pixel data in images. It preserves transparency and a higher level of compression, keeping the file size smaller while preserving the high quality of images. Unlike its predecessor, it has not gained universal acceptance and it is largely used in professional imaging environments such as medical diagnostics or digital cinema production. Do not use `.jpeg2000` when creating PDF/A-compliant files.

  - ZIP compression refers to the `.tiff` lossless format used for compressing large-file-size images used in print only. They cannot be used on the internet as they are not supported by browsers.

- **Output** provides choices to create a new PDF, append an existing one, or save multiple files.

- The gear icon next to **OCR** lets you choose one of 42 languages and provides a choice for **Editable Text and Images**, which creates a new custom font that closely resembles the original while preserving the page background using a low-resolution copy. The **Searchable Image** option deskews the original image if needed and places a text layer over it.

- Metadata such as document title, author, keywords, and others may be added.

- Scanned pages may automatically be made compliant with the **PDF/A-1b** standard designed for archiving PDFs. This ensures they meet internationally recognized formats and that documents can be preserved for viewing over a very long time.

Important note

PDF/A-1b is a version of PDF designed for archiving that meets basic levels of conformance. PDF/A compliant means your file meets the requirements of the PDF/A format. The most basic PDF/A requirements are as follows: all content is embedded (fonts, colors, text, images, and so on) and does not contain audio or video. The file is not encrypted. It follows standards for metadata, does not contain JavaScript, does not contain references to external content, and is not an XFA form created in LiveCycle Designer.

Creating a digital image of a paper page through scanning is the first step in creating a quality PDF. Options selected will affect how clean and sharp pages look. This will also have an impact on how accurately OCR will render live text in an invisible layer.

In the following section, we will discuss the options available to enhance both the visible content of a page (ink on paper) and text output after OCR conversion. We will start the process with a scanned or photographed page, where conversion or enhancements were not applied.

Enhancing a scanned image through OCR

Scanned pages and saved images may be enhanced in many ways. This section will guide you through those choices.

The process begins with clicking the **File | Create PDF From File…** option. Then, select and open the desired file.

The file is in the process of conversion at this point. Until it is saved, the title bar area filename is only temporary. You may also open a file that was already converted to PDF but no enhancements have been applied yet. It is a good idea to know what you're working with before you begin the process. Here are two methods to find out whether any enhancements have been applied to a document:

Figure 2.3 – Acrobat selection and hand grabber tools

The Acrobat default options from the **Select & Zoom Toolbar** displayed at the top of the screen are the **Selection** (the black arrow) and **Panning** (the hand grabber) tools, similar but meant for specific functions. The Selection tool (the arrow) changes its appearance as you move it over different areas of a page. We will use it to examine the page using one of these methods:

- **Method #1**: Use a selection tool and move it over the page. If it is an image-only file, your cursor will have the shape of a crosshair even when positioned over the text area. When you click anywhere on the page, the entire page will be selected, since it is only a bitmap image at this point. This means that no enhancements have been applied yet.

- **Method #2**: We can test searching the text from the **Edit | Find** menu options or use the *Ctrl + F* keyboard shortcut (or *Command + F* on Mac). A search dialog box will open, as in this screenshot:

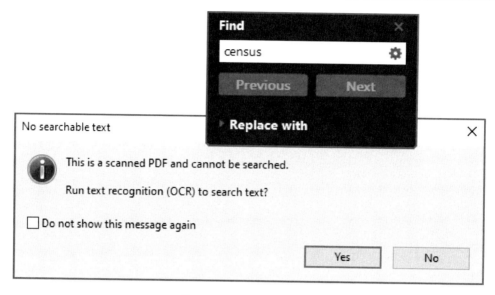

Figure 2.4 – Scan .pdf alert

Type a word of text that you see on the page in the **Find** field and click the **Next** button. The **No searchable text** alert appears giving you a choice to run text recognition (OCR):

- Choosing **Yes** will automatically perform the scan.

- Choosing **No** will give another alert saying **Adobe Acrobat has finished searching the document. No matches were found** for the phrase that you searched.

The alerts appear only when no enhancements have been applied to the scanned document and the page still contains only an image of text.

> **Important note**
>
> Acrobat offers to begin OCR immediately after you use the search function. Choosing the **No** option at this point is the *better* choice. Rather than depending on default settings, you will have access to options and more precise control of the scanning process using the **Scan & OCR** tool.

Now that we confirmed that the page is only a bitmap image, we can begin the process of applying enhancements using the **Scan & OCR** tool options.

If the tool is not visible in the **Tools** column on the right, open **Tools** in the bar directly below the menu:

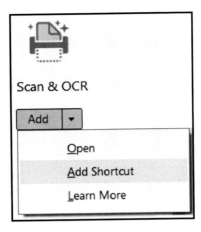

Figure 2.5 – Scan & OCR tool options

- Adding a shortcut will place the tool in the column of other tools from now on

- Clicking on the shortcut will open a toolbar at the top of the screen:

Figure 2.6 – Scan & OCR toolbar options

The **Insert** dropdown allows you to add another page using the **From File…** or **From Scanner** option.

The **Enhance** dropdown gives the **Scanned Document** and **Camera Image** options. Enhancement choices and their meaning are consistent with options covered in detail in the earlier discussion on scanner settings in the *Scanning document pages* section:

- The **Scanned Document** settings let you choose which page to enhance if you work with a multipage document. **Optimization Options** gives separate output settings for color or grayscale images and monochrome, typically text pages. **Filters** and **Text Recognition Options** can also be changed.

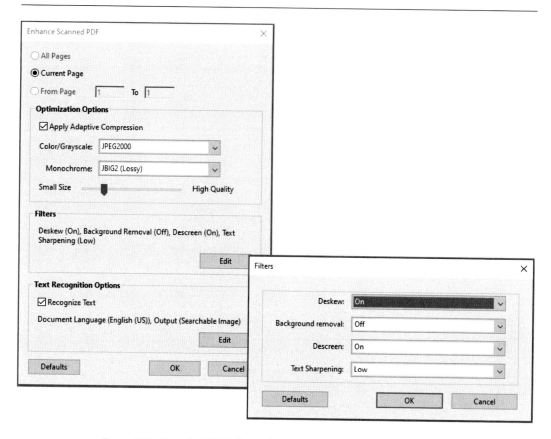

Figure 2.7 – Scan & OCR | Enhance | Scanned Document | Filters options

- The **Camera Image** choice gives you more options. In addition to recognizing text, it adjusts the contrast level of the background image. Settings contained in this function are especially useful when a document is a photo with skewed edges, a typical problem when taking pictures rather than scanning pages (*Image 1*):

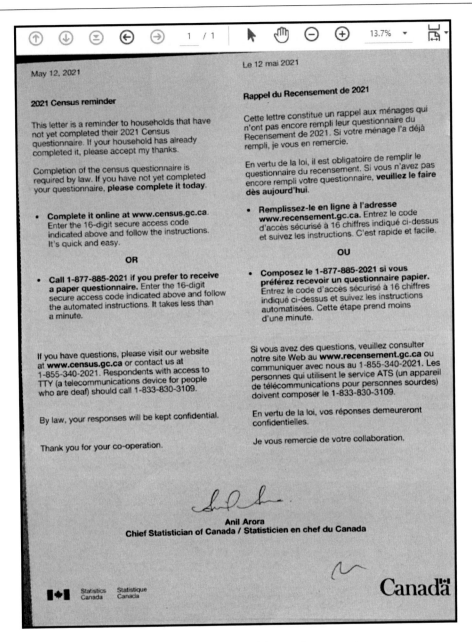

Figure 2.8 – Image 1: page with no enhancements

- Choosing the **Whiteboard** setting will give you the highest contrast for text pages with no photo images: white background for black text, as in forms or memos. Selecting the **Auto Detect** or **Document** options balances the contrast between text and images on the page. You can manually adjust the edges by sliding the corner blue handles (*Image 2*):

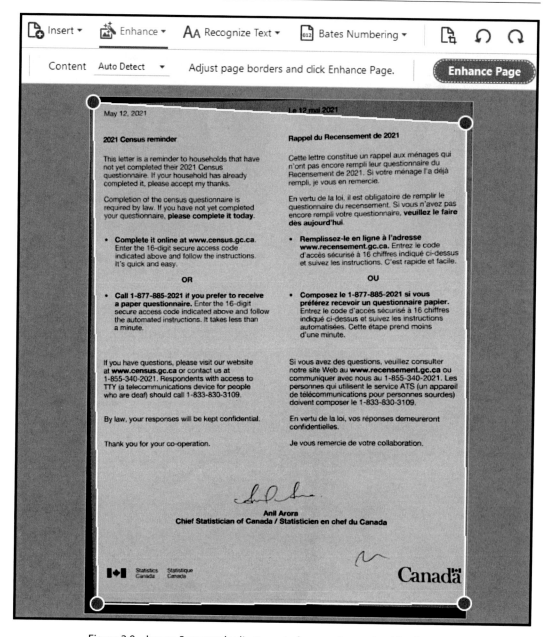

Figure 2.9 – Image 2: manual adjustment of page edges using blue handles

- After you click **Enhance Page**, the contrast is greatly improved, and the edges of the page are adjusted and aligned as a true rectangle (*Image 3*). The **Adjust enhancement level** slider at the top allows you to further control the level of contrast helpful to improve the quality of the visible text while balancing the quality of photos on the page. Ready for the next step?

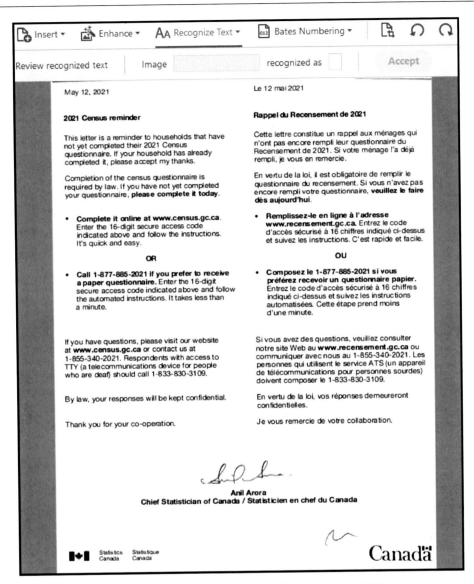

Figure 2.10 – Image 3: result after enhancement and OCR

You can now click on **Recognize Text**, which will give you choices for one or multiple files. After you make a selection, another toolbar opens with more options:

- You can select a language for the OCR engine to identify the characters. Not all text is in English. Can you see French on the sample page? In fact, you can expand the language choices to use Asian languages and right-to-left Hebrew if needed. Normally, the locale chosen at the time of installation determines the local language.

- You can adjust settings for output and resolution for this document only. When you click the **Recognize Text** button, OCR analyzes bitmaps of text and substitutes those areas with words and characters. If it is uncertain, the phrase is marked as suspect. Suspects appear in the `.pdf` file as the original bitmap of the word, but the live text is included on an invisible layer and highlighted by red-bordered temporary rectangles, making it easy to spot problem areas, as seen in this screenshot:

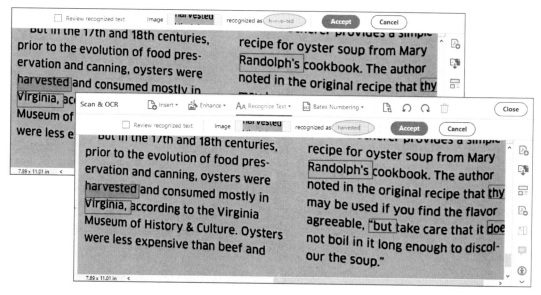

Figure 2.11 – Correcting recognized text

- Use **Correct Recognized Text** from the **Recognize Text** toolbar option to correct the suspects in this invisible layer. Using the toolbar field and highlighted areas of the page, you can type the correct text. If there are no suspects, you will see an alert saying **Acrobat didn't find any text needing correction**.

Important note

The OCR accuracy level will vary depending on the document type, scan quality, and enhancements applied. Additionally, the **Language** setting may affect the reliability of the OCR results, with English being rather stable, but other languages may need more attention. To ensure acceptable quality of text recognition output, it should always be checked for suspects.

We can now test the usefulness of using OCR and other enhancements. Do you recall the file test at the start of our discussion? Now that we have applied enhancements, we will repeat testing the document with the same two methods mentioned earlier – *Method #1* and *Method #2*. Note the differences in results:

- **Method #1**: Use a selection tool and move the cursor over the page. If it is *not* an image-only file anymore, your cursor will have the shape of a crosshair only on the margin and photo areas if there are any. Over the text area, the cursor changes to an I-beam, and when you click on the text, the insertion point signals that you can work with the text. It can be searched, selected, copied, and so on.

- **Method #2**: Test searching the text from the **Edit | Find** menu or use the *Ctrl + F* keyboard shortcut (or *Command + F* for macOS). Type a word of text that you see on the page in the **Find** field. Acrobat finds all phrases on the page and in parentheses tells you how many it has found. Click the **Next** or **Previous** button to find all instances.

So, now your document has been enhanced. Improved contrast and straightened edges make it much easier to read, and OCR made it searchable for text. The next section will show you how to take advantage of those newly added features.

Searching and using content in the enhanced PDF

Now that the document contains live text, you can find any phrase by selecting the **Find | Replace with** options and then entering the text in the field. If needed, you can also replace those phrases with different text, or you can change their formatting. Here are the steps:

Figure 2.12 – Find/Replace with dialog box (Ctrl + F or Command + F)

1. Type text in the **Find** field. The **Options** button will open a menu so that you can refine the search to whole words only, case sensitive, and include bookmarks text, or use the **Open Full Acrobat Search…** option. If no refinements are needed, click the **Next** or **Previous** button.

2. Open the **Replace with** field by clicking the small pointing *triangle* on the left.

3.   Type the replacement text.

You can see that the **Edit PDF** tool with all formatting options opens in the **Tools** column. We will discuss in detail all the edits that can be done using this tool in *Chapter 4, Modifying and Editing PDF Files*.

4.   Replace the selected text by clicking **Replace**.

Great job! Taking some time to apply enhancements really paid off. The file is much more functional now and you learned how to take advantage of the enhancements. It does take quite a bit of effort to produce high-quality scanned pages. But it is worth it. In *Chapter 5, Remediation for Accessibility in PDF Publications*, we will add even more features to the scanned document and learn how to make it compliant with accessibility standards.

There is one more thing that needs to be discussed. No one wants to have beautiful pages posted online that readers can't access because the file size is too large. In the next section, we will explain what optimizing is and why it is important in scanned PDFs.

Optimizing a scanned document

Optimizing scanned pages means finding a balance between image quality and file size. Text-heavy pages contain much less bitmap information than color pages with photos and charts.

> **Important information**
>
> The process of creating PDFs discussed here should only be used when no digital version of the publication exists in a file format that could be edited in an authoring application, such as **Microsoft Word** or **InDesign**. We assume you work with paper copies with no trace of the electronic files that created them.

Acrobat performs multiple tasks all at once when we scan a page. Selections made before scanning discussed earlier can deliver great results. This is a good time to look at the file size of the finished, optimized PDF and compare it with our initial file, before any enhancement, including optimization, was done.

Use the menu to open the **File | Properties…** options, then click on the **Description** tab at the top of the dialog box.

The bottom-left area of the dialog box will display the file size. Our sample file initially had **1.33 MB** of data. All those color bitmaps added up to quite a size. And this was only one page. Imagine a file size of 200 pages. You can do the math…

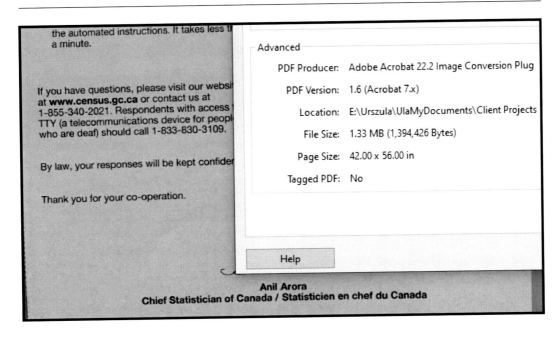

Figure 2.13 – File size before optimization

On the other hand, the completed, functional, and optimized file had **61.60 KB** – just a fraction of the initial file size, yet much easier to read on screen and much more functional with a layer of live text that can be searched. If you emailed me a copy, I would rather open the optimized file.

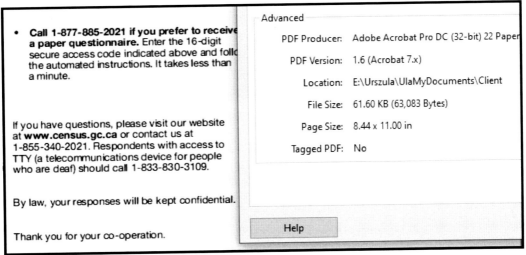

Figure 2.14 – File size after optimization

In review, how did we get here? We selected the **Scan & OCR | Enhance | Camera Image | Whiteboard** options, where Acrobat converted the background to white and the text to black.

In documents that have a mix of text and photos, it is helpful to know that a default setting for the **Enhance Scanned PDF | Optimization Option** options is **Apply Adaptive Compression**. This algorithm divides each page into black-and-white, grayscale, and color regions and chooses a representation that preserves the appearance yet highly compresses each type of content. Scanning resolutions at 300 dpi for color and grayscale and 600 dpi for black-and-white content and/or for pages with very small font sizes provide the best image quality-to-file size balance.

Summary

The scanning of printed pages will continue since paper publications, especially older archives, preserve mountains of information that needs to be available to a wider audience. Online distribution requires that PDF files can be searched, opened globally, and available for a very long time. From the very first step of scanning or taking a photo to a final searchable document, this chapter guided you on how to do it to get the best results.

You learned about the different scanning options, how to enhance a page that originated as a bitmap image, and finally, how to make text searchable, and why it is important to optimize a .pdf file.

In the next chapter, we will go through the process of creating PDF files as a final output in a disciplined workflow using **Microsoft Office PDFMaker**, where fully featured PDFs are produced and exported from fully featured authored files. As you examine the final output, you will enjoy knowing that to accomplish all that, you do not need new tools. You already have them! And it will take no time to do it.

3
Converting Microsoft Office Files to Adobe PDF Using PDFMaker

Most .pdf files originate from an application where the content editing and layout setting are done. In this chapter, we will focus on **Microsoft (MS) Office for Windows**, and specifically **MS Word**, since it is the most common tool used for adding, editing, and formatting text, placing charts and photos, inserting tables, providing page navigation through headers and footers, and providing other visual elements that make a completed publication. As the last step, a PDF output is created.

We will explore how different choices made during this process will affect the code and, therefore, features of the final PDF. We'll cover the following topics in this chapter:

- From authoring content to PDF output
- Understanding PDFMaker (Windows only)
- Evaluating content prepared for PDF conversion
- Testing and comparing converted PDF files

Please note that the authoring and PDF export options in Adobe InDesign, which is a commercial layout software, will be discussed in *Chapter 10, Integration with Adobe InDesign*.

Information on how to export to .pdf documents created in MS Office for Mac is covered in *Chapter 13, Acrobat Pro Tools, Shortcuts, References, and Mac Notes*.

From authoring content to PDF output

Stories, articles, and news published online and on paper all originate with someone typing text. Formatting the text can be done automatically, as in books and other high-volume publications, or manually by an individual writer, editor, or graphic designer. Images and charts may be added and then organized on pages in the desired layout. We refer to this stage in a document production process as **authoring**.

Once authoring is completed, the conversion to PDF begins. Selecting options such as **Create PDF** or **Save as PDF** launches a PDF conversion engine that produces a digital page as a result. The settings selected by the user will convert elements of the layout and other building blocks used in the authoring software during document production to corresponding properties in the PDF and features accessed in Acrobat. For example, MS Word comments are converted to PDF notes and formatting styles may be used to create PDF bookmarks and accessibility tags.

There are two commonly used paths to the final .pdf file: printing and exporting/ converting. Thus, it is important to understand the process from the very beginning. Please take your time to examine the following flowchart:

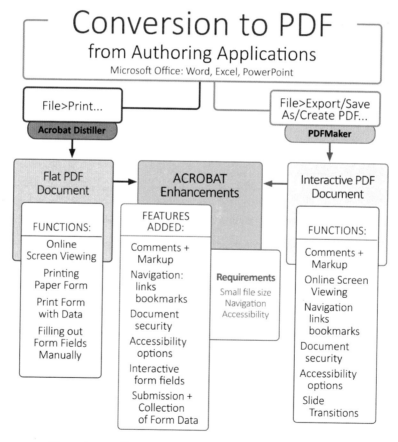

Figure 3.1 – Different methods used to create a final .pdf file

This diagram shows how conversion to .pdf format is done using different methods yielding different results. The red boxes in the preceding diagram show a file printed to a virtual printer, using **Acrobat Distiller** to produce a .pdf file. When this process is selected, the file is created with a focus on the distribution of physical ink on paper by a printing device, such as a desktop printer or a commercial printing press. We also refer to that file as flat, as it has no interactive elements.

On the other hand, the green boxes on the right of the diagram show the process when **PDFMaker** is used to create a .pdf file. When this process is selected, interactivity is the focus of document conversion. As a result, the file meets the needs of online readers who interact with a publication using a keyboard and mouse. We refer to this .pdf file as interactive.

The middle boxes in the diagram under the **Acrobat Enhancements** header refer to features added using Acrobat to change a flat PDF to an interactive PDF or to edit interactive elements.

> **Important note**
> The **Print to PDF** process is different from **Convert to PDF** and gives different results. A detailed comparison will be discussed later in this chapter in the *Testing and comparing converted PDF files* section.

Not all .pdf files are created equal. The features listed in *Figure 3.1* make a rich, functional PDF as opposed to a flat PDF. Both look the same on screen, but a well-constructed PDF contains much more interactivity.

Scanned PDFs, discussed earlier, start as a bitmap image that can be enriched so that the text can become live for searches, and conversion to a synthesized speech by accessibility devices. Still, these are basics in terms of PDF functionality.

If you're reading a physical book, you only expect to see the content. A much more interactive experience is expected when the same publication is viewed on a screen.

Depending on the purpose, an onscreen publication should contain at least some of the features listed here:

- Navigation through links, bookmarks, and buttons
- If the flow of text on pages is too large for a screen, such as tablets or smartphones, it should be converted for displaying Liquid layout to avoid zooming in and out
- Accessibility features for software and devices operated by users with physical impairments
- Forms with fillable fields that may include validated and calculated data submitted using a button
- Security to ensure the document is secured against malicious content
- Audio and video for multimedia presentations

- Interactive 3D imaging
- Authors and copyright owners of material available online want to ensure protection from unauthorized changes or reprints

To address the need for interactivity in a publication, we will next learn what PDFMaker is and what role it plays in the process of conversion to PDF in MS Office applications.

Understanding PDFMaker

To include the most relevant interactive features in a .pdf file, it is important to build the source file in an authoring application correctly and then preserve those features on exporting to PDF. We will begin by understanding the conversion process in PDFMaker.

PDFMaker is an engine that creates .pdf files while preserving interactive features built into a document in the authoring software. PDFMaker is part of the **Acrobat Professional** and **Standard** installations. It is not installed with the free **Acrobat Reader**.

All MS Office applications, such as **PowerPoint**, **Excel**, and **Word**, display an **Acrobat** tab in the ribbon with buttons that open dialog boxes with PDF settings:

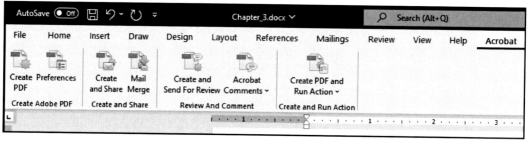

Figure 3.2 – Acrobat ribbon options in MS Word

PDFMaker changed over time

In **MS Office 2003** and earlier, PDFMaker used **Adobe PDF Printer** to create a **PostScript** file. Then, the Adobe PDF printer interfaced with the **Adobe Acrobat Distiller** application to create a .pdf file.

Since **MS Office 2007**, **2010**, **2016**, and **365**, PDFMaker uses the **Adobe PDF Library** to convert MS Office documents to .pdf files. This updated core technology from Adobe gives IT developers the ability to expand functionality when rendering, extracting, and printing the content of .pdf files. Acrobat Distiller or Adobe PDF Printer can be used independently to create .pdf files.

PDFMaker is also available in **AutoCAD** and **Lotus Notes**. Following installation, controls appear in the software interface. Some features are not available in certain versions of the authoring applications.

Next, we will focus on an MS Word document as an example of building and exporting a fully featured PDF. You will understand how the authoring process in an MS Word publication affects features desired in a final .pdf file. You will learn how the settings in PDFMaker relate to a document's text formatting, thus appreciating the importance of using styles.

PDFMaker settings for desired PDF output

All the settings that control the process of conversion to PDF are found in **Preferences**. We will explore the options and learn how to adjust the PDFMaker settings for the desired level of interactivity in a .pdf file. You'll need to click on **Preferences** to open the PDFMaker dialog box:

- The **Settings** tab displays general options organized into two groups:

  - **PDFMaker Settings** is used to manage the image quality of document pages. These options are only selected in PDFMaker but may be edited in Acrobat Distiller, which is a component of Acrobat. Distiller will be discussed in detail in *Chapter 11, Using Acrobat for Professional Publishing*:

    - Checkboxes allow authors to name and review each newly created .pdf file. In batch processing, when many PDF files are created in one step, the **View Adobe PDF result** and **Prompt for Adobe file name** options may be turned off.

    - The **Convert Document Information** option preserves metadata entered in the Word document properties (**File** | **Info**).

    - The **PDF/A Compliance** options allow the creation of PDFs that comply with the PDF/A standard for archiving.

  - **Application Settings** allows you to control how interactive components of the .docx file should be converted. Please note these checkboxes:

    - The **Attach source file** option for embedding the MS Word file into the resulting PDF.

    - **Create Bookmarks** along with the **Bookmarks** tab can be used to specify how to create and organize bookmarks.

    - The **Add Links** option will only work if corresponding features in Word were incorporated.

    - The **Enable Accessibility and Reflow with tagged Adobe PDF** option should be always checked. More on this when discussing accessibility in *Chapter 5, Remediation for Accessibility in PDF Publications*.

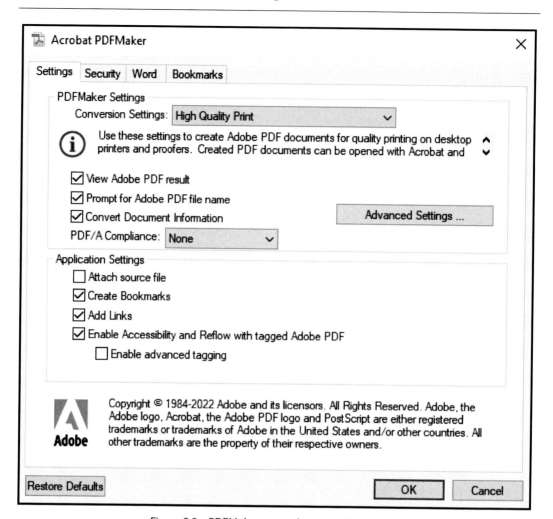

Figure 3.3 – PDFMaker general settings dialog box

- Select the **Security** tab, where passwords may be added to prevent unauthorized viewing or editing of the PDF. Editing permissions may allow printing or not, and control what changes are allowed. The choices include five options and are self-explanatory. Note the checkboxes to allow text access for screen reader devices. Even if access to editing a PDF is restricted, accessibility should be available.

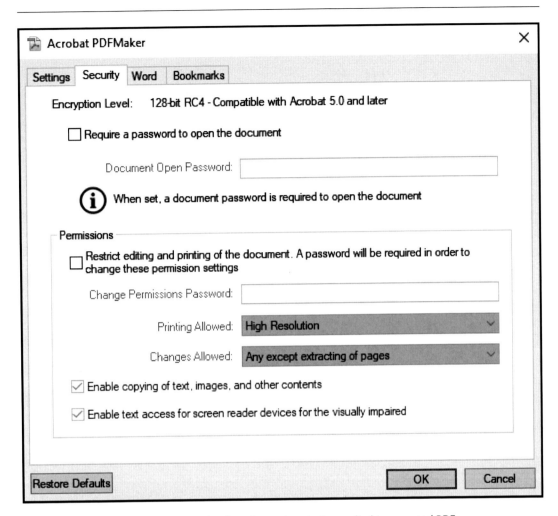

Figure 3.4 – PDFMaker Security options to be applied to exported PDF

- Select the **Word** tab now. This and the **Bookmarks** tab are unique to MS Word. Word and Acrobat share options for the editorial markup of content. Also, footnotes and endnotes in Word become PDF links. Finally, signatures in a Word document become signature fields in the PDF if requested.

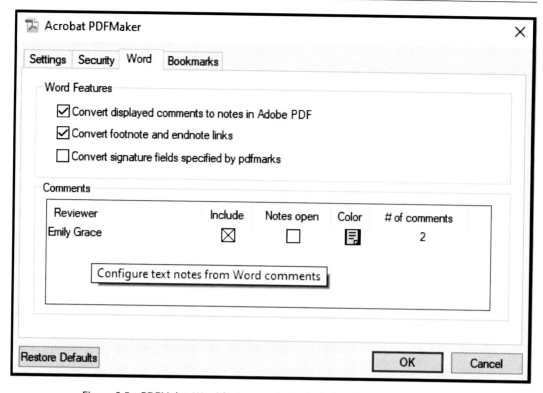

Figure 3.5 – PDFMaker Word features to be included in the conversion to PDF

- Select the **Bookmarks** tab. Word is the only MS Office application that uses styles for formatting. In addition to visual formatting, such as fonts, color, and paragraph alignment, styles identify paragraphs that will become sources for the text of links and bookmarks on exporting to PDF.

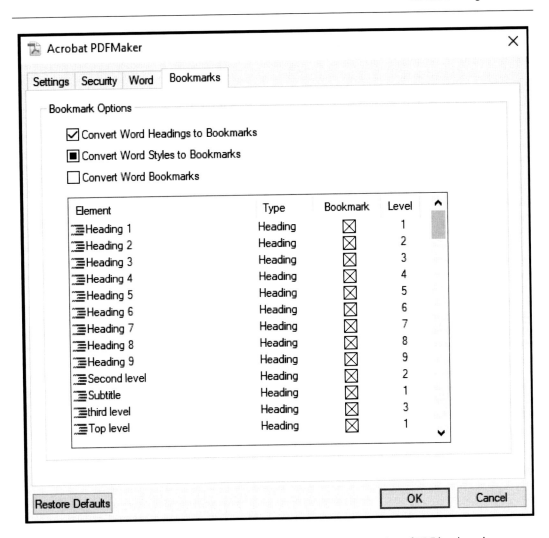

Figure 3.6 – Selection of paragraph styles for the automatic creation of PDF bookmarks

This is a powerful feature that automates the creation of bookmarks, a basic navigation tool in Acrobat. It is especially useful in long documents since books and reports on a screen appear as a single, flat page. Bookmarks give readers options to find and mark desired page(s). If you've ever tried to read a user guide online for any application, you'll appreciate the value of bookmarks.

Bookmarks can only be automatically created if the .docx file is properly formatted using styles. In the next section, we will expand on understanding MS Word styles and their value during the authoring process.

Evaluating content prepared for PDF conversion

In this section, you will learn how to evaluate the impact of document formatting in the original MS Word file on the final PDF output. To say that this information is important is an understatement. Following proper guidelines saves countless hours of repairing a final .pdf file and provides the consistency in formatting expected of a professional document.

Many documents are simple one-page memos or letters. Automation of formatting in this kind of file may be done by using a template. Manual formatting is also common when a document is short, typically one or two pages. *Manual formatting* refers to applying font settings by highlighting the desired text and clicking on the font options in the **Home** ribbon of Word.

Formatting long documents, such as books, reports, magazines, or proposals, should be done in a disciplined, consistent manner. To accomplish this, it is critical to use styles. Styles are also necessary for building a structure of a publication to comply with accessibility requirements. More details on this are discussed in *Chapter 5, Remediation for Accessibility in PDF Publications*.

The process of formatting with styles should begin very early, even for publications that are eventually completed in other commercial layout applications, such as Adobe InDesign or **FrameMaker**.

MS Word provides authors with paragraph and character styles. Paragraph styles group different types of paragraphs and allow the consistent application of these options:

- Headings, which can be assigned levels in the document structure. This will affect bookmarks, accessibility tags, and **Table of Contents** (**TOC**) entries.

- Lists, both numbered and bulleted.

- Figure captions, which may contain labels and automatically updated numeric values. Using proper styles will automate the creation of lists of figures and cross-references exported as links to corresponding pages.

- Footnotes and endnotes, which not only provide text formatting but also are automatically placed on a page or at the end of a document.

- Each style may be modified by the authors (if authorized), who can select the following:

  - Font settings, such as family, type, size, and color.

  - Paragraph settings, such as alignment, indents, spaces before and after controlling the amount of space between paragraphs. Adding extra space with a numeric value is a much better technique than tapping the *Enter* key (*Return* key on macOS) multiple times.

Here is an example of an MS Word-style dialog box with just a few paragraph settings defined for the title of a document:

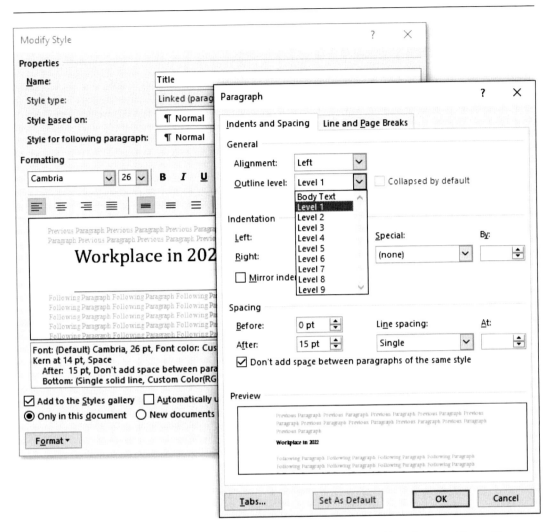

Figure 3.7 – MS Word dialog box to edit the title paragraph style used in a document formatting

In addition to font options and paragraph alignment, please note the connection between the title paragraph style outline level, in this example, **Level 1**, and the bookmark level in Acrobat. *Figure 3.6* shows, in the **Level** column, how PDFMaker interprets paragraph style outline levels.

As you can see, some time may be required to plan a publication. Someone may have already created a template with all the formatting options already set up. Using these options properly will make the difference between having a rich, interactive, and accessible `.pdf` file or a flat file in need of enhancements in Acrobat.

The next section will give insight into how, in a few steps, you can check whether good formatting has been used in a Word document before it is converted to PDF.

Recognizing the formatting type in an MS Word document

If your document is already created, how do you know whether it was formatted properly using styles? Here are the steps to check:

1. Open the **Styles** pane by clicking the small button under **Styles** in the **Home** ribbon:

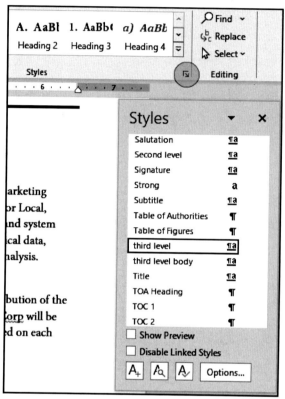

Figure 3.8 – MS Word Styles pane

The placement of an insertion point in the text will highlight a style used in the formatting of that specific paragraph.

2. Click in a different paragraph and see a style highlighted again. The label may have changed if a different style is used.

3. Click on different headings in the document and check which style is used to format each one.

> **Important note**
>
> If there are no changes in the highlighted labels in the **Styles** pane as you click in different paragraphs, and the only label highlighted is **Normal**, it means that the document is *not* using styles, regardless of how the formatting looks in the page layout.

Here is another method to quickly see not only whether styles are used but how consistently they are used:

1. Click **File** at the top left of the screen.

2. Click on **Options**.

3. In the dialog box that opens, select **Advanced**.

4. Scroll until you see the **Display** group of settings.

5. Find the **Style area pane width in Draft and Outline views** field and type 1".

6. Click **OK**.

7. Return to your document page and in the **View** ribbon, select **Draft**.

You will see all document style tags displayed on the left. Here is an example:

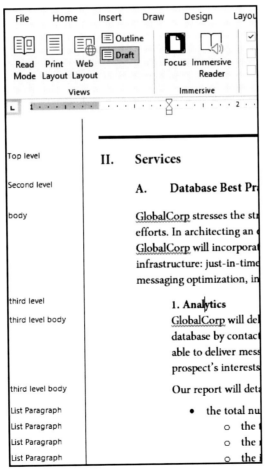

Figure 3.9 – The Draft view revealing styles used in document formatting

In the left area of the screen, the **Styles** pane displays tags for each paragraph of content. You can click on the tags to select the paragraphs. At a glance, you can see whether a document has been properly structured with styles or not. If the only tag displayed is **Normal** (or any other one defined as a body text tag), it means that the document does not have the required structure to deliver full functionality when exported to PDF.

> **Tip**
> Holding the *Shift* key while clicking tags will allow you to select multiple paragraphs.

We reviewed the process used while authoring a document in Word and the options selected in PDFMaker that make the best use of the settings applied during authoring. We will now address the final step: making a `.pdf` file.

Testing and comparing converted PDF files

Once the authoring process is complete, the author has the choice to create a `.pdf` file using the **PDFMaker | Create PDF** options or **Adobe PDF Printer (Acrobat Distiller)**. We will compare the results of both methods.

Exporting to PDF using the PDFMaker function

The following process will describe the option of converting a document in a way that incorporates settings selected in the PDFMaker preferences:

1. In the **Acrobat** ribbon tab, click **Create PDF**.
2. Select the desired folder and type the filename.
3. Click **Save**.

The process of conversion is quick; while it is happening, you will see a progress bar like the following:

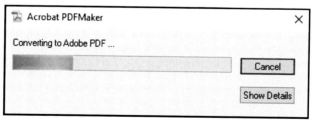

Figure 3.10 – PDFMaker conversion progress bar

If the **View Adobe PDF result** checkbox was selected in the **Preferences** dialog box, (see *Figure 3.3*), the new PDF opens in the Acrobat application set as the default for `.pdf` file viewing (see *Figure 1.3* and *Figure 1.4* for macOS).

Acrobat, like many other applications, uses metadata to preserve and update information about many aspects of a file, such as the date of creation and modification, keywords, the author, the title, and the file size. In our example file, the metadata reveals information about when and how the PDF was created:

1. Select the **File | Properties…** options from Acrobat's top menu to open the **Document Properties** dialog box.

2. Confirm that the **Description** tab at the top is selected and read the **Application** info. You can see that **Acrobat PDFMaker 22 for Word** was used, as seen in this screenshot:

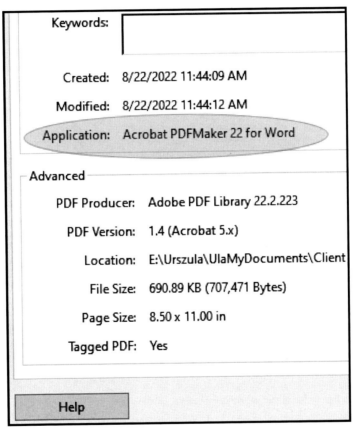

Figure 3.11 – Document properties displaying the application that created it

In the next section, we will create a PDF using the **Print to Adobe PDF** function and compare the effects this method has on the final PDF.

Exporting to PDF by using Adobe PDF Printer (Acrobat Distiller)

In this example, instead of using the Acrobat ribbon options, we will print the same document to **Adobe PDF Printer**, which is a virtual printer driver commonly used for conversion to PDF. The settings selected in the PDFMaker preferences for our example document remain the same. Here are the steps for exporting to a .pdf file using Adobe PDF Printer:

1. Select the **File** option and click **Print**.

2. From the **Printer** options, select **Adobe PDF**.

3. Select the desired folder, type the filename, and click **Save**.

The process of printing again is quick but while it is happening, you will see a different progress bar. It represents the process being done by Acrobat Distiller.

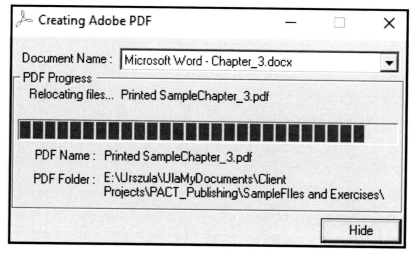

Figure 3.12 – PDF printing using the Acrobat Distiller conversion progress bar

Again, the new PDF opens in Acrobat, allowing you to examine the resulting file. We will once more open the document properties, following the same process as before:

1. Select the **File | Properties…** options from Acrobat's top menu options.

   Then, the **Document Properties** dialog box opens.

2. Select the **Description** tab at the top and read the metadata, revealing that the application used was **PScript5.dll Version 5.2.2**, as seen in the following screenshot. The application name refers to the PostScript image file creation process, which we will discuss in *Chapter 11*, *Using Acrobat for Professional Publishing*.

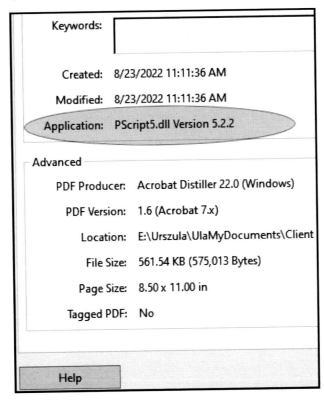

Figure 3.13 – Document properties displaying the application that printed the .pdf file

Both .pdf files came from the same authoring environment, but the conversion process selected was different for each one. Please review the **conversion to PDF workflow** chart in *Figure 3.1*.

In the next section, we will compare the differences in the resulting PDFs side by side.

Comparing PDF document conversion results

The following table provides a comparison of features included in a .pdf file depending on the conversion process selected. In both instances, the original Word document was properly constructed using paragraph styles and the PDFMaker settings were the same:

	Document converted using the PDFMaker Create PDF function	**Document printed to Adobe PDF Printer**
Application used	PDFMaker	Acrobat Distiller
Bookmarks	All levels are created automatically based on selected styles	None
Hyperlinks	Created automatically if present in a document and in footnotes and endnotes	None
Navigation	Created automatically for TOC and buttons	None
Accessibility tags	Document structure created automatically based on styles	None
Comments and review	Converted to interactive live review options	Displayed exactly as seen on the screen, not editable in Acrobat
Searchable text	Yes	Yes

Table 3.1 – Side-by-side comparison of functionality in PDFs created using different methods

As you can see from the table, many features are missing in a flat PDF created by printing. It is possible to add full PDF functionality and missing elements. Adobe Acrobat Pro and Standard are designed to do that. However, this method of adding interactivity is called **repair**. Repair is always manual and tedious and implies flaws. Additionally, every new version of the same publication will have to be repaired all over again.

On the other hand, properly constructed and exported documents will automatically include interactive features. A new version of the publication will also contain the same functionality.

Please don't repair your .pdf files; build them right the first time. You just gained the skills to do it!

> **Important note**
>
> PDF files may also be created using the MS Office application's **Save As | PDF (*pdf)** or **Export | Create PDF/XPS Document** options. This works in environments where Adobe Acrobat is not installed on a desktop. Although bookmarks and accessibility tags can be created on export, the major limitation of this process is that comments and markup are not converted to Acrobat annotations and markup.
>
> This chapter focused on the PDFMaker options that work over a PostScript-described page layout to create an Adobe PDF rather than an XPS PDF.

Summary

This chapter explained the process of creating a final PDF with the functionality needed for online viewing. We stepped through the PDFMaker settings to understand how the construction of a Word document gives choices that users may select for inclusion on export. We also compared how using different methods to convert a file to a .pdf file will give different results.

This should be the final output for a publication. Nothing is final in the digital world, though, and all too often we must fix or modify a document after the final version is created.

Fortunately, Acrobat Pro and Standard provide a wide range of editing tools. In the next chapter, we will explore how fixes and updates can be applied to content in a PDF publication.

4

Modifying and Editing PDF Files

Authors, graphic designers, layout artists, and other professionals spend countless hours producing publications. Once completed, these documents may be printed directly to a paper printing device, or they may be exported to a .pdf file. Some authoring applications, such as InDesign, provide settings to further optimize the final .pdf file either to fit commercial paper printing needs or to make it meet online distribution standards that allow printing as needed.

At this point, a .pdf file is meant to be a final document. However, there are many instances when changes or improvements still need to be made. Reasons for these changes vary. Authors may provide content late in the production cycle, such as covers for books, or good production practices may have not been followed and the final PDF needs to be enhanced further by adding navigation or accessibility features.

In this chapter, we will learn how to use Acrobat tools to make improvements by adjusting both the order and content of pages. We will cover the following topics:

- Adding and organizing pages and page numbering
- Adding, editing, and formatting text and images
- Creating and editing bookmarks and links
- Creating headers, footers, and watermarks
- Introduction to accessibility tags

> **Important note**
>
> The editing options considered in this chapter are extensive, yet they are not to be confused with authoring. Acrobat is *not* an authoring application, so any changes in the content are considered fixes, repairs, or touch-ups. None of the changes performed in Acrobat will be reflected in the source documents.

We will now learn how to organize PDF pages by placing them in the correct order and assigning relevant page and/or section labels. You can use any multipage .pdf publication.

Adding and organizing pages and page numbering

Some publications are very long, and their sections may be completed by different authors. Each part may be exported to PDF independently and they all may need to be combined into one file in Acrobat. Some pages may need to be replaced with updated content. None of these edits are possible in paper documents, but PDF gives us so much more flexibility.

Organizing the order of document pages may be done in the **Pages** pane or using the **Organize Pages** tool. We will use the **Pages** pane, where the **Options** menu will be our starting point for edits.

Pages navigation pane and options

First, if it is not opened already, we will open the **Pages** navigation pane. Follow these steps:

1. Click in the middle of the gray bar on the left side to open the pane icons.

2. When you see the icons for available panes, click the **Pages** icon to open the **Pages** pane with numbered page thumbnails appearing in the column, as seen in the following screenshot:

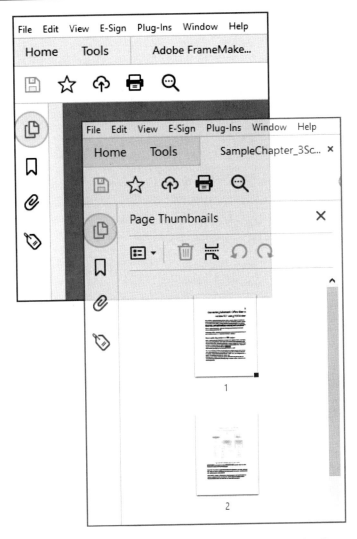

Figure 4.1 – Pages pane opened displaying page thumbnails

Next, we will explore editing options available in the **Pages** pane by clicking on the **Options** button to reveal a menu. The button is highlighted in the following screenshot:

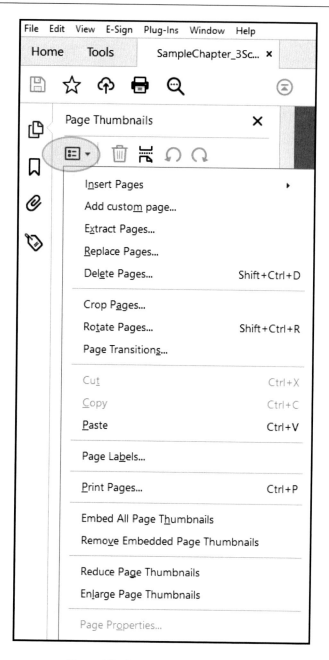

Figure 4.2 – Pages pane options menu

Please take some time to examine the choices. They are self-explanatory. We will cover just a few examples that will illustrate the richness of the changes to document pages that can be made using this tool.

Using the **Pages** pane is a convenient and intuitive way to manipulate the order of pages:

1. To resize the pane width, position the cursor on the vertical edge between the pane and the page area.

2. When you see a double-sided arrow, click and drag to the right. You will see thumbnails arranged in multiple columns. This is helpful if you work with a very long publication.

3. Click on a thumbnail to select a page and display it in the main area of the screen.

> **Important note**
>
> The selection of page thumbnails signals to Acrobat which pages will be affected by functions chosen in the **Options** menu. Keep this in mind when extracting, deleting, cropping, or rotating any pages and when changing the page properties.
>
> To select multiple pages, hold the *Shift* or *Ctrl/Command* key when clicking on different thumbnails.

In the next section, we will learn how to add, insert, extract, or delete pages in a document. We will also reorganize the order of the pages.

Adding and removing pages

Removing pages is the simplest task. Here are the steps to do so:

1. Select the thumbnail(s) and either tap the *Delete* button on your keyboard or select the trashcan at the top of the **Pages** pane.

2. Confirm your choice by clicking **OK**. The page(s) will be gone forever.

There is no undo option for this action, so use it wisely. Well, you can use the **File | Revert** options from the top menu but you will lose any unsaved work.

More advanced options involve inserting, extracting, and adding a custom page (there is a new **Add custom page** feature in the subscription-based Acrobat Pro). We will explore these menu options next.

Inserting pages

Here are the steps for inserting pages:

1. Select a thumbnail in the **Pages** pane and from **Options** (or right-click), select the **Insert Pages | From File…** options.

2. Locate a .pdf file to be the source of the inserted pages and click **Open**.

3. A dialog box opens where you can specify where to place the inserted pages:

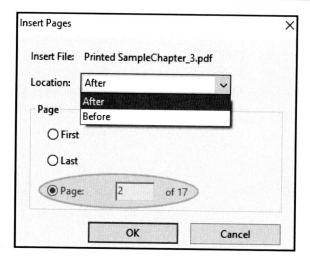

Figure 4.3 – Dialog box for positioning inserted pages

Please note that the first choice for the **Before** or **After** position is the page that you selected prior to opening this menu.

4.   To finish the insertion of pages, click **OK**.

Now we will extract two pages from the document.

Extracting pages

In a situation where you do not need all pages of a document but only one or a few, you may extract that page and reuse it after saving. It will become an independent .pdf file. Here are the steps to extract two pages:

1.   Holding the *Shift* key, click on pages 2-3 in the **Pages** pane, and from **Options** (or right-click), select **Extract Pages…**:

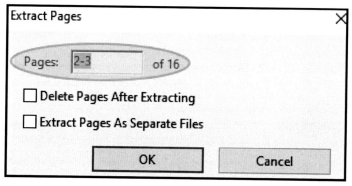

Figure 4.4 – Dialog box options for extracting pages

Please note that the first field in the **Extract Pages** dialog is populated with the page numbers that you selected prior to opening this menu.

2. If you select **Delete Pages After Extracting**, these pages will be removed from the original document and only the new file will contain them.

3. In our example (we selected two pages), **Extract Pages As Separate Files** will create two new one-page PDFs. This is useful if a publication has graphics or diagrams that need to be treated as individual figures placed in other applications.

4. To finish the extraction of pages, click **OK**.

We will now explore a different method to insert pages into a document – **Add custom page**. This is useful when a publication is complete, but a cover page that does not exist as a separate `.pdf` file yet needs to be designed and added. This is a new feature added to the subscription-based Acrobat and gives you access to several templates to get started. We will review some of these options.

Adding custom pages

We'll follow these steps for adding custom pages:

1. Select the first page in the **Pages** pane and from **Options**, select **Add custom page…** (if you use the **Organize pages** tool, select **Add custom page** from the toolbar at the top of the screen).

Important note

We discovered that some Acrobat versions use different labels for the **Add custom page** function, such as **Design a new page** or **Add cover page**. They are exactly the same. Have they done this just to check whether we are paying attention? Roll your eyes if you want to. This is not the first time that identical tools or options have been named differently in the same software. This makes me think of paragraph styles/tags/formats.

---

2. You need to be online to make this work. A **Customize Page** sub-application powered by Adobe Express opens with templates and/or options for text, adding photos, shapes, or backgrounds. You may want to explore this feature if it is useful in your projects. At this point, you are in full authoring/design mode. Once finished, you click **Add** and the new page is inserted into your publication. You can't go back to customize the page editing settings, though, once it is added. If you need to change the new page, use the same tools as for the rest of the pages in the PDF.

Quite a fun and great way to kill some time on Friday before leaving the office!

Now that we have added pages, we need to move them to the correct positions and update thumbnail page labels to match the page numbering assigned in the authoring application.

Moving pages and updating page numbering

Page numbering is typically a function of an authoring application, and it is automatically done during the production stages. The traditional term for a page number in a printed book is *folio*. If a publication is entirely produced as one file and exported to a .pdf file, there should be no need to update page numbers (if only!).

Many final PDF publications, however, are a result of combining multiple PDFs or adding pages as we did in the earlier example. This may result in at least two different outcomes:

1. Page numbers in a document appear in the wrong order, are missing, are duplicated, or have gaps in the sequence
2. Page numbering is missing altogether and needs to be added in Acrobat

We will first update pages that appear in the wrong order and need the page labels to be edited to reflect sections in the publication.

Moving pages in the Pages pane

When a new .pdf file is created and opened in Acrobat, the **Pages** pane will always display page numbers below the thumbnails, beginning with 1 and ending with the last page number. Each thumbnail is always assigned a numeric label and it is always in the correct order. It may be referred to as an **integer** that increases by 1. The **Pages** pane from the **Options** menu refers to these numbers as page labels (some older versions of Acrobat may still use **Page numbering...** as a menu option):

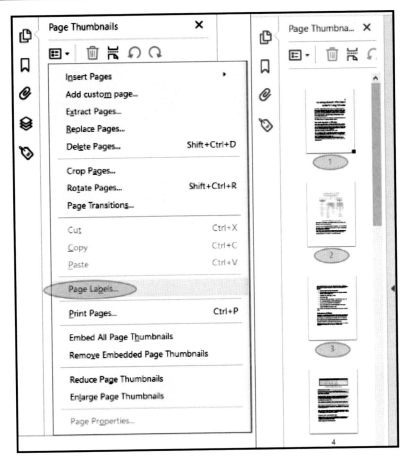

Figure 4.5 – Pages pane – Options | Page Labels…

In documents where these page labels do not match the page numbers in the footer or header of the document's actual pages, do the following:

1. For pages in the wrong order, click to select the page thumbnails (hold the *Shift* key to select multiple) and drag to move them to a location corresponding with page numbers in the page footer or header. Numbers on the document page rule! It is the thumbnail that needs to be moved to get the correct label, which will be updated automatically.

2. For pages where a page number is missing or duplicated, you will need to manually add or change the page numbers using the **Add Text** tool. We will show how to use it in the *Adding new text on a page* section.

3. For page numbers that are missing and creating gaps in the page numbering on many pages (in the footer/header area), you can use the **Header & Footer** function. We will use this feature in the *Creating headers and footers* and *Creating watermarks* sections.

> **Important note**
>
> Updating page number labels affects only the page thumbnails in the **Pages** pane.
>
> To add or change page numbering on the actual document pages, you need to use the **Edit PDF** option and then the **Add Text** or **Header & Footer** feature.

In the following sections, we will update the page labels to address the need for section numbering.

Section numbering

In long documents, content is often divided into sections. The Introduction, Acknowledgements, **Table of Contents** (**TOC**), Index, or Appendix sections may have page numbering displayed in a style different than the regular body page numbers. They may even include a prefix.

The sections in our example use lowercase Roman numerals, such as i, ii, iii, and so on. We will update the thumbnail page labels to reflect the numbering of the publication pages. Here are the steps:

1. Select the page thumbnails that will get new section labels.

2. Click to select the **Pages** pane, then click on the **Options** menu.

3. Click on **Page Labels…**.

4. When the dialog box opens, select the numbering style in the **Numbering** group of choices. If needed, also add a section prefix and change the **Start** number.

5. Don't forget to check which pages will receive new labels. The fields are at the top of the dialog box in the **Pages** group. As you can see again in the following screenshot, selecting thumbnails before opening this dialog box makes the label changes more intuitive.

6. You can repeat this process for all other sections, if needed:

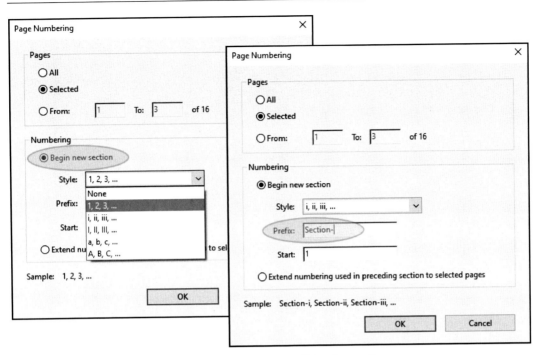

Figure 4.6 – Page Numbering dialog box options

> **Important note**
>
> If you expect the PDF to be updated repeatedly, you should leave updating section numbering to the very end of editing. None of the changes in the **Pages** pane done in Acrobat can be transferred from one version of a PDF to another. In fact, no content edits performed in a PDF document can be automatically applied to another one.

In addition to working with the **Pages** pane, you can accomplish the same tasks using the **Organize Pages** tool. We will briefly review it next.

Working with the Organize Pages tool

The **Organize Pages** tool is an expanded way to see all page thumbnails on the screen, rather than in a column on the left. Click on **Tools** at the top of the screen and locate it among the Acrobat tools. If you like using it, select **Add** from the menu. The shortcut will be now placed in the panel on the right.

Let's explore how you can organize pages using this function:

1. Click the **Organize Pages** tool to open all functions available. Page thumbnails now replace the actual pages in the main area of the screen. To make it easier to recognize the content, look for the slider at the bottom of the screen. This will help you adjust the thumbnails to the desired size.

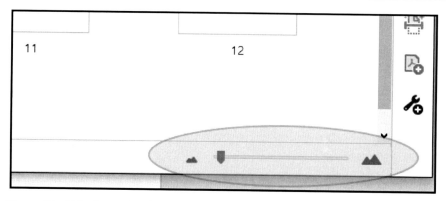

Figure 4.7 – Slider located at the bottom right of the screen for resizing page thumbnails

2. You can click and drag pages to the desired location, the same way we did in the **Pages** pane.

At the top of the screen, available options are represented in a toolbar:

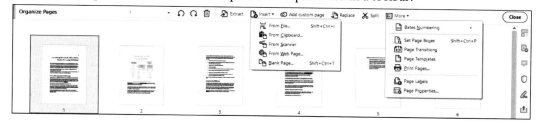

Figure 4.8 – Organize Pages tool menu options

You can see that there are a few more choices available here than in the **Pages** pane's **Options** menu. One of them is **Split** for dividing document pages into smaller PDFs.

> **Important note**
>
> It is worth repeating that the vast quantity of options in Acrobat creates a need to access them in many ways. My approach in this book has been to use both menus and tools. The presented examples will use menus, and when helpful, the tools will also be mentioned. When a tool is the best way to work, examples will be based on the options contained in it.

We will next address the problem of missing or duplicated page numbers in addition to making changes to other areas of page content, such as body text and images.

Adding, editing, and formatting text and images

Just as reorganizing pages in a `.pdf` file may be necessary, a publication may also need changes made to its text and images. We will focus now on the **Edit PDF** tool, located in the column on the right side by default, and its toolbar options.

Click on the **Edit PDF** tool in the column to open it. A new toolbar appears at the top of the screen. Click on each dropdown to explore the options.

The labels on tools help identify functions available after a tool is selected. Here is a brief overview of each tool:

- The **Edit** tool allows you to select the text and delete, format, or replace it with new text. It is also used to select an image so you can move, resize, or delete it.

- The **Add Text** tool allows you to start typing text anywhere in a blank area of the page.

- The **Add Image** tool opens a dialog box to locate a new image and place it on a page.

- The **Link** tool is for creating new interactive links to specific destinations in a document or modifying existing links.

- The **Crop Pages** tool is for changing the page size, by removing some of it through cropping.

- The **Header & Footer** tool is for adding and editing headers and/or footers, including auto page numbering and dates.

- The **Watermark** tool allows you to add a transparent image or text that clearly identifies copyright or security status, for example.

- The **More** button contains options to modify the page background, by adding color or an image, and **Bates Numbering** for legal documents.

> **Important note**
>
> You cannot do any editing or formatting using the **Select** tool: it's a black arrow on the left of the hand grabber in a toolbar. *It is for selecting and copying only.* Copied text using *Ctrl + C* or *Cmd + C* may be pasted in another area of the PDF or a file created by a different application, such as Word or InDesign. The same applies to images; they can be selected, copied, and pasted using this tool but not resized or moved.

Opening the **Edit PDF** tool also opens the **FORMAT** panel on the right. Dotted lines appear on the page to represent boundaries of text frames that can be resized or moved. The panel contains extensive formatting options for text, such as font, font style, size, and color. You may also format paragraph alignment and make bullets or numbered lists with different styles. When text is selected or new text is typed, text formatting options become available; when an image is selected, image-related options become available.

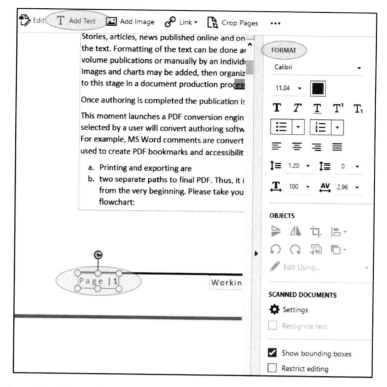

Figure 4.9 – Text and image formatting options when the Edit PDF tool is used

In the next few sections, we will improve a publication using different options from the **Edit PDF** tool.

Adding new text on a page

Do you recall adding page numbers in our earlier discussion? The **Add Text** tool is perfect for manually adding a few page numbers if they are missing from document pages. Again, this is for documents that mostly have page numbering in place already, but due to changes, some page numbers are missing. Take a look at *Figure 4.9* and then follow these steps:

1. Click on the **Add Text** tool.

2. Position your cursor on the blank area of the page where the page number should be placed.

3. Click and start typing.

4. Select and format the text using the **FORMAT** panel on the right.

Use the same process to add and format new text in any area of the publication. This could include headings, adding photo captions or credits, or labels for form fields.

Next, we will go through the steps to add a new image to a page.

Adding a new image

If a page is missing a photo, a logo, or a chart, it may be fixed by using the **Add Image** tool. Here are simple steps:

1. Click the **Add Image** tool to select it.

2. A dialog box opens, allowing you to locate the desired image. You can only choose one image at a time, though there is no limit to how many images you can add. The most common supported formats are .gif, .png, .jpeg, and .tiff.

3. Select the image and either double-click or click **Open**.

4. Your cursor will now display a thumbnail of the image. We refer to it as a loaded cursor. Click the mouse key to unload it. The new image is now placed on the page. Its top-left corner is positioned at the location where you clicked.

   These steps are very similar to working with the layout in InDesign, which is a graphic design application. An image file can be selected in the file browser and then precisely sized and positioned on a page. Through the process, the cursor gives more visual feedback to the user, thus the loaded and unloaded cursor terms.

5. To move the image, click on it and drag it around the page:

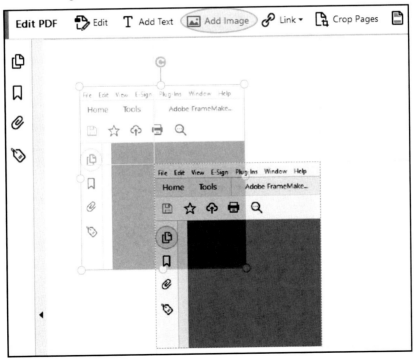

Figure 4.10 – Stages of positioning an image on a page

6. To resize the image, position your cursor over one of the round handles, then click and drag that handle.

7. Green **smart guides** that become active while you hold your mouse button and move the image are temporarily shown and are a great help in aligning images to margins, text, or other graphics on the page. Once you release the mouse button, the guides disappear.

Replacing an image

Some images, for example, charts, may need to be updated by replacing them. To do that, follow these steps:

1. Select the **Edit** tool and click on an image that needs to be replaced.

2. Right-click and select the **Replace** context menu option.

3. Locate a new image in the dialog box that opens.

4. Click **Open** to complete the task.

5. To adjust the formatting of the image, such as crop, rotate, or stacking position (**Bring to Front** versus **Send to Back**), use the **FORMAT** panel options on the right.

    For more advanced image editing options, right-click and choose **Edit Using | Adobe Photoshop** or another software installed on your system.

    Now, you are in full authoring mode. Hopefully, these additions to your document are only touch-ups. Any formatting is only applied to a single object; no text or object styles are available. You cannot place multiple images at once, as you would in InDesign, so hold on to your original authoring files and applications as Acrobat is not replacing them.

6. Close the **Edit PDF** tool before we move on to the next topic.

We will now move on to working with interactive navigation in a .pdf file: bookmarks and links.

Creating and editing bookmarks and links

In this section, we will understand the purpose and process of creating and editing bookmarks and links.

Navigating a paper book requires page numbers, running headers and footers, or tabs. We can see all the pages as we turn them. A PDF, however, is just a flat image on the screen, so functionality to find the content that a reader is looking for is provided by bookmarks or links in addition to the obvious, such as scroll bars and page navigation toolbars.

Working with bookmarks

Bookmarks are so important that they have their own navigation pane, which is available by default. They are a bit like a TOC in a document that may not have one. At a glance, a reader may get an idea about the volume of content. Click on the **Bookmarks** icon to open the pane:

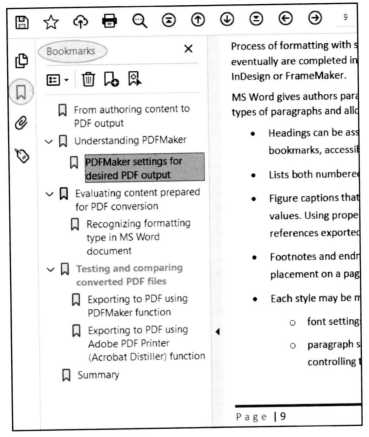

Figure 4.11 – Bookmarks pane

As you see, bookmarks may represent headings or other information that you want to provide quick access to, they may be organized by levels, and they may be even highlighted by a non-default color to create bookmarks within bookmarks for topics that you do not want to miss.

Clicking on a bookmark takes you to the destination, just like a link does. How do you create bookmarks? The best approach is to go through the proper process before and during the export to a .pdf file in an authoring application, such as Microsoft Word. We covered details of the workflow in *Chapter 3, Converting Microsoft Office Files to Adobe PDF Files Using PDFMaker.*

However, if we need to edit bookmarks after a `.pdf` file is created, here is the process:

1. With the **Bookmarks** pane still open (as in *Figure 4.11*), click on a few bookmarks in a document that contains them and confirm that the main area of the screen displays a page that represents the description for the selected and highlighted bookmark. This is a **bookmark destination**. If the content of a page matches a bookmark, nothing needs to be done. However, if nothing happens after clicking a bookmark or the wrong page is displayed, you need to fix the bookmark, meaning you need to set a new destination.

2. Select the bookmark that needs to be fixed. Scroll and/or zoom to the desired destination for the bookmark and click on the **Options** dropdown to reveal the pane menu (or right-click) and choose **Set Bookmark Destination**, as shown in the screenshot:

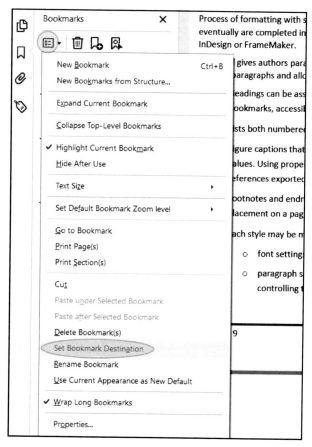

Figure 4.12 – Bookmarks options menu

We successfully changed where in a document a bookmark takes us. Now, we will learn how to add new bookmarks either in a document that has none or where some areas of the document are not bookmarked.

Creating new bookmarks

When a document is missing bookmarks, you can add them manually. Here are the steps:

1. Before you create a new bookmark, locate a page that will become its destination. Set the magnification level, and if needed, adjust the view. When you see page content displayed correctly, move to the next step.

2. From the **Options** menu, select **New Bookmark**. You can also use the *Ctrl + B/Cmd + B* shortcut or the bookmark button if you don't want to use the menu.

   If the bookmark is to a heading or specific text, then selecting the heading will automatically name the bookmark with the selected text. Or you can type the bookmark name to replace *Untitled*.

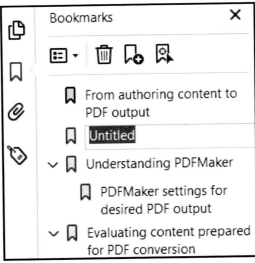

Figure 4.13 – A new bookmark being created

3. Give the bookmark a name/label, then press the *Enter/Return* key to save it.

   You created a new bookmark. Its destination is what you see in the main area of the screen. Now, you can test it to make sure it works.

4. Click on a different bookmark, then again click on the bookmark you just made. Confirm that it works as expected. You successfully added a new bookmark.

5. Repeat the steps for adding new bookmarks.

Bookmarks can be set to a page or a specific view, which may be an area of a page. This is especially useful for very large page sizes, such as architectural drawings or posters. They may also be reordered and rearranged hierarchically by clicking and dragging in the pane. A horizontal line hints where the bookmark's new position will be when you release the mouse key.

Setting bookmark properties

We will now add formatting to highlight or emphasize a particular bookmark. It will be easy to spot it among the other bookmarks and quickly find a desired page in the document. This is very useful when a publication is very long, and you need to mark specific topics to return to. This could also be a way to alert readers that they need to look at a specific area of the document. Follow these steps to do so:

1. Click on a bookmark and then right-click it to reveal a context menu.

2. Click on **Properties….**

3. Select a color and/or style and click **OK** to save the changes:

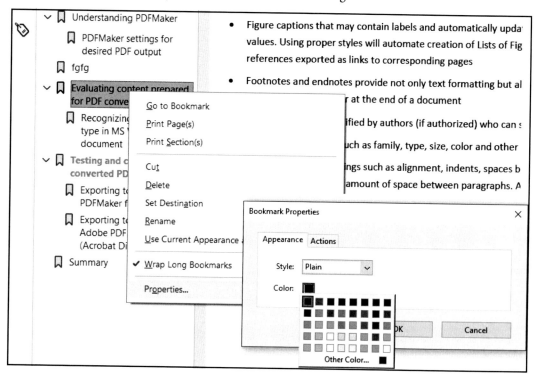

Figure 4.14 – Bookmark properties for an individual bookmark

The bookmark now reflects new formatting and stands out from the rest. There is no limit to how many bookmarks may be individually formatted.

We have accomplished fixing a bookmark that did not work correctly and added a new one to the list. Our next task will be working with links.

Working with links

Links are clickable areas on a page. Unlike bookmarks organized in a pane, links appear randomly in a document. Typical links on pages are the following:

- TOC or index entries
- Cross-references
- Footnotes and endnotes
- Links to web addresses

A well-designed and correctly exported `.pdf` file will inherit links created during the authoring stage. For example, if an author properly constructs a document and generates a TOC or an index, all entries become clickable links in the `.pdf` file. If TOC entries were typed as regular text, they'd need to be enhanced in Acrobat using the **Link** tool.

Like bookmarks, links take you to a destination. We will review and create a new link now using these steps:

1. Open a `.pdf` document with a generated TOC or use our example file, `Chapter_3SampleTOC. pdf`.

2. Click **Edit PDF** in the **Tools** pane on the right to open it again. All text on the page is inside frames that are represented by dotted lines.

3. Click on the **Link** dropdown and select **Add/Edit Web or Document Link**. You will now see rectangles with solid black lines, but only on some text. As you move your cursor over the rectangles, they are detected, and small handles that enable you to adjust the size and position of the clickable area appear on the corners. This is how clickable links are represented when the tool is active. Notice that the text frames with dotted edges disappear, as shown in *Figure 4.15*:

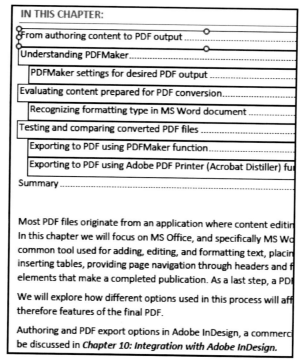

Figure 4.15 – Clickable link detected on a page; one entry is missing its clickable region

4. Now that you recognize where the links are located, let's test them. To do that, select the hand grabber from the top toolbar. Notice that all link rectangles have now disappeared.

5. As you hover with the cursor over TOC entries, you will see it changes to active, and when you click a link, the destination page is displayed on the screen. Quite predictable!

6. Now, move your cursor over the area where we expect a link, in our example in *Figure 4.15*, a TOC entry: **Summary**. Notice that your hand grabber cursor does not change and if you click, nothing happens. The TOC does not have a link on the entry, therefore the cursor would not change, nor would anything happen if you clicked on the text.

7. Select the **Link** tool and you can see that there is no rectangle over that entry. Similarly, if you are working with your own example file and there is no interactivity where you expect it, select the **Link** tool to see whether there is a rectangle over that region. If there is not and you would want there to be a link, it needs to be created, which we will do next.

> **Important note**
>
> Links in Acrobat are not based on text (like in HTML code for browsers) but are clickable regions, most commonly rectangles. Sometimes, these rectangles are too small or too large.
>
> Use the **Link** tool to resize the regions by clicking and dragging the round handles. To select multiple links, hold the *Shift* or *Ctrl/Cmd* key and click on the links that you want to add to the selection.
>
> To align, center, or distribute them, right-click and select the context menu options.

We will now create a new link to the **Summary** heading (see *Figure 4.15*):

1. Select **Add/Edit Web or Document Link**.

2. Click and drag to create a rectangle over the **Summary** TOC entry. As you click above and to the left of the word **Summary** and then drag so that the blue transparent region covers the clickable area; it gives you an idea of the dimensions and the position of the new link:

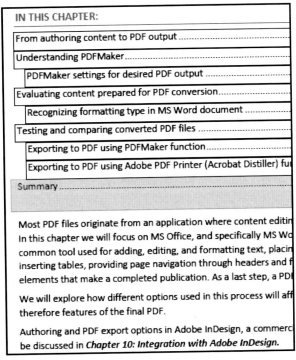

Figure 4.16 – Creation of a clickable link in progress

3. When you release the mouse, the **Create Link** dialog box opens. The **Link Appearance** group of choices allows you to specify how readers see an active link before they release the mouse. The **Link Action** group defines the type of destination for a link. We will keep the defaults.

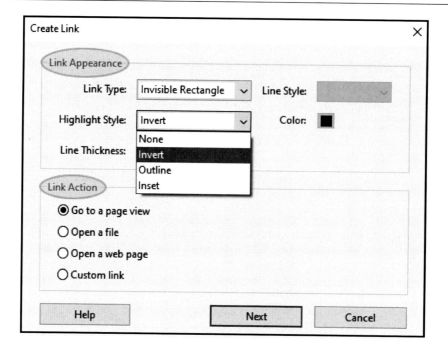

Figure 4.17 – Create Link dialog box options

4. Click the **Next** button. A new dialog box appears. If you tend to ignore the content of long instructions or alerts in dialog boxes, I have full empathy, but this one (*Figure 4.18*) needs to be given some thought. So, let's go through it together.

You are in the process of creating a link **destination**, meaning setting up a view of a page for a reader after a link is clicked, *not* the view of a page where the link is on. Before you click anything in this box, you must find the page or a specific page view using any method listed in this alert.

Our link is to take us to the *Summary* page; so, we scroll till we find it. The dialog box remains in place until you find and adjust the view of the target page. When you are done, you are ready to click **Set Link**:

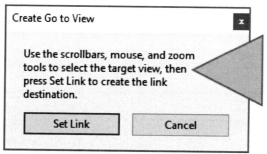

Figure 4.18 – Setting a link destination

5. Acrobat takes you back to the page where the text of the link is located, in our case, the **IN THIS CHAPTER** page heading, as in *Figure 4.15*. The **Summary** entry now has a rectangle representing a clickable link region. Let's test it.

6. Select the hand grabber tool. Notice that all link rectangles are now gone. When you hover over the text of our new **Summary** link, the cursor changes. When you click, the destination **Summary** page opens on the screen. Congratulations! The new link works perfectly.

We have stepped through the process of creating one link. For more links, simply repeat all the steps for each new link. Unless, of course, you prefer to have them created automatically during authoring. I think I am repeating myself now…

We will also explore how to fix a link that takes you to a destination that you want to change. You will work with **link actions**. Here are the steps:

1. Select **Add/Edit Web or Document Link** again and double-click on a link to open the **Link Properties** dialog box. For existing links, there are two tabs.

2. Click the **Actions** tab, then the action displayed in the **Actions** window, and select the **Edit** button. You will have two dialog boxes open, as shown in the screenshot:

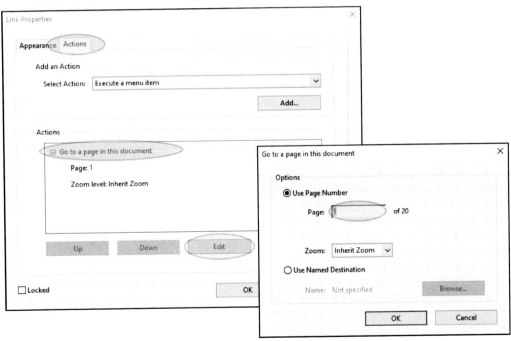

Figure 4.19 – Editing link destination in the Actions tab

3. The second dialog box presents settings associated with the selected action. You can now change the page number.

4.   Click **OK** twice to close both dialog boxes.

5.   You can also **Use Named Destination**. Destinations need to be created in the **Destinations** pane (**View** | **Show/Hide** | **Destinations**) prior to editing the link. This option may be especially helpful for charts, endnotes, and cross-references.

Instead of selecting a page number, when editing a link or bookmark, click **Used Named Destination**, then the **Browse** button, which opens a list of destinations to choose from.

We have learned how to create and edit interactive navigation in a PDF using bookmarks and links. We will move on now to creating navigational page elements, that is, headers and footers, using another feature-rich tool – **Header & Footer** – and explore its options.

Creating headers and footers

In this section, we will explore the reason and process for the creation of headers and/or footers in Acrobat.

Creating headers and footers in Acrobat ties the elements of the publication together by combining individual `.pdf` files into one. Many books and journals are created this way, allowing many authors to contribute.

> **Important note**
>
> We will focus on footers, but the same steps and principles apply to headers. Adding headers or footers should be done at the end of editing the document after all the pages have been organized and their location in the publication has been finalized.

When all document pages are in place, the page numbers, dates, and text of the footer can be added. Here is the process:

1.   In the **Edit PDF** toolbar, click the **Header & Footer** | **Add...** options to open a large and options-rich dialog box. Please take time to look at different groups of choices. It is easy to miss margin settings located in the top-right area while looking at the preview at the very bottom of the box. *Figure 4.20* already has footer text in place, but we will now do it together step by step.

Our footer will have chapter title text, the date, and page numbers with the page count.

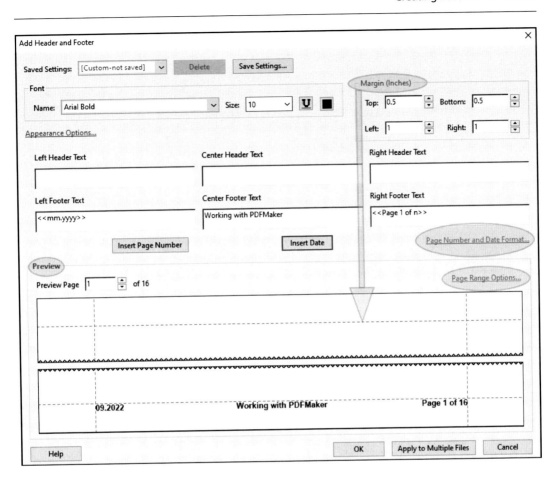

Figure 4.20 – Add Header and Footer dialog box

2. Click in the **Center Footer Text** field and type Working with PDFMaker. The footer text is centered on the page.

3. Change the text formatting using the **Font** selections at the top. Select **Arial Bold**, size **10** pt, and a dark red color.

4. We will now set the format for the date and page numbers. Click in the **Left Footer Text** field, then click the **Page Number and Date Format…** link. It opens a dialog box with choices for adding the date and page numbers. Set **Date Format**, then set **Page Number Format** and click **OK**:

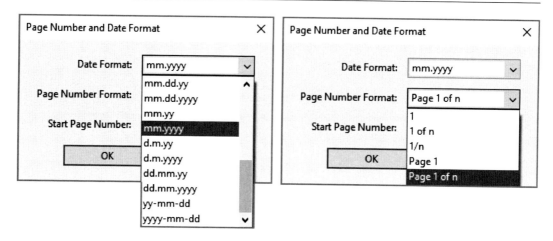

Figure 4.21 – Header and footer Page Number Format and Date Format options

5.   Once the format is set, you can complete the footer. With your insertion point still in the **Left Footer Text** field, click the **Insert Date** button and look at the **Preview** area.

6.   Click in the **Right Footer Text** field, then click the **Insert Page Number** button. Since we already made formatting selections earlier, our footer fields have placeholders, and the **Preview** area displays the date and page numbering as it will appear on pages.

7.   The last step is to set the **Page Range Options…** options. Click it to open the options dialog box and specify on which pages the new footer should be placed, then click **OK**:

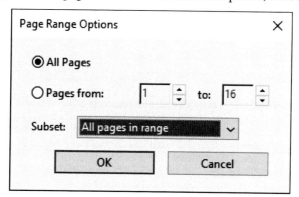

Figure 4.22 – Header and footer Page Range Options

8. You can test the footer placement on each page by clicking through the **Preview Page** field to advance to any page.

9. If you are fully satisfied with the new footer, click the *big* **OK** button. *Big* because it closes all the **Header & Footer** functions and completes the process of placing all the footer components on the page.

> **Important note**
>
> When Acrobat adds a footer, it is not an auto adjusting footer as in a Microsoft Word document. Pages added later in Acrobat will not automatically get the new footer.
>
> Also, if you change the order of pages, the page numbering will not be automatically updated. You will need to either update the footer or remove it and create a new one. The same applies to headers.

Earlier in this chapter, we added page numbers in the footer area by simply typing them on a page using the **Add Text** tool. Exploring the options in **Headers & Footers** allows you to apply fixes to many pages with missing page numbers.

We will now review the reasons and options for creating watermarks.

Creating watermarks

Watermarks have a surprisingly long history. They have been used since the 13th century, only on paper at that time. A mark of varied thickness was created while the paper was still wet, which is why it is called a *watermark*. In the digital world, watermarks refer to transparent images or text placed over page content, often to alert readers to a specific status of the publication. Version revision, confidential information, and copyright protection are among the uses of watermarks.

We will now step through the process of creating watermarks in a `.pdf` document:

1. Click the **Watermark** dropdown from the **Edit PDF** tool.

2. Select **Add…** to open another large dialog box. Acrobat has many of those.

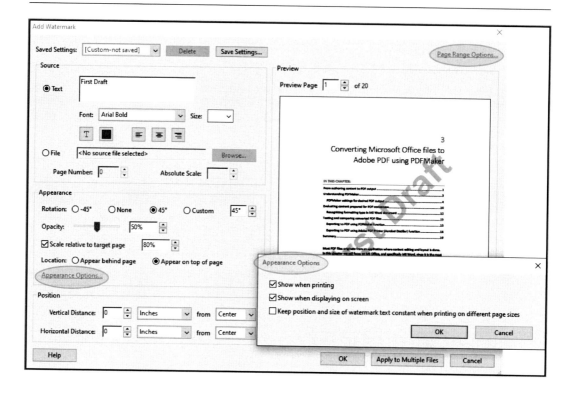

Figure 4.23 – Add Watermark dialog box and options

Take some time to look through the options:

- You can add typed text or place an image

- The text can be formatted with fonts, color, and alignment

- The font size should be left without a value as a default setting since the **Appearance** group of choices gives much better control of the watermark settings

- The **Appearance Options** dialog box allows you to specify when the watermark is to be displayed: when printing, on the screen, or in both instances

3. When the text and formatting of the watermark are complete, you can preview its placement on all affected pages using the **Preview Page** area.

4. The **Page Range Options…** option further specifies which pages should receive the watermark.

5. Happy with everything? Click **OK**. *Oh, if life could be this easy!*

We have covered some of the most important functions of Acrobat that allow you to edit a .pdf document's page content. You may explore the remaining functions available in the **Edit PDF** tool, such as additional options of the **Link** tool or the **More | Background | Add...** options.

We will now move on to introduce accessibility in PDF publications. We no longer need the **Edit PDF** toolbar, so click **Close** on it.

In the next section, we will understand PDF accessibility tags and their functions.

Introduction to accessibility tags

Accessibility of information for readers with physical impairments was recognized as a necessary function of Acrobat in its **1.4 version** released in 2001. It followed the addition of **Section 508** to the **Americans with Disabilities Act** (**ADA**). A lot has changed since then, including awareness and support from the business community and government guidelines and laws.

It has been a challenging road for the PDF format since it began its existence as an image, a means to preserve visual integrity with an emphasis on visuals. Unlike content presented through browsers based on text code, .pdf pages must be described so that speech synthesizers used by readers with a visual impairment can read the content. To address this challenge, PDF accessibility tags were created, allowing us to build the text-based structure of a publication.

We will discuss the process of adding accessibility to a .pdf file in greater detail in *Chapter 5, Remediation for Accessibility in PDF Publications*. As an introduction, we will now explore the **Tags** pane and options in a .pdf file that do not need to be remediated or repaired.

Accessibility in a .pdf file should be built right from the start during the authoring stage. A good document construction in Word through the use of paragraph styles and lists and generating referenced content such as a TOC prepares it to be fully accessible when converted to a .pdf file. We reviewed good practices in *Chapter 3, Converting Microsoft Office Files to Adobe PDF Files Using PDFMaker*.

We will examine Acrobat features and document content independently to see how compliance with public guidelines is accomplished and how all users benefit from it.

Acrobat accessibility features

Acrobat as an application is used by readers with impairments and as such contains settings to accommodate accessibility. Here are the most important ones:

- The Accessibility **Tags** pane and options allow refining the logical structure.
- The **Accessibility Checker** feature provides a detailed report of a PDF document's compliance with accessibility standards.

- The Accessibility tool with multiple functions that accommodate the remediation of a PDF.

- The **Read Out Loud** function is especially useful for authors who do not have expensive software that converts text to speech. You can access it from the **View | Read Out Loud** menu. Additional settings can be accessed through the **Edit | Preferences | Reading** group of choices (**Acrobat Pro | Preferences | Reading** on Mac).

- Some readers with a visual impairment need to change the background of pages for greater contrast and Acrobat accommodates that in the **Edit PDF | More | Background | Add…** options.

If a publication is not accessible, Acrobat features alone do not sufficiently compensate for the lack of accessibility features built into a document. We will now examine what makes a .pdf file accessible.

Document accessibility features

Accessible .pdf documents will contain these components:

- **Document structure** with accessibility tags organized in a logical order, presenting all content on the pages.

- The **language** of the document is defined.

- **Fonts** used are conforming to Unicode standards, including those used as bullets.

- **Alternate text** descriptions for images, especially those without captions.

- **Background** decorative images are tagged as such.

- **PDF forms** must be navigable using the *Tab* keyboard key with all fields described and tagged.

- **Tables** are simple and used for presenting data only. *Simple* means that merged cells are not used for headers and header cells are clearly identified.

This was a brief overview of features that accessible .pdf files must have. The remediation process will give us the opportunity to review all these features in detail, which we will see in the next chapter.

We will now examine a document that is accessible and complies with the **Section 508 accessibility standards**:

1. Open the **Tags** pane on the left:

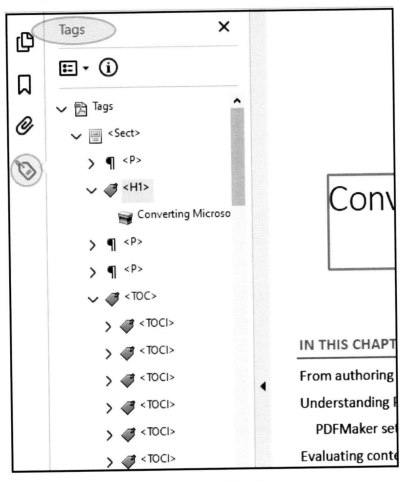

Figure 4.24 – PDF accessibility Tags pane

2.   Open the **Accessibility** tool options:

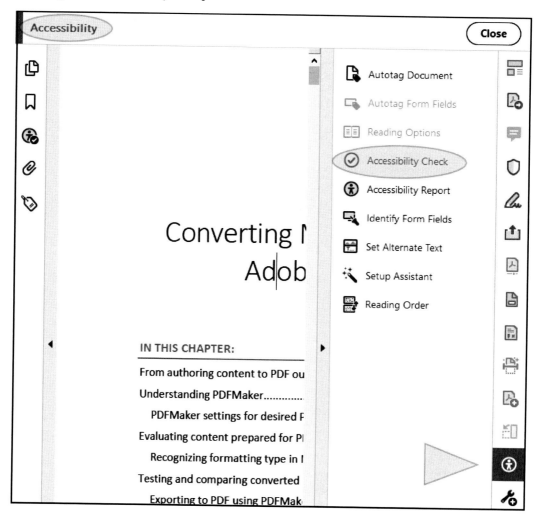

Figure 4.25 – PDF Accessibility tool panel and options

3. Click **Accessibility Check** and run the report without any changes to settings. Click **OK** to close the dialog box. The report about the document will appear in a pane on the left:

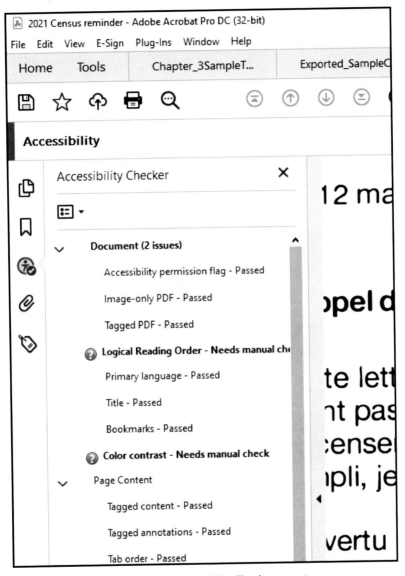

Figure 4.26 – Accessibility Checker report

4. One last check for accessibility in our example is in the document metadata. Click the **File |**
Properties... options and select the **Description** tab. The lower left area displays **Tagged PDF:**
Yes, which confirms that the document has accessibility tags:

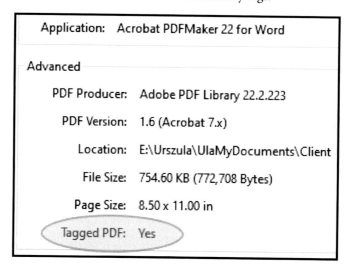

Figure 4.27 – File properties with metadata confirming a tagged PDF

We have explored tools that assist in evaluating the level of accessibility in a `.pdf` document. You
have learned what tags are and the reason why they need to be included in a document.

Summary

In this chapter, we learned about many tools that Acrobat offers allowing us to fix and update content
in a PDF publication. We added and organized pages, created new sections, and updated page labels
in the **Pages** pane. We corrected and added page numbers on the document pages.

We learned how to edit images or add new ones. We created new bookmarks and links. We also
unified a publication created from different sources by applying a footer. Finally, we reviewed features
in Acrobat that help to ensure that a `.pdf` file complies with accessibility standards.

In the next chapter, we will expand our discussion on accessibility. We will go through the entire process
of remediating a `.pdf` file so that the result will meet the high standards of Section 508 compliance.

5

Remediation for Accessibility in PDF Publications

This chapter will provide an overview and the steps needed to make PDF publications accessible. International standards define the purpose and legal requirements for the information presented online to address the unique needs of readers with visual, hearing, and motor skill impairments. Part of the solution is specialized software and devices to convert visual information to synthesized speech, or an alternative format that is perceivable to those readers. It all starts with PDF accessibility tags.

You will learn what accessibility is, how to include accessibility features when authoring a publication, and how to test and remediate it if needed. The following topics will be considered in this chapter:

- What is accessibility in a PDF publication?
- The principles of building an accessible document during the authoring stages
- Understanding the **Tags** pane and tags
- Working with accessibility tools

The next section will focus on understanding why we need accessibility in PDFs and what public guidelines or laws digital publications must comply with.

What is accessibility in a PDF publication?

Federal agencies, private businesses, and public bodies have become almost entirely reliant on information provided in an electronic format in day-to-day operations. We have embraced technology at work and in our personal life. Consider how we use it every day. Could you do your job, regardless of what it is, without the computer, the telephone, the tablet, the printer, or the fax machine?

Information distributed for viewing on the screen must be made available in formats that provide equal access to persons with disabilities. To address these needs, global standards have been developed and adopted. There are two main organizations that develop recommendations, publish guidelines, and promote accessibility globally:

- The **World Wide Web Consortium** (**W3C**) initiative **WAI** (short for, **Web Accessibility Initiative**) published *Web Content Accessibility Guidelines (WCAG)* that developers can refer to when writing software that will comply with accessibility for the web.

- The **International Organization for Standardization**) (**ISO**) published *ISO 14289 specification for PDF/UA (PDF/Universal Accessibility)*. The standard specifies features that a .pdf document must have to ensure that assistive technologies can access and convey its content and meaning to impaired readers.

The guidelines provided by these organizations are incorporated into regional standards and legal requirements.

In the USA, all **Electronic and Information Technology** (**EIT**) that is developed, procured, maintained, or used by the federal government must be accessible, as required by **Section 508 of the Rehabilitation Act of 1973**. Other countries also have laws and guidelines for accessibility. For expanded information on how accessibility is implemented legally in many countries see *Chapter 13, Acrobat Pro Tools, Shortcuts, References, and Mac Notes*.

> **Important note**
>
> If a person with a disability discovers that a federal agency has failed to comply with Section 508, they can file an administrative complaint or a civil lawsuit.

Disability overview in the United States

There is growing awareness of the need for accessible design. As people are living longer, the population ages, and many people deal with temporary disabilities due to accidents or illness, with the number continuing to grow. It is easy to understand why accessibility is an important issue.

As of 2020, an estimated 61 million, or 26% of adults in the United States, live with a disability that affects their ability to perceive and provide information. Considering the number of affected readers and the range of their needs, addressing them benefits everyone.

In general, it is expected that digitally distributed information should be equally available to everyone, including those with these disabilities:

- **Visual impairments**, such as blindness, low vision, and color blindness

- **Hearing disabilities** with different degrees and categories of hearing loss

- **Motor skill impairments**, such as paralyzed or limited use of hands

Section 508 addresses compliance with all methods and devices that are part of information technology. This includes websites, telephones, ATM kiosks, printers, fax machines, and so on. Our discussion narrows the focus to publications that are distributed electronically as PDFs. This applies to both documents available on the web, and internal networks of government or public organizations.

It is helpful to understand how disabled readers use different tools to access information online. We will explore this topic next.

Accessing online content by people affected by disability

To address the unique needs of readers with impairments, both software and hardware tools are produced that work as add-ons to user computers. Here are some of them, both software and hardware-based:

- **Screen readers**: People affected by blindness can listen to online content. Software programs called screen readers convert text and other information into synthesized speech. Common screen readers include **JAWS**, **NVDA**, and **VoiceOver**. Screen readers also allow users to navigate through content in many ways. Here are some functions beyond simply reading text:

  - Users can let the screen reader read everything from top to bottom, one line at a time, or press the *Tab* key to navigate through links and form fields.

  - They can also navigate via headings, from one region to the next, by bookmarks or other methods.

  - Smartphones and tablets come with built-in screen readers that allow touch or swipe gestures to navigate through content.

  Screen readers cannot extract the meaning of images. That is why **alternative text** (the `alt` tag) must be provided. Similarly, a sighted user can scan a page and quickly determine how it is organized and differentiate content based on visual design. A screen reader can't do this. However, pages that are structured properly and include proper code, (`H1`, `H2`, `H3`, and so on tags) make it possible for a user of screen reader devices to have an equivalent experience.

- **Dictation**: Navigation, typing, and other interaction with online content are possible through the use of speech recognition software.

- **Specialized keyboard**: Screen reader users do not use a mouse. Instead, they typically use a keyboard as the primary means of navigating the web. Functionality in a publication that only works when using a mouse or touchpad/touchscreen makes it inaccessible. This issue doesn't just affect screen reader users – some sighted users may only use a keyboard due to motor disabilities or other reasons.

- **Screen Braille Communicator** (**SBC**): Readers affected by the condition of being both deaf and blind depend on a specialized device that translates digital text into braille dots through tiny, raised dots on each key. Users place their hands on the device keyboard so that the text can be read with their fingers. When accessing web content, these Braille devices are used, allowing users to access text content, including alternative text for images.

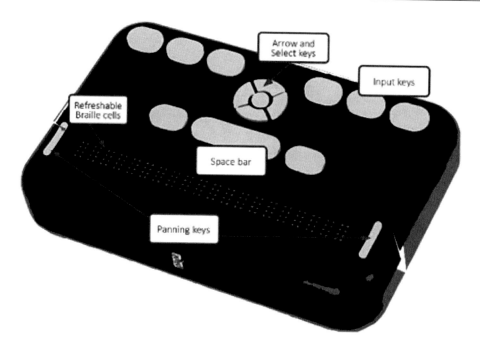

Figure 5.1 – A diagram of a Braille display reader

You may wonder now how we connect these devices with the work of authors and graphic designers. Having a bit of insight helps us to write and design publications in a way that makes them more accessible. In the next section, we will discuss some principles that should be followed when designing a publication, long before it becomes a PDF.

Principles of building accessible documents

As we discussed in previous chapters, a PDF document is the final product of work done in other applications where both text and images are placed and organized on pages. Here are some guidelines for authors to consider:

Principle	Reason
Provide equivalent alternative text	Alternative text (`alt` text) provides a description of non-text content. It is especially helpful for people who are blind and rely on a screen reader to have the content of images read to them.
Charts and diagrams should include expanded text	The expanded description should convey the meaning of data presented in a chart or a diagram. For a very long description, a link can be provided to a different area of the publication with expanded text.

Create a logical document structure	Document structure in .pdf pages is built using tags for headings, lists, and other elements. Keyboard navigation also depends on the document structure.
Provide headers for data tables	To make data tables accessible, row and column header cells need to be properly tagged. (`<th scope="row">` and `<th scope="col">`) make it possible to identify the meaning of corresponding data cells (`<td>`), allowing screen reader users to understand and navigate a table. Longer tables should have `Summary`.
Ensure users can complete and submit all forms	Every form element (text field, checkbox, dropdown list, and so on) needs an associated label and description. Users must be able to submit the form and recover from errors.
Write links that make sense out of context	Every link should make sense when read by itself. Phrases such as *click here* must be avoided.
Ensure the accessibility of PDF, Word, and PowerPoint	PDF documents and other non-HTML content must be as accessible as possible. If you cannot make it accessible, consider using HTML instead or provide an accessible alternative. Reference to a publication printed on paper may be necessary.
Allow users to skip repetitive elements on the page	Each page should provide a method to skip navigation or other elements that repeat on every page. Headers and footers on printed pages, used by sighted readers, should be tagged as background to avoid needless repetition in the document structure.
Do not rely on color alone to convey meaning	Although color is an important aspect of page design, it should not be used alone to convey meaning. People affected by different types of color blindness will have difficulty perceiving information. For example, well-designed train maps or charts will incorporate patterns in addition to color.
Make sure the content is clearly written and easy to read	Write clearly, use clear fonts, and use headings and lists logically. Simplify, simplify, and simplify again.

Table 5.1 – Guidelines to consider

Obviously, each publication needs to meet the needs of its intended audience. The principles listed here can be implemented without compromising the overall purpose, look, and feel of a document. In fact, if followed, they will improve the quality of all published materials.

In the next section, we will briefly review the tools that MS Word, a common authoring software, provides to implement the principles listed previously.

MS Word authoring for accessibility

Accessible design demands an understanding of how content, layout, and formatting work together to minimize remediation in Acrobat. Here is a brief review of MS Word tools. You will also find a more detailed discussion on authoring for accessibility in InDesign in *Chapter 10, Integration with Adobe InDesign*.

The accessibility-aware process needs to start at the very beginning of editing, as it affects both the editorial and formatting aspects of a document. In addition to incorporating the principles of building accessible documents discussed earlier, here is a formatting checklist to follow:

- Use paragraph styles, especially for headings. When properly set up, they will export proper-level heading tags, such as `<H1>`, `<H2>`, and `<H3>`.

- Use proper lists, both bulleted and numbered, for a complete proper structure of tags such as `<L>`, `<LI>`, `<Lbl>`, and `<LBody>`.

- Use a generated table of contents and index (rather than typing them manually) for automatically created `<TOC>` and `<Index>` sets of tags in a structure and automatically tagged links.

- Add alternative text tags and identify document language during authoring, rather than in Acrobat as a remediation step.

- Use tables for data only; do not use them for layout. Avoid merged cells. Complex tables can be simplified by breaking them into multiple simple tables with a heading above each. The proper nesting of table tags is `<Table>`, `<TR>`, `<TH>`, and `<TD>`. The `<THead>`, `<TBody>`, and `<TFoot>` tags are optional but must be child elements of the `<Table>` tag. Tables must have headers.

- Enter values in MS Word document properties, especially `Title` metadata.

- Use PDFMaker to preserve accessibility on export to `.pdf`.

Following these guidelines will result in an accessible final document with minimal or no need for remediation in Acrobat.

Now, we will step through the tools available in Acrobat that help to ensure that a publication complies with accessibility standards.

Understanding the Tags pane and tags

Accessibility in PDFs begins with tags. Since PDF document pages were initially just **PostScript** files meant for viewing on a screen as read-only content, it was necessary to come up with a method to describe each portion of a page's relevant information in both text and images and to build a logical structure for an entire publication, so that text-based screen readers could use it when converting code to synthesized speech.

Tags in PDFs look similar, and some may have the same meaning as HTML tags, but they should not be confused as being the same. Unlike HTML tags that mark up and organize countless lines of text that are eventually interpreted, formatted, and displayed on a screen by a browser, PDF accessibility tags do not control the appearance of a document. They simply describe the type of content on a page.

While the tagging order in HTML is also used to order the tagged content in the browser this is not the case in PDF. In PDF, the order in which the content is positioned in the page layout is independent of the tagging structure. In other words, the tagging structure in PDF is invisible only when a page is displayed; additional tools are needed to visualize it. In *Chapter 13, Acrobat Pro Tools, Shortcuts, References, and Mac Notes,* you will find a complete list of **PDF tags** and their meaning.

Several issues need to be resolved for a document to become accessible. Here are some that we will discuss next:

- Without tags, a document is not accessible. Tags need to be added to a document if they are not included.

- A document may have some tags, but not all content on a page is included or structured correctly in the tagging structure.

- Tags may not be consistently and properly used. For example, text in headings may be tagged as paragraphs or headings that do not follow proper nesting.

- Tags in document structure may need to be reorganized to simulate the logical reading experience of a sighted user, especially when the page layout includes columns, independent sidebars, or articles. For example, a footnote in the tagging structure should be positioned within a paragraph element, rather than after the last paragraph of text on a physical page.

Let's now get familiar with tags, the **Tags** pane, and its options.

Working with the Tags pane

The **Tags** pane contains tags, containers with text or graphic content, and/or alternative text descriptions. When a tag is selected, the corresponding content on a page is highlighted, as shown in the screenshot in *Figure 5.2.* Note the <P> tag selected in the **Tags** pane, highlighted in blue, and the corresponding paragraph of text on the page that is highlighted by a purple rectangle. As you click on each tag, a different area of the page will be highlighted similarly:

- The <P> tag contains a container with text that screen reader software and devices access and convert to synthesized speech.

- The <Figure> tag contains a container with an image displaying dimensions.

- As you scroll through the example file, you can see a <L> tag, a <H1> tag, and many <P> tags. Clicking any of them finds corresponding content on a page and highlights it:

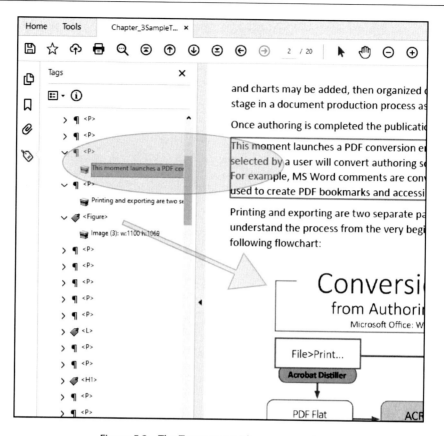

Figure 5.2 – The Tags pane with some open tags

As you can see, this document has different tags organized in a logical structure, and a device using it reads the content to a physically impaired user – simple enough. However, our world is about to become much more complicated. We will remediate documents that have problems. We will fix a PDF that has no tags at all.

Adding tags to an untagged document

There are two main reasons why a PDF file may not have any accessibility tags:

- It was **created from a scan**, a process we discussed in *Chapter 2, Creating and Enhancing PDF Files from Scans*, and tags must be added in Acrobat.

- It was **printed to PDF**, a process we discussed in *Chapter 3, Converting Microsoft Office Files to Adobe PDF Using PDFMaker*, resulting in a flat PDF. Again, tags must be added in Acrobat if the source document is not available.

We will now work with an example file created from a scan, where the OCR process added searchable text to the document, allowing us to complete the process of making the document accessible.

Important note

Remediation of `.pdf` documents created from scans presents a particular challenge, as there are many methods for adding tags, including third-party software. A choice in this chapter is to use the **Tags** pane menu options, as they automate the entire process using Acrobat Pro exclusively. The results of this function in the same document almost always vary from one computer system to another. Steps listed as examples simply reflect the process in general, as recorded using a specific file.

Another method for tagging a document is using the **Reading Order** tool. One tag at a time is added by click-dragging the tool over content in the page layout.

You, as the reader, may see different tags on your system than those in screenshots, but it is the meaning of each tag that matters and needs to be conveyed accurately. Examples will show the overall process.

We will start by adding tags. Here are the steps:

1. Open a file that was enhanced, using the process discussed in *Chapter 2, Creating and Enhancing PDF Files from Scans*. Adding accessibility tags must happen *after* OCR recognized text on a page.

2. Open the **Tags** pane, which will display the **No Tags available** alert, as shown in the screenshot:

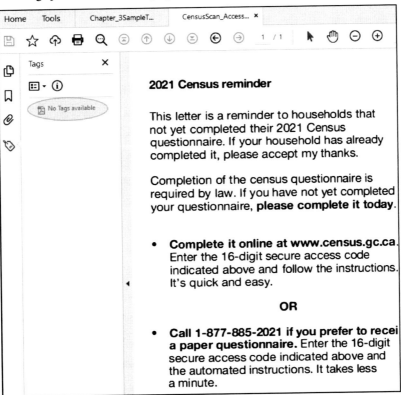

Figure 5.3 – The Tags pane in a document with no tags

3. Select the **Tags** pane menu options and click on **Add Tags to Document**:

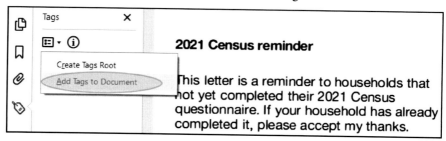

Figure 5.4 – The Tags pane options allowing you to add tags

4. A report appears in the pane. It explains the assumptions made by Acrobat when tagging the page content. Extensive hints help authors new to the process of adding tags.

5. Click on the **Tags** pane to see all the tags added to the document:

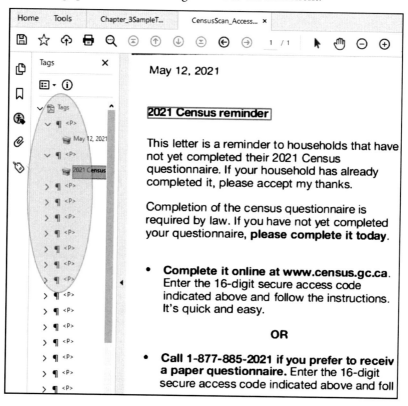

Figure 5.5 – New tags added to the document

As you scroll through the pane, you will see that Acrobat recognized all text as body paragraphs and tagged it with <P> tags. Next, we will refine the tags assigned by Acrobat.

Tip

To open all the tags in the **Tags** pane, hold *Ctrl* or *Option* on the macOS keyboard while clicking on the bracket. All the tags will open, revealing all the details of the document structure.

To change a tag, you can simply click on it twice, and when the tag name is editable, type a new name inside the brackets.

Other ways to rename a tag are to *select a tag | right click | Properties | type or select a tag from dropdown*, or *select a tag | click pane menu options | Properties | type or select a tag from dropdown*.

To add a new tag to the structure, select the **Tags** pane menu and click on **New Tag…**, or right-click on a tag, and from the menu, select **New Tag….**

Use *Adobe Acrobat Predefined PDF Accessibility Tags* in *Chapter 13, Acrobat Pro Tools, Shortcuts, References, and Mac Notes*, as a reference for a complete list of accessibility tags and their meaning.

Editing and moving tag

Formatting of text in a document suggests its tag, but Acrobat does not always recognize the content accurately. This is when the **remediation** process begins. A human reader must convey the meaning of text on a page, relying on the meaning of a tag. This is always done manually, as it is a somewhat editorial process. Here are the steps:

1. Click on a small bracket to the left of the first tag to reveal its content:

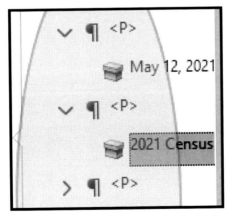

Figure 5.6 – Open tags revealing their content

2. Since this is the title of the document, the second <P> tag should be changed to <H1>.

3. Slowly click twice on the <P> tag that contains the **2021 Census reminder** text, and when the tag is editable, change it to <H1>.

4. Click on another tag to accept the change.

This was a simple change. We will now expand on the process of building a proper structure in a document. Bulleted and numbered lists are often poorly tagged during remediation. We will address that and go through the steps to fix our bulleted list structure, which is missing a few tags.

The content of two paragraphs on a page (see *Figure 5.4*) indicates that they should be tagged as a bulleted list, rather than body paragraphs. We will change the tags and build the correct structure for this portion of the text:

5. Proper nesting of content in a list requires the following order of tags:

    I.   `<L>`

    II.   `<LI>`

    III. `<Lbl>`

    IV.   `<LBody>`

    Here is the meaning of these tags: `<L>` is a list, `<LI>` is a list item, `<Lbl>` and `<Lbody>` are subelements to `<LI>`, where `<Lbl>` stands for a label and can be a number, bullet, letter, and so on, and `<Lbody>` stands for the list item body and contains the information about the list item.

6. Slowly click twice on the `<P>` tag that contains bulleted text and change it to `<L>`.

7. Right-click on the container and select **New Tag…** from the menu. A dialog box with options appears. Select **List Item**, as shown in this screenshot:

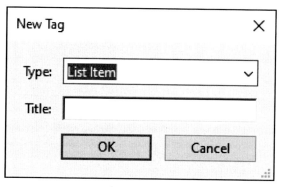

Figure 5.7 – The New Tag dialog box

If tags automatically close, just open them again by clicking on the brackets.

8. The new tag is empty and needs to be positioned properly. *Any tag will be moved into the desired position the same way.* Click, drag, and nest it below the `<L>` tag, as shown in this screenshot:

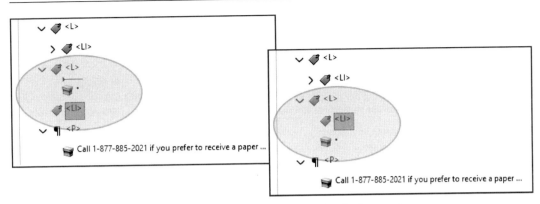

Figure 5.8 – Moving a tag to a new position in the structure

9. Now, you need to create a `<Lbl>` tag. Right-click on the container with a bullet again and select **New Tag…** from the menu. Select **Label** from the dialog box.

10. Move and nest the `<Lbl>` tag under the `<LI>` tag.

11. Move and nest the container with a bullet under the `<Lbl>` tag.

12. The `<P>` tag that follows should be changed to `<LBody>`, since the text in it is the content of the bullet. Slowly click twice the `<P>` tag and change it to `<LBody>`.

13. Nest the `<LBody>` tag under the `<LI>` tag but below the `<Lbl>` tag. It is easier to move our tags when they are closed by clicking the structure brackets first. You should have a final structure that looks like this:

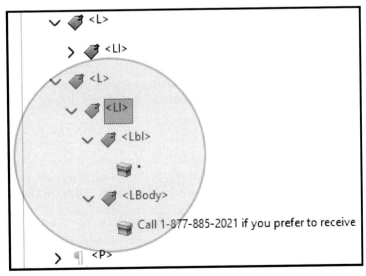

Figure 5.9 – Tags in a proper structure for a list

106 Remediation for Accessibility in PDF Publications

> **Tip**
>
> In programming, references to the position of elements in a document structure are taken from family relationships. A tag that contains another tag is its parent, making the nested tag a child. Two or more nested tags under the same parent are called siblings. Moving tags to a specific level in a structure defines the parent, child, or sibling relationship. Tags containing multiple levels of nested tags become ancestors to descendant tags. Tags always nest containers with text or graphics.
>
> The *UNDO* or *Ctrl/Command* + *Z* function works only in newer versions of Acrobat. When you work with the **Tags** pane, proceed cautiously, and save your file often. If something happens that makes it hard to recover (for example, you lose lots of tags), select the **File | Revert** options. The most recently saved version will allow you to start again.

Was that tedious? Well, only the first 100 times. Once you get some practice, it is not that bad. Please do not forget that remediation is repair, so we are *repairing* a document. You were prepared for this, weren't you? Renovations are for the brave.

The process of adding, editing, or moving tags is the same for any tag. You may want to practice the steps in our example a few times, and the process will then become more obvious. As you move the tags, watch the highlighted area on the body page.

Here is how you can do it:

- To test the logical order of the structure, select a tag and tap on the *Up* or *Down* arrow keys of the keyboard. This will simulate how screen reader software moves through page content.
- If highlights on a page appear randomly rather than progressively, as you move through tags in the structure, you may need to adjust their order.
- Simply repeat the process of changing the position of tags, as we did in our exercise, and then test the logical order again.
- If you have enough tags but they do not accurately reflect the type of content, you can simply change their name by typing rather than using the **New Tag…** options.

We will now retag some content that will leave us with empty tags that need to be deleted.

Deleting empty tags

Take a closer look at the screenshot in *Figure 5.10* that shows a `<L>` tag selected, but only one line of the list paragraph is highlighted. The `<P>` tags under the `<L>` tag are lines in a single paragraph. We will move the containers with each line of text to nest them properly in the `<LBody>` tag. They need to be positioned so that the text can be read progressively line by line.

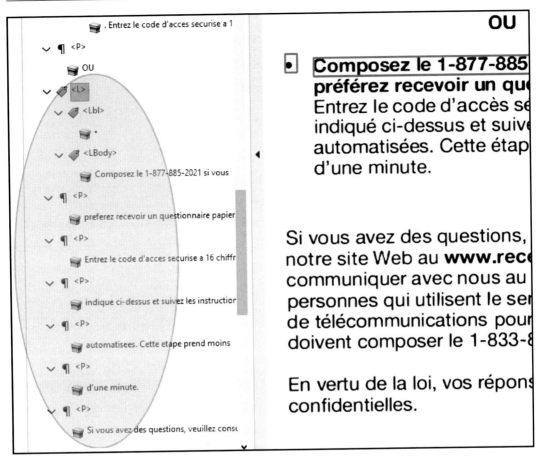

Figure 5.10 – Tags that do not reflect the content correctly

1. Click and drag a container (not the `<P>` tag) with the text **preferez recevoir un questionnaire** and position it under the container with the text **Composez le 1-877-885-2021**.

    The `<P>` tag is now empty, and it does not have a bracket on the left that would indicate more content. Change it to a `<LI>` tag that needs to contain both the `<Lbl>` and `<LBody>` tags.

2. Move and nest the `<LI>` tag under the `<L>` tag.

3. Move and nest the sibling `<Lbl>` and `<LBody>` tags under the `<LI>` tag.

4. Repeat *step 1* by clicking and dragging the containers with text and placing them under other containers nested in the `<LBody>` tag.

5. Do this until all the text of the bulleted paragraph is highlighted when you click on the `<LI>` tag. Compare the following screenshot:

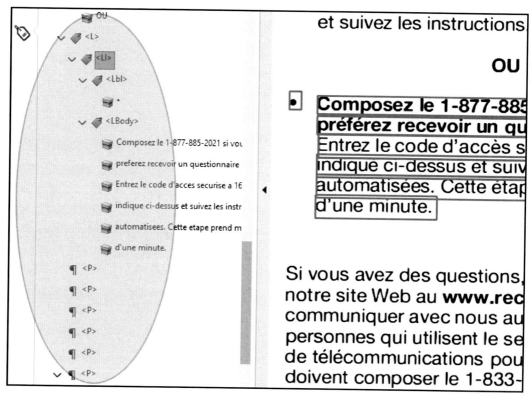

Figure 5.11 – Content moved to a proper tag, leaving some empty tags

6. You can see that we are now on the left with many empty `<P>` tags. They need to be deleted.

7. Select the tags (you can hold the *Shift* key to select many) and tap the *Delete* key on the keyboard. If you have many empty tags and are confident that they are no longer needed, you can also use the **Tags** pane menu and select the **Options | Delete Empty Tags** options.

8. Save the file.

The next section will address tagging content that should not be part of a structure, such as decorative graphics and background.

Artifact or background content

When a PDF document is designed with accessibility in mind and exported to .pdf correctly, all navigational and decorative elements of a printed page are tagged as background automatically. Logos, design elements such as borders or boxes, or lines contained in a footer or a header will not enter a document structure.

However, we are stepping through a remediation process, and Acrobat cannot tell the difference between meaningful information on a page, a background, or decoration. This is when a human author or editor needs to assign a proper tag. We will work on such an example next:

1. Our file was sourced from a scan, and a meaningless scribble was tagged as `<H1>`, as shown in the following screenshot:

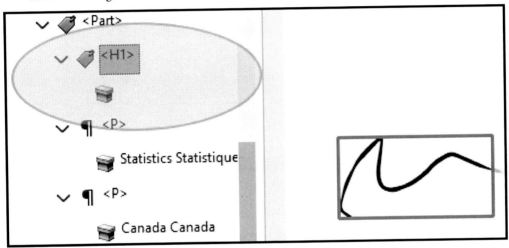

Figure 5.12 – Content with no meaning is tagged as a heading

2. We will change the tag to a background or artifact (both terms mean exactly the same in Acrobat). Select the container under the `<H1>` tag and right-click to open the menu. See the following screenshot:

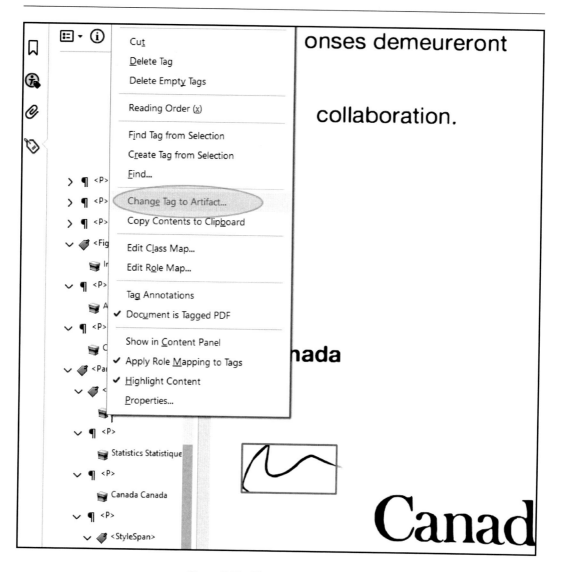

Figure 5.13 – The tag context menu

3. Click on **Change Tag to Artifact…**, which opens a small dialog box, as shown in the following screenshot:

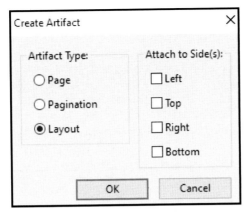

Figure 5.14 – The Create Artifact dialog box

4.   Select **Layout** and click **OK** to close the dialog box.

> **Tip**
> **Page** artifacts are print production aids placed outside a document page, such as cut marks and color bars.
>
> **Pagination** artifacts are page features, such as running heads, page numbers, or Bates numbering.
>
> **Layout** artifacts are purely cosmetic typographical or design elements, such as footnote rules or decorative ornaments.

5.   The page highlight on the scribble disappeared and the `<H1>` tag is now empty. Select and delete it by tapping on the *Delete* key. We conveyed to Acrobat that this was not information, so it will not make the screen reader app look for the heading. Computers are only as smart as we tell them, aren't they?

Great job! You just stepped through an advanced process of adjusting the logical order of tags in a document structure. Keep in mind that if you delete a tag that is not empty, your document will fail the accessibility check by flagging untagged content on a page.

We have worked with tags that give meaning to text, but what makes screen readers stumble the most is the image content. Images must be described, and we will do that next by adding an **alternative text description** to an image already tagged as `<Figure>`.

Adding alternative text to a figure

Our page contains a signature, but it is just a scan, so Acrobat assigned it a `<Figure>` tag, as shown in the following screenshot:

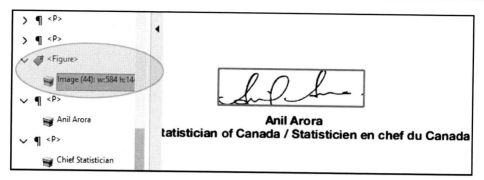

Figure 5.15 – The <Figure> tag in a structure

We will add a text description of the signature image so that a screen reader can identify the content to an impaired user:

6.   Select the Image container (not the <Figure> tag) and right-click to open the menu.

7.   Click to select **Properties…**, which opens a dialog box with the **Alternate Text:** field, where you can type the description of the image content:

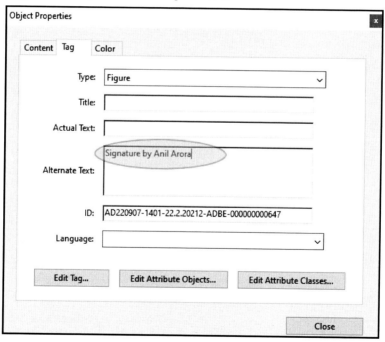

Figure 5.16 – Adding an alternate text description in the Object Properties dialog box

8.   Type Signature by Anil Arora and click **Close** to accept the change.

Selecting an image tag and adding an alternative text description is one of a few methods. If there are many images that need descriptions, you can use the **Set Alternate Text** function or the **Reading Order** tool, both available in the **Accessibility** tool panel. Just a reminder again, *do* save your file often. The **Undo** function when you work with the **Tags** pane is not available in older versions of Acrobat.

To complete the structure and tags in this example, add a few more tags as needed. When completed, we will specify the properties of a group of tags. The process is described in the next section.

Grouping tags

Usually, document language is set for an entire file in **File Properties…**. However, some documents may contain multiple languages, and a screen reader needs to have this information to read the content correctly. A few tags are available to group content, such as the following:

- **Division element** (`<Div>`): A basic block-level element or a group of block-level elements
- **Section element** (`<Sect>`): A general container, such as Division
- **Article element** (`<Art>`): A continuous body of text, such as an article
- **Part element** (`<Part>`): A part element splits a large document into smaller parts; it can also group smaller parts together, such as article, division, or section elements

A detailed explanation of the meaning of all PDF tags is in *Chapter 13, Final Overview of Acrobat Pro Techniques, Shortcuts, and Online User Support*.

Our document is in two languages, so we will add two `<Art>` tags that will allow us to set the language of the text in the left column to **English** and the text in the right column to **French**. Here are the steps:

1. Select the top `<P>` tag in the structure, right-click, select **NEW Tag…**, and then choose **Article** from the options.
2. Nest `<Art>` under the `<Tags>` tag.
3. Select all tags containing English text in the left column (click on the first `<P>` tag in the structure, hold the *Shift* key, and then click on the last `<P>` tag that includes text in the left column).
4. In one step, click and move the tags to nest them under the `<Art>` tag.
5. Click the `<Art>` tag again to select it, then right-click to open the menu, and choose **Properties…**.
6. Select **English** from the **Language:** options, and then click **Close** to update the tag.
7. Repeat *steps 1–6* with tags containing French text in the right column, and select **French** as a language.
8. Save the file.

We will now explore more methods and tools to make a PDF accessible.

Working with accessibility tools

We have learned how to modify tags, add alternative text to figures, and edit a document structure using the **Tags** pane and its options. To help us evaluate the level of compliance with accessibility standards, Acrobat provides additional tools. They include the following:

- **Accessibility Check**, formerly the **Full Check** tool (the name was changed in the May 2022 version). The

- The **Reading Order** tool (the **Touch Up Reading Order** (**TURO**) tool in older versions of Acrobat) allows us to add tags to page content that is not tagged. It also gives us access to the **Table Editor**.

- **Making PDFs accessible** is an action that guides you through some basic options with instructions. The process automates some tasks and provides shortcuts to relevant accessibility settings in a document. It can be found in the **Action** wizard tool.

- The **Set Alternate Text** function finds all figures and displays alternative text. It also allows us to convert a figure to an artifact/background.

Accessibility Checker

The **Accessibility Checker** is a starting point for evaluating potential problems with document accessibility that need to be addressed. It is very detailed but relatively easy to understand. In this section, we will use it but not go into too much detail.

The following steps show how an accessibility report is created:

1. Select **Accessibility Check** from the **Accessibility** tools column on the right.

2. The **Checker Options** dialog box opens. If this is the first time you are seeing it, take time to review the details. If your settings are set at default (most options are checked), click **Start Checking**.

3. A detailed report is displayed in the pane on the left. Our example file needs quite a few fixes, and they are flagged as **Failed**, as shown in the following screenshot:

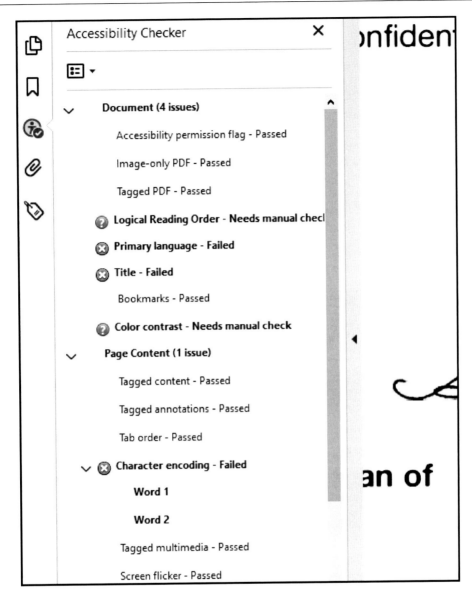

Figure 5.17 – The Accessibility Checker report showing issues to fix

Acrobat provides two methods to fix the problems:

- Right-clicking on each flagged entry and choosing **Fix** gives access to choices or fields to fill in with information. You will also see in this menu an **Explain** option that launches a browser and opens the online help where the error is described.

- Working with **Document Properties**, which allows more thorough edits.

We will use **Document Properties**, which allows us to evaluate all the relevant fields, including those that may need to be corrected or were missed. The following steps will take you through tabs related to accessibility settings that need to be changed:

1. Select the **File** | **Properties** options from the menu to open the **Document Properties** dialog box.

2. Click the **Description** tab to open it:

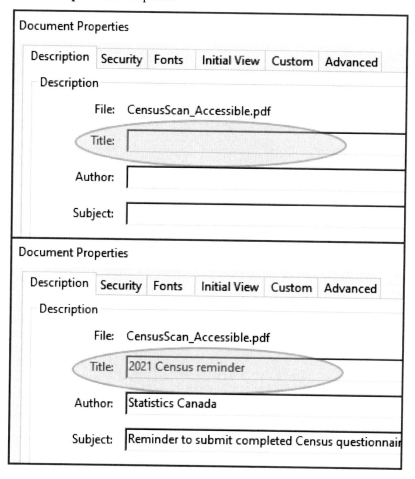

Figure 5.18 – The document Title field

Screen readers use text in the **Document Title** field to identify publication content. When this field is left empty, a filename is read by the screen reader, making it hard for a user to identify the publication content. **Author**, **Subject**, and additional metadata should also be filled in, although the Acrobat accessibility checker does not flag these when blank.

3. Next, select the **Initial View** tab to open it:

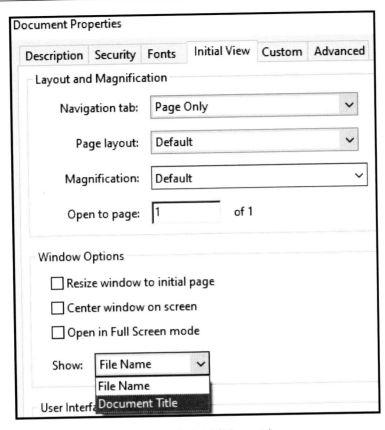

Figure 5.19 – The Initial View settings

4. Select **Document Title** from the dropdown in the **Window Options** group of settings. This will ensure that a screen reader uses the text that we typed in the **Document Title** field of the **Description** tab. The setting will also display the same title in the application title bar, as seen in the following screenshot. Interesting, right?

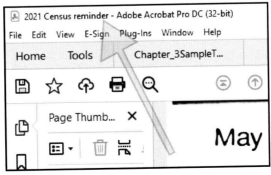

Figure 5.20 – The Initial View settings results – the document title displayed in the application title bar

5.   Finally, we will set the **Language** field. Select the **Advanced** tab to open it, and select **English**
from the **Reading Options** group of settings. Setting a language this way ensures that the entire
document is read in English by a connected device.

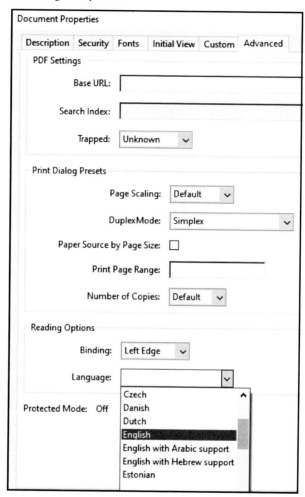

Figure 5.21 – Advanced settings – choosing a document language

We have addressed some of the issues flagged by **Accessibility Checker**. We will now run it again
and compare the results:

1.   Select **Accessibility Check** from the **Accessibility** tools column on the right again.

2.   The **Checker Options** dialog box opens. Click **Start Checking**. A detailed report displayed in
the pane on the left shows different results. Compare it with *Figure 5.17*. You can see that the
flagged issues were fixed.

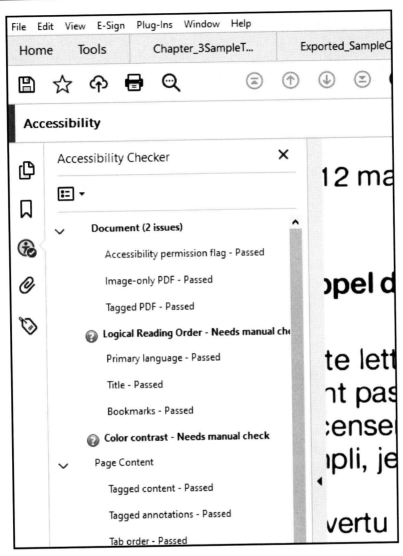

Figure 5.22 – The Accessibility Checker report showing the resolved issues

All items marked here as **Passed** meet the Section 508 accessibility standards. The **Logical Reading Order** alert reminds an author that the document structure and tags need to be checked by a human editor, so that they truly reflect the type of content on a page and convey the progression of the information correctly.

Next, we will work with another Acrobat tool that helps to fix accessibility issues, **Reading Order**, also known in earlier versions as the **TURO** tool.

The Reading Order tool

The Reading Order tool allows you to see the flow of content on a page, rather than the structure in the **Tags** pane, and perform many functions related to tagging content on pages. You can do the following:

- See the way text flows if it is read using the **View | Read Mode** options

- Tag content on a page

- Edit tables using the **Table Editor**

- Quickly identify figures with missing alternative text and either add a description or change the tag to **Background/Artifact**

We will explore the **Reading Order** tool panel. Options become active only after content on a page is selected. Here are the steps:

1. Select **Reading Order** from the **Accessibility** tools column on the right.

2. **Reading Order** opens with all buttons grayed out and inactive.

3. Click and drag over page text or a graphic, as instructed at the top of the tool. Here is a screenshot of the result after selection:

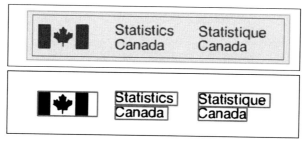

Figure 5.23 – Page content selected with the Reading Order (formerly TURO) tool

4. The selected page content is highlighted in purple and can be assigned a tag using the buttons that become active:

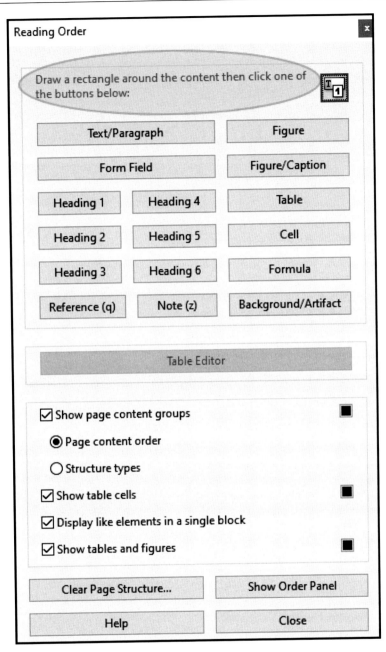

Figure 5.24 – The Reading Order tool with active options

5. Click **Background/Artifact**, assuming that the type of content in our example can be considered as visual branding and is not conveying meaningful information.

> **Important note**
>
> The **Reading Order** tool is not meant for screen readers. It is an author's or designer's tool to quickly find problems with missing descriptions or untagged page content. Screen readers depend on tags and structure. Adjusting the logical reading order of a document using this tool can lead to you potentially losing existing tags.
>
> The numbers appearing on shadowed frames when the tool is active are hints only. If text or graphics conveying information on pages are not shadowed by any frames at all, confirm in the **Tags** structure that the tags are missing. Use the **Reading Order** tool only to add tags to untagged content, and be sure to monitor the **Tags** pane for the position of all tags in the structure. Is this complicated? Yes, a little bit…

As you can see, accessibility tools in Acrobat are used for many reasons. Documents that require remediation also vary greatly. It takes some practice to feel comfortable with the process.

You have learned how to remediate a document. Now, here are the steps necessary to make a scanned document accessible:

1. Enhance pages using the **Scan & OCR** tool.
2. Recognize text with OCR.
3. Add accessibility tags using the **Tags** pane options.
4. Refine the document structure by changing tags from body text to headings.
5. Tag background images, scribbles, and navigational elements as **artifacts**.
6. Add alternative text to images that convey information.
7. Run **Accessibility Checker** to confirm that all necessary elements and settings are included (title, language, and so on) and fix errors.

Once all these tasks are completed, you can have the satisfaction that a person who cannot see the text of a publication on a screen can perceive and interact with it using devices they are familiar with. This is possible only because you took the time to remediate a file and make it accessible. Good job! You just changed someone's world for the better.

Summary

In this chapter, we learned what PDF accessibility and the Section 508 guidelines binding in the USA are. We reviewed what accessibility compliance guidelines are from a legal perspective.

We learned about impairments that restrict access to electronic information and explored methods that affected readers use to access information. This helped us to understand how publications need to be designed and published so that the support devices that those readers depend on can extract meaningful content. The principles of accessible document design were reviewed, and we looked at methods used to implement them.

Finally, we learned how Acrobat assists in evaluating the level of compliance, such as Accessibility Checker, and how to use tools to repair a document in need of remediation.

In the next chapter, we will move on to another rich function of Acrobat – a document review cycle. In our interconnected world, physical notations are a major limitation to efficient communication, so I know you will enjoy using the tools we will explore, which I use daily.

6

Using Acrobat in a Document Review Process

You will now be introduced to possibilities consistent with the reality that the use of paper and ink in a business office should be in decline thanks to sufficient tools to convey information digitally. This includes editorial markup during the publishing workflow. Instead of a multitude of copies being printed on paper for each version review, Acrobat allows you to use specific commenting/markup tools and a document comparison feature to communicate needed edits.

Editors do not make changes to the `.pdf` file using Acrobat, but communicate ideas, provide feedback, or suggest changes to content created and edited in the authoring application.

We will take a close look at the commenting tools and types of reviews possible based on **Adobe Document Cloud**. In *Chapter 10, Integration with Adobe InDesign*, we will also explore **Creative Cloud**-based direct collaboration and review process options for graphic designers working with InDesign.

In this chapter, you will learn the purpose of different commenting and markup tools, how to customize them, and how to use them in editorial responses, which will enable you to choose the best process for editorial feedback. We will also cover how to include users of free Adobe Acrobat Reader in the review process.

While reading, you will assume different roles related to reviewing a document. You will use tools used by clients who request projects, authors, designers, reviewers, and editors. Roles will change, and to keep confusion at bay, I will attempt to clearly state who uses which tools and why. The content of the chapter can be divided into these segments:

- Overview of available comment and markup tools in the desktop version of Acrobat
- Exploring and understanding different PDF document review workflows
- Working with some comments and tools in specific scenarios in an email-based review
- Adding stamps

- Exploring a shared group review workflow
- Including Acrobat Reader users in a review process

To start, please examine the flowchart shown in *Figure 6.1*, which will give you a perspective on how you, the reader, will change roles while exploring the information contained in this chapter:

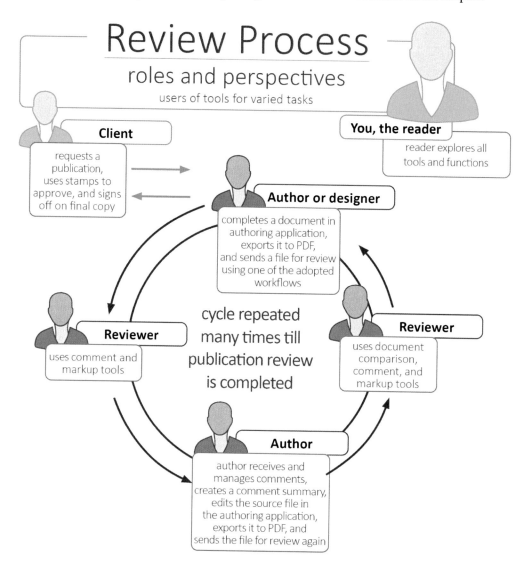

Figure 6.1 – Reader assuming many roles while exploring review functions

The next section will introduce commenting and markup tools.

Overview of comment and markup tools

The concept of markup or commenting comes from the world of editors, who review authors' or designers' work and mark corrections that need to be done in a document. It is a critical part of the publishing process and allows many experts to contribute to creating a high-quality final publication. Traditionally, the markup was done using red pencils and yellow (or another color) highlighters so that areas that needed attention were not missed. The marked-up copy was returned to an author who produced a new version of the publication after incorporating edit changes. The process could be repeated many times before the final content was ready for publishing.

How important is a review? If you watched *The Devil Wears Prada*, a 2006 comedy and now a classic, you get the idea. Instead of a thick book delivered in the middle of the night, though, we can use reviewing options available in Acrobat that will let you do everything without ever leaving your desk. Or a comfy armchair.

Let's look at the commenting tools contained in the **Comment** toolbar.

Comment tool in desktop Acrobat

The **Comment** panel on the right of the screen opens a toolbar at the top with a wide range of tools, many selected from a dropdown. We counted 21 of them. Some offer an **auto-edit** function, which means that when comments are imported and accepted in the original source document, updates are automatically merged with content, with no need for the author to copy and paste each editing change manually. Auto-edit that deletes, inserts, or replaces text significantly saves time, eliminates the potential for new typing errors, and works well in InDesign and FrameMaker.

Each document may have multiple reviewers. By default, the name you log in to the computer is used as the reviewer's identity. To allow different editors to use their names as temporary defaults, rather than changing each comment name as it is made, you need to adjust the application **Preferences** default settings. Here are the steps to allow changes to the reviewer's name in the document, rather than using a default login name:

1. Select from the top menu the **Edit | Preferences… | Commenting** options (**Acrobat Pro | Preferences | Commenting** on macOS).

2. In the **Making Comments** group, deselect the **Always use Log-in Name for Author name** checkbox. This setting will allow name changes to be applied to all commenting and review tools as needed.

3. Click **OK** to accept changes.

> **Important note**
> If your scenario does not require system sharing, you can skip adjusting **Preferences**.

Each commenting tool is highly customizable at any time during the review process. In the next section, we will review those options so that you can choose the ones that work best for you.

Click the **Comment** panel on the right area of the screen. A long toolbar containing over 20 tools will appear at the top of the screen. Quite arbitrarily, I split the toolbar into two screenshots to fit the page. Here are the text markup tools (*Figure 6.2*) and page markup tools (*Figure 6.3*):

Figure 6.2 – Text markup tools

The text markup tools, as seen in *Figure 6.2*, located on the left area of the **Comment** toolbar when you look at the monitor, are specifically designed to be used in text markup.

> **Important note**
> I often find that the text markup tools are underused by editors who default to using **Sticky notes**, meant for general comments. Hopefully learning how to use the text markup tools properly will change that.

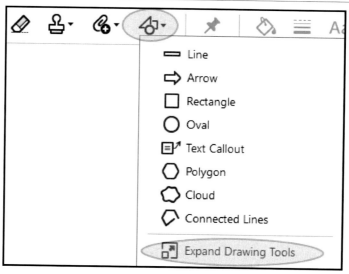

Figure 6.3 – Page markup tools with the Drawing Tools menu (expanded, tools will move to the toolbar)

The **Drawing** tools shown in *Figure 6.3*, located on the right of the tools in *Figure 6.2* in the **Comment** toolbar, are meant to be used for **Page Markup**. These tools should be used to mark images and layout, allowing you to add comments in a way that makes them stand out very clearly from the reviewed page.

Let's now take a closer look at each one of the tools, beginning with controlling how they behave. This is done by setting tool properties.

Setting properties for commenting tools can be done in many ways. Here is a list of possible methods for you to choose from:

- A floating **Properties** toolbar opens when you press *Ctrl + E/Command + E*. You can keep it open if you need to make frequent changes to your tool properties. The toolbar activates properties for each tool selected:

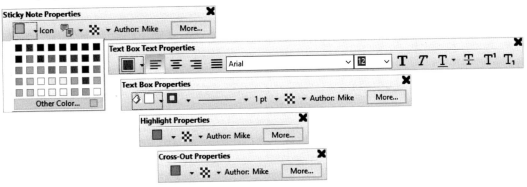

Figure 6.4 – Markup tools, properties toolbar variations

If you have enough space on your monitor or—even better—more than one monitor, using the preceding method to change tool settings is very efficient since the **Properties** toolbar stays open, allowing for a quick adjustment to an active tool.

- Another method is setting choices available in the **Properties** dialog box accessed from **context menus** selected while a tool is active. All tools can be customized following these steps:

  I.   Select a tool from the toolbar and use it in the document by clicking or click-dragging on the page area.

  II.   Right-click on the icon or marked area to open the context menu and select **Properties…**.

  III. In the dialog box that opens, select the **Appearance** tab, and configure the icon, color, opacity, line style, and so on. Options will vary depending on which tool was used:

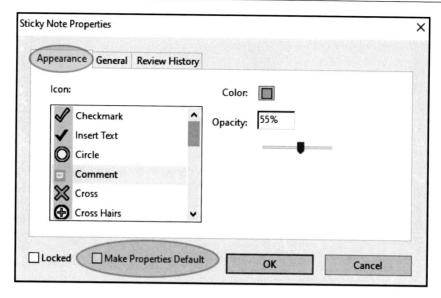

Figure 6.5 – Example: Tool properties dialog box

IV.   Click to select the **General** tab, and confirm or change the name in the **Author:** field if needed. The name change is possible only if allowed in Acrobat **Preferences**, as outlined earlier.

V.   For a one-time change, click **OK** to accept. If you want the new settings to be applied from now on, click the **Make Properties Default** checkbox field and then click **OK** to accept.

• Finally, one more method for setting properties and text formatting in comments is to use the **Comment text properties** toolbar, usually automatically activated after comment text is typed or selected. If it is not open, click the last icon on the right of the **Comment** toolbar:

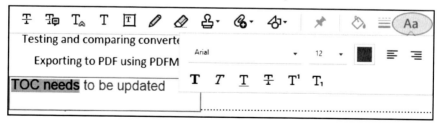

Figure 6.6 – Text properties toolbar for comment text formatting

We learned how to set tool properties, and now we will review the purpose of the most common tools.

Understanding text markup tools

Editorial markup falls into two main categories: text and page. Text markup tools work with text, where errors are marked for correction by the author. When selected, you can click-drag individual characters and entire paragraphs of text on a page, resulting in a unique styling for each type of edit. This is very intuitive and feels a lot like using a physical highlighter or a pen. What is even more important is that using text markup tools conveys more accurate feedback. Each character—such as a comma, period, or hyphen—can be marked as deleted or inserted.

Using these tools allows auto-edits when comments are imported from a `.pdf` file to a source document if supported by the application. For any of the tools in this group to work, the text needs to be selected. If a document originated as a scan, text markup tools will only be available after **optical character recognition** (**OCR**) makes the text searchable. For details on how to do this, see the *Enhancing a scanned image through OCR* section of *Chapter 2, Creating and Enhancing PDF Files from Scans*.

The following review will help you understand the purpose of the respective tools:

- Though included in this group, the **Add Sticky Note** tool stands on its own and is not meant to be used in the text, though often it is. It is for general comments only placed anywhere on a page. It has a note icon that appears on the page and a pop-up note for your text message. You can add a sticky note anywhere on the page or in the document area. While this tool is most intuitive and common, it should be avoided for text markup as it obscures content and cannot be inserted in a line of characters, making the correction imprecise.

- **Highlight Text** tool: This highlights text and may include a comment but does not allow auto-edit changes. You can press the *Ctrl* key and drag the selection (also known as *Ctrl-drag*) to mark up a rectangular area—for example, text in a column.

- **Underline Text** tool: This indicates which text the comment refers to, somewhat like the **Highlight Text** tool. It is good for marking text as is done in traditional proofreading where underlining indicates the need to set the text in italics or bold. It works with *Ctrl-drag* to mark a rectangular area.

- **Strikethrough Text** tool: This deletes text with no replacement. The selected text will show as a red strikethrough line, which can be changed to any color. The text will be deleted when the edit is accepted by the user in a document authored in a compatible application, such as InDesign or FrameMaker.

- **Replace Text** tool: This is the most versatile text markup tool in Acrobat. Edits made with the **Replace Text** tool can be accepted (auto-edited) back into the text layout in InDesign or FrameMaker. It performs three functions in one tool:

  - **Replace**: Used to select and highlight old text. When the mouse key is released, you can type replacement text in the popup.

  - **Insert**: Used to place the cursor at an insertion point and type new text in the popup.

  - **Delete**: Used to select and highlight text. When the mouse key is released, the markup shows as a red strikethrough, meaning that the text should be deleted.

- **Insert Text** tool: This inserts text without deleting any existing text. Markup edits with this tool can be accepted as auto-edits. Be careful and consistent when adding or removing spacebar spaces, since auto-edits will include or exclude all the literal characters.

- **Add Text Comment** tool: This is for typing text anywhere on the page without a frame around it. Very useful when filling out a flat `.pdf` form that lacks interactive fields for data input. Here is how you can use this tool, a bit like using a typewriter on a page:

  - Select the tool, click anywhere on the page to place the cursor, and you are ready to type any amount of text.

  - To change the text formatting, locate the **Text Properties** icon in the **Comment** toolbar and choose from the toolbar properties that you want to be changed. The text properties are applied to the entire comment text.

  - This tool does not allow auto-edits, making it similar in function to the **Add Sticky Note** tool, but you can read the comment on the page, rather than in a popup.

> **Important note**
>
> The **Add text comment** tool should not be confused with the **Edit** or **Add text tools** from the **Edit PDF** toolbar. Those tools are meant to permanently change `.pdf` text content, not just mark up a page.

- **Add Text Box** tool: This allows you to precisely position the rectangular area of a comment. You can also see the comment on the page, like a Post-It paper note rather than in a popup. Here is how you can use and customize it:

  - Select the tool, click or click-drag on a page, and type your comment text inside a rectangle. You'll notice that the text wraps automatically within the box. The default settings for this tool create a frame with a red border, white fill, and red text. You can change all these properties.

  - With the typed text highlighted, click the **Text Properties** icon in the **Comment** toolbar, then choose from the toolbar properties that you want to be changed. See *Figure 6.6* for this. Not all text in this comment must have the same formatting. Different properties may be applied to characters within the same textbox.

- Select the font, font size, and color for the text. You can also open **Text Box Text Properties** (*Ctrl + E/Command + E*) to expand text formatting options for paragraph alignment and font styles.

- To change the textbox, click the edge of the box. You should see a blue bounding box with round handles. Drag one of the handles to resize the box.

- Right-click to open the context menu and select **Properties…** to change the border and fill options. You can also use the **Properties** toolbar.

To change the text of the existing comments, double-click the markup, select the text, and edit it. If you need to change text formatting, select the text, and choose options from the **Properties** toolbar. You can also paste a block of text by copying the text on a page or in any application and pasting it into any comment. To delete any markup, select it to see the bounding box and handles, and press *Delete*.

Understanding page markup tools

Additional tools are available to markup page layout or objects on a page other than text. These will include photos, charts, header and/or footer areas, or regions on oversize pages containing large technical drawings. As with text tools, when selected, you can click-drag to mark areas on a document page. The following is an overview of these tools:

- **Use Drawing** (or **Pencil**) tool: This creates free-form drawings, and the **Erase Drawing** tool erases the drawing pencil tool's free-form drawing. Useful when careful selection of markup needs to be made—for example, with maps.

- **Add Stamp** tool: This applies stamps, functioning like a rubber stamp. You can create custom stamps based on a pixel image of your choice. Very useful for logos, alerts, or quick signatures not requiring security verification.

- **Add a New Attachment** tool: This adds a comment that also contains an embedded attached file or audio recording. You can either attach an audio file or record your spoken voice message into the audio comment.

Acrobat offers nine drawing tools. You may want to review again *Figure 6.3*. The tools are meant to draw the author's eye to the area where an edit is expected. Double-clicking after the markup was drawn will open a popup where you can type the expected corrections or explanation. Properties can be changed using the methods listed earlier.

Here is a list of these tools and the reason why you need them. The comment included with each markup provides instructions for edits required in the source file:

- The **Line** tool to draw straight lines. Conveys the idea to separate page content visually.

- The **Arrow** tool to create arrows to draw the eye to a very specific area on a page where edits are expected.

- **Rectangle**, **Oval**, and **Polygon** tools to create simple square, circular, and polygonal shapes. Odd shapes in markup are easy to spot. The comment included with the markup provides a reason for edits in the area.

- The **Text Callout** tool is very helpful when you need to precisely point to an area to edit with easy-to-see comment text. It works by click-dragging on a page. A box opens to type your comment, such as the **Add Text box** tool. The **Text Callout** tool does not have a pop-up note; its shape is a rectangle with text and a pointer that has three parts:

  - A textbox

  - A knee line

  - An endpoint line

Resize each part by dragging a handle. The knee line can be resized in one direction only—horizontally or vertically. The textbox expands vertically as you type so that all text remains visible. Here is an example of **Text Callout** markup:

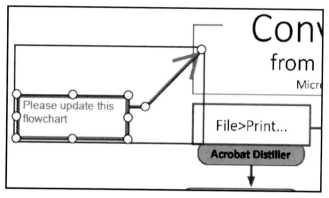

Figure 6.7 – Text Callout tool markup

- The **Cloud** tool creates closed shapes that are very easy to notice even in the most complex page layout, such as a busy catalog or advertisement.

- The **Draw Connected Lines** tool creates shapes with multiple line segments. It gives you a free-form shape, very useful when a marked area is irregular—for example, an outline of two bedrooms and a hallway in a technical drawing.

Tip

To keep a tool selected so that you can add multiple comments without having to select it each time, click the tool you will use in the **Comment** toolbar, then click the **Keep Tool Selected** icon (it looks like a pin). Continue using the selected tool. When done, select a different tool such as a hand grabber.

The rich set of tools and customization options likely will address the needs of any project. Using the tools is very intuitive—just take time to play with each one of them. In one afternoon, you will probably discover which tools are especially useful to you.

We will now take a larger view of the editing process and discuss the review cycle and choices that are available in this area.

Email-based group review workflow

The review cycle typically begins when an author or a designer has completed the project and exported it to .pdf. The file is then sent for feedback to editors. Editing may involve checking for typos and grammar, but also for the accuracy of content, credits for artwork, compliance with accessibility standards, and so on.

Depending on how demanding the publication is, the editing process will vary. In this section, we will review the process for both a relatively simple project where only one or two editors provide comments and a larger publication with input from many subject matter experts.

The flowchart in *Figure 6.8* illustrates two types of review cycles:

- **Email-based review**: We will bypass the discussion on methods of transport of the .pdf file under review since they vary greatly. Email-based simply means a final version of a publication exported to .pdf gets delivered to the involved editor or many editors. It could be done using email, accessing files on a shared network drive, or through the organization's **content management system (CMS)**. Our focus instead is on functions related to the document and commenting tools using a version of desktop (laptop) Acrobat.

  This process can be briefly described this way: the author completes the final document in the authoring application, exports it to a .pdf file, then sends it for feedback from reviewers, receives the comments, and changes the source document, repeating the process multiple times as needed. Multiple editors' comments can be received by the author/a review initiator individually, so if many subject matter experts need to provide feedback and see one another's comments, the review becomes linear: one editor must complete the markup before the next one can see it and then move on with theirs. See the left side of *Figure 6.8*.

- **Shared review**: This process depends on the .pdf file being shared on **Adobe Cloud**. The markup is browser-based and done collaboratively, thus everyone must have access to Adobe Cloud but does not need to have the Acrobat application installed—a web browser is sufficient. For expanded information on this workflow, see the *Shared group review process using Adobe Cloud* section.

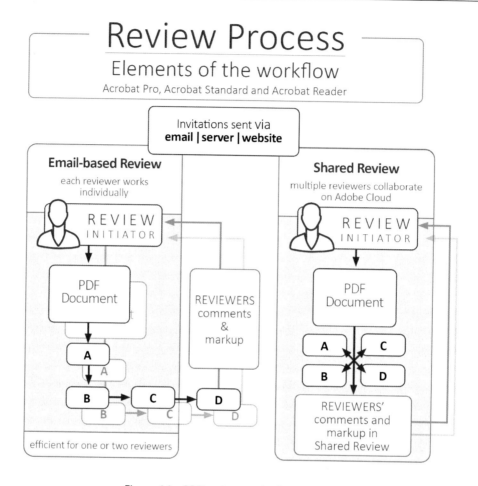

Figure 6.8 – PDF review methods comparison

It is worth repeating that the review process happens outside of authoring, even though many edit changes can be done in Acrobat. The purpose of a review is to communicate changes that should be incorporated into a source document in the authoring application. Thus, multiple versions of a `.pdf` file may be necessary before a final version is ready for distribution or print.

In the next section, we will step through functions in a typical review process using just a few tools. You will also learn how to create and keep copies of edit trail using **Comment Summary** and **Compare Files**.

Working with comments

We will now add a few examples of comments to a `.pdf` document that will be used in the email-based rather than shared review. (More details on the differences are under the *Shared group review process using Adobe Cloud* section.)

You can open any multipage PDF file for this exercise. I assume that you remember all the tools and ways to use them since we just covered them. If you need to recall any of them, just go back a few pages in this chapter.

Here are the steps for commenting on a publication:

1. Let's add a general comment to a page. Select the **Add Sticky Note** tool and click on a page. A symbol appears on the page, and on the right, a comment box in the **Comment** panel is ready for text.

2. Type this inside the comment box: `This is a first review of the document.` Click **Post**.

3. Select the **Add Text** tool, click on the left margin of the page, and type `This paragraph information needs to be updated.`

4. Scroll a few pages and select the **Replace Text** tool. Click-drag over some text and type `Replacement text.` Click **Post**.

5. Find an image or a table in your `.pdf` file, select the **Text Callout** tool, click-drag to create a frame, and type inside it: `This image has a newer version posted this morning.` Click on a page to accept the comment.

6. Move to another page, select the **Rectangle** tool, click-drag over a paragraph, then type in the comment box on the right: `This paragraph should be moved to the next section.` If you clicked before typing, double-click the rectangle markup to open a popup or activate the comment area in the **Comment** column and then type your text. Click **Post** to accept the comment.

We have just added markup to a document. All comments neatly appear in the column on the right sorted by **Page** by default. Clicking on a comment in the column takes you to a page where the markup is placed. If you want to remove a comment, simply click on it and press the *Delete* key.

When the **Comment** tool is closed, the column with comments disappears. You can still see the content of each comment either as a popup or a tip. If you want to use popups to work with rather than the column on the right, you can change settings in **Preferences**. Here are the steps:

1. From the top menu, select the **Edit | Preferences | Commenting** options (**Adobe Acrobat** I **Preferences ...** on macOS).

2. Choose your settings in **Pop-Up Open Behavior**:

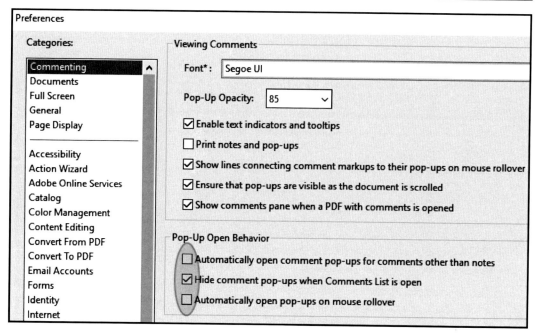

Figure 6.9 – Comment popup preferences

3. Select the behavior you prefer. **Automatically open comment pop-ups on mouse roll-over** will allow you to read and type replies to comments directly in the popups, with the **Comment** column closed.

4. Click **OK** to close **Preferences** dialog box.

In the next section, we will move on to managing the volume of comments.

Managing comments

It may be a challenge not to miss the review details in publications that require extensive feedback provided by many reviewers. Managing the comments and markup is very important both for the author who gets feedback to act on and for the editors who keep track of their edits.

We will now explore how to manage the comments using the **Comment** panel options:

*   You can sort them by page, author, date, type, and so on. Here is a screenshot with the **Sort** menu open:

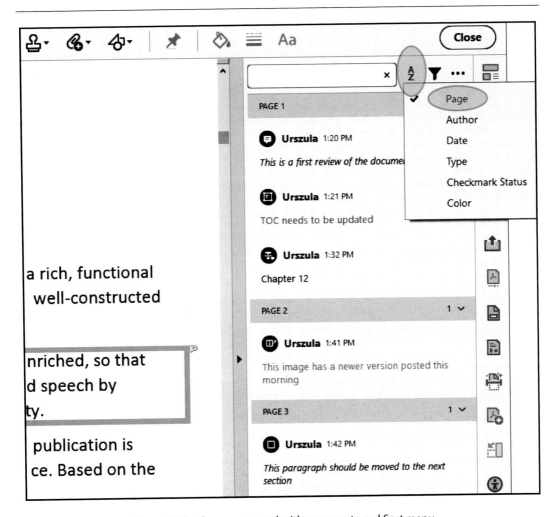

Figure 6.10 – Comment panel with comments and Sort menu

The default sort order is by page, but it is easily changed by clicking on a different menu option.

- You can also **filter** comments by clicking the filter icon next to the right. Clicking a filter will leave these comments visible and hide the rest. You can filter reviewers and types of comments. Combining the choices in the **Sort** and **Filter** menus will make the displayed volume of comments more manageable if you have dozens of them. Here is a screenshot:

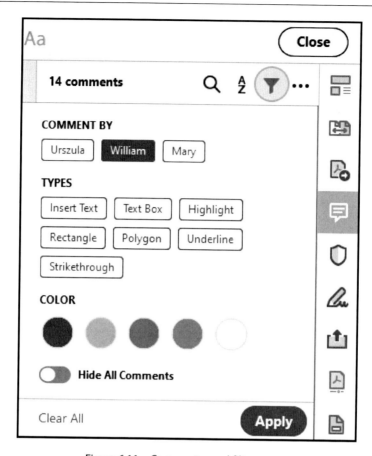

Figure 6.11 – Comment panel filter menu

When marking up changes is finished, it is time to create a **comment summary**, a new, independent .pdf file that can be saved and preserved as an edit trail. We will create a comment summary next:

1. Click three dots (options) in the **Comment** panel to open the menu and select **Create Comment Summary…**.

2. A dialog box opens with choices for the summary layout. Select the second option, as shown in this screenshot:

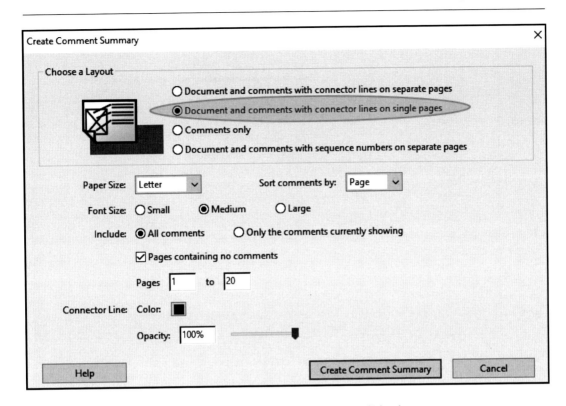

Figure 6.12 – Create Comment Summary dialog box

3.   Click on the **Create Comment Summary** button. A brand new `.pdf` file is created, displaying publication content on the left area of the page and a detailed report of all comments on the right, sorted by the choices you made earlier in the **Sort** menu.

Black lines help you find the location of the markup on a page since the document is flat and the **Comment** panel is empty. None of the comments can be easily deleted. The report can be saved for future reference:

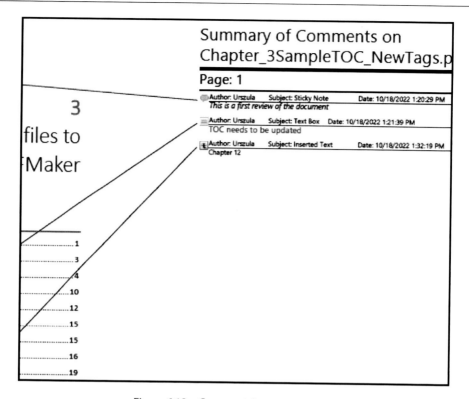

Figure 6.13 – Comment Summary report

You created a **Comment Summary** report for your records.

We will now move to complete the review cycle by sending feedback to the initiator of the review. Acrobat gives you a few methods, which we will explore next.

The most obvious one is to send the entire .pdf file back to the person who requested the review. Comments then can be read, responded to, or acted on. The drawback of this method is that if the document file size is large, and more than one editor is involved, we may run into bandwidth issues. Security may also be a concern. So, we will now explore a more efficient method that involves sending comments and markup only using a .fdf file.

> **Important note**
>
> **Portable Document Format** (.pdf) refers to what we see on the screen such as formatted text and images but also all background code that makes a publication, such as fonts, scripts, accessibility tags, and so on. All the content can make the file size large.
>
> **Forms Data Format** (.fdf) refers only to the content of form fields and markup in Acrobat. It is strictly a text data file, creating a very small file size.

When a reviewer wishes to send comments, they can save bandwidth by exporting only the comments in a format that the reviewer can import into the original PDF file.

We will now go through the process of exporting comments—a function performed by reviewers—and then we will learn how to import them—a function used by an initiator of the review. This is useful for consolidating comments from several reviewers into one PDF file so that they can be imported as comments into the authoring application:

1. Return to a `.pdf` document that contains comments and markup in the **Comment** panel.

2. Click on three dots (options) to open the panel menu and select **Export All to Data File…**.

3. Before you click **Save** to accept, look at the **Save as type:** dropdown in the dialog box. It should look like this:

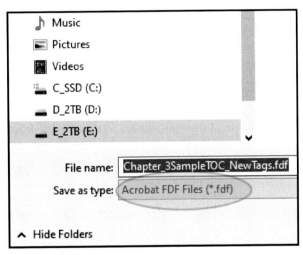

Figure 6.14 – Saving comments and markup as .fdf

4. After the file is saved, you may want to compare the file sizes in the file browser. A complete `.pdf` document with comments is much larger than a `.fdf` file containing markup only. Here is what my browser displayed:

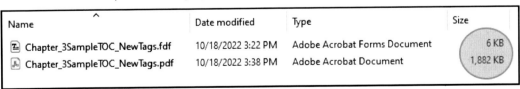

Figure 6.15 – File size comparison: .fdf (6 KB) versus .pdf (1,882 KB)

> **Tip**
>
> If you don't see `.pdf` and `.fdf` file extensions, change the file browser setting using the **View** options, then click the checkbox for **File name extensions**.

You can now send either file back to the initiator of the review who can receive comments in either format if auto-edits are not expected.

This brings us to the next step: we will assume a role of an author or initiator of the review and receive the comments and markup using a reliable and rather simple method of importing comments to the initial `.pdf` file, as shown in the **Email-based Review** area of *Figure 6.8.*

Importing comments

Just as publications vary, so does the method for receiving comments, since the adopted process of accepting or rejecting changes depends greatly on the software that the author uses to produce a publication. The volume of markup will additionally influence the process, especially if multiple editors have submitted their feedback. There are two main methods to accept comments:

1.   Importing the comment data file into the original `.pdf` file that was sent out to the editors. Submitted feedback will serve as a guide for an author who makes changes to the source document.

2.   For applications that support direct import of markups, such as InDesign and FrameMaker, an author will import comments directly into the source file and accept, reject, or reply, implementing the auto-edit function. More on this in *Chapter 10, Integration with Adobe InDesign.*

We will work with the first method. Here are the steps:

1.   Open a `.pdf` file with comments that you already added and exported to `.fdf` earlier.

2.   Select all comments. To do this, click on the first/top comment in the panel, press the *Shift* key, and click on the last/bottom comment in the panel.

3.   Tap the *Delete* key or right-click and select **Delete** from the context menu. All comments should be gone. The `.pdf` file is now the same as it was at the time of initiating the review before any markup was added.

4.   Save the file, close it, and open it again. Why? Well, to simulate the lengthy editorial process in a few minutes.

You are an author now and ready to make changes to the source document. First, you need to import the comments saved in the `.fdf` file created earlier (or files received from the reviewers):

1.   Open the **Comment** panel and click the three dots for the panel menu.

2.   Select **Import Data File….**

3.   In the dialog box, select the `.fdf` file and click **Open**.

4. All comments and markup are now placed both on the document pages and in the column of the panel. If you were the author, you would have received a `.fdf` file from each editor, then to receive the comments, you would repeat *steps 2* and *3* till you had imported everyone's feedback.

5. You can import all comments from multiple reviewers in one step. Select all the `.fdf` files holding the *Shift* or *Ctrl/Command* key.

As you apply requested changes following instructions in comments, you may set a status option for each comment to help you remember which task has been completed or to communicate with reviewers. Here are the steps:

1. Select a comment in the **Comment** tool column, then click the comment options menu (**…**). You will get a few self-explanatory choices, as shown in the screenshot:

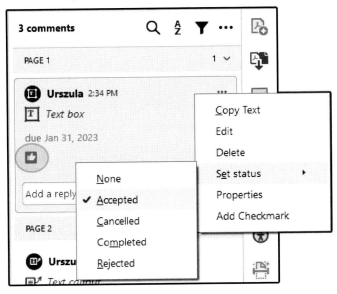

Figure 6.16 – Comment status options

2. Click **Set status | Accepted**. A small icon appears on the left of the comment area. As you move through document updates and accomplish editing tasks, you can set the status of each comment. Status icons remain visible so that you can see editing progress at a glance.

If another round of edits is needed, you would repeat the process of initiating the review and receiving feedback.

After each round of edits to a source document is applied, you would create a new version of the `.pdf` file. You may want to compare the changes in the older and newer version and keep the report for future reference. Earlier, we explored **Comment Summary**; now, we will look at the **Compare Files** function, which is very helpful as a landmark in showing what changed in a document along the production process.

Using the document comparison feature

To use this feature, two .pdf versions of the same document are needed. An earlier one can be compared to a newer one. Here are the steps:

1. Open a .pdf file that you would like to work with.

2. Select **Compare Files** from **Tools** if not available already in the tool column in the right area of the screen.

3. A new screen opens, allowing you to choose two files and select options.

4. Select the newer file using the dropdown. Both filenames will be shown on the screen.

5. Click **Settings** to open the dialog box. Here is a screenshot:

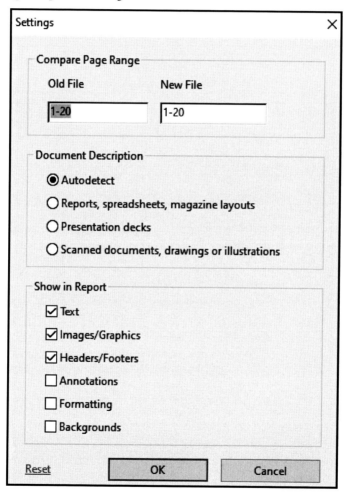

Figure 6.17 – Compare Files option settings

You can choose to compare only a portion of a file if you change the range of pages in the **Compare Page Range** fields. Selecting one of the **Document Description** options will tell Acrobat how to determine results. Here are the choices:

- **Autodetect** allows Acrobat to choose a type of document.

- **Reports, spreadsheets, magazine layouts** tells Acrobat that this is a continuous story, and the content may reflow across pages.

- **Presentation decks** treats each slide or page individually and matches ones that are similar. Then, the content of each matching page is compared. This setting identifies pages that moved, such as slides in a presentation.

- **Scanned documents, drawing or illustrations** allows each scanned page to be treated as a bitmap image, and the pixels are compared. This option should be used to compare images or architectural and technical drawings.

You can further tell Acrobat which components of the document should be compared, by selecting options in **Show in Report**.

6. Click **OK**, then click **Compare**.

7. A new `.pdf` file auto-named **Compare Report** opens, and a toolbar becomes available to help you navigate the results.

Saving the report will allow you to keep a trail of edits for future reference. The files that you compared are not affected.

In the next section, we will explore stamps, often added toward the end of the review cycle.

Adding stamps

You are an author again in our scenario. Finally, you have incorporated all the required editing changes, the publication is completed, and it's exported to `.pdf` one last time. You may now need to request final approval from the client or boss before the publication is posted online or sent for print. They could use a stamp tool to convey visually that the publication is, in fact, approved. In contracts or forms, a visual mark may be placed not to miss the fields for signatures or initials.

To help with that, the **Add a stamp** tool is available.

> **Important note**
>
> Custom stamps may also be used to place seals or logos. The timing of placing a stamp is very flexible; it simply depends on its message. Dynamic stamps—such as **Approved**, **Reviewed**, **Revised**, and so on—included as defaults and containing the time and date of placement imply that they should be used at the end of the review cycle.

Stamps are very intuitive and easy to use. Here is a screenshot of the options:

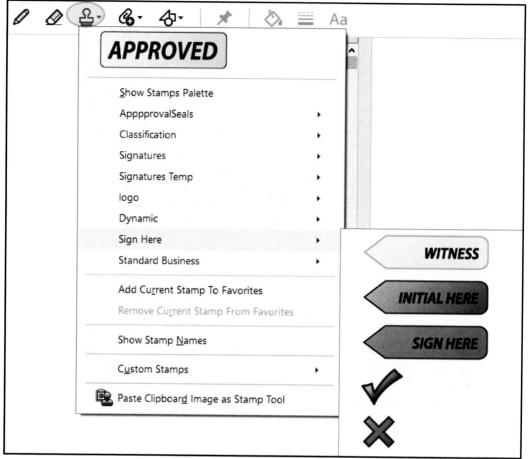

Figure 6.18 – Add a stamp menu

When you scroll through choices, you will see many default stamps:

- Dynamic stamps include a name and date.
- You can add custom stamps using text or images from any file converted to a `.pdf` file. This is especially useful when a logo or seal needs to be placed in a document.

  Keep in mind that stamps are markup, and they can be copied and pasted into another document if a `.pdf` file is not secured. We will discuss document security and digital signatures in *Chapter 8, Adding Digital Signatures and Security Settings*.

> **Important note**
>
> Images of **signatures** may be saved as stamps for quick use in many documents that do not require certification or signature validation. A word of caution, though: they can be copied and pasted into another document if the `.pdf` file is not secured. To prevent unauthorized use, you can print the file to the **Adobe PDF** virtual printer to create a flat `.pdf` copy of the signed document. *This method does not replace digital signatures.*

We discussed the purpose and settings of available commenting and markup tools, then we used some of them in a review process based on the use of Acrobat installed on a desktop (laptop). Distribution of the document and submission of feedback depended on email, thus it was an email-based review. We exported and imported comments using a `.fdf` file to address file size issues, and finally, we compared two versions of a document.

In the next section, we will understand the key differences between **email-based review** and **shared group review** processes.

Shared group review process using Adobe Cloud

Shared group review is a separate process of distributing `.pdf` files for review and gathering feedback. Available tools are similar but not as extensive as desktop applications. Many features are still evolving. The key aspect of this method is that the process happens fully online using Adobe Cloud (or Creative Cloud).

To review the cycle differences, please look at *Figure 6.8*. Editors can see each other's notes and can communicate with one another throughout the review process. When the markup is completed, the author can retrieve feedback and make changes to a source document. **Text auto-edit is not available in this process**.

> **Important note**
>
> At the time of writing this book, tools and options for shared review are still under development, with a goal for future release versions to imitate all the capabilities of `.pdf` commenting of desktop Acrobat.

We will now explore the process and options of this workflow. It begins with an existing `.pdf` document that needs to be shared with others for the purpose of commenting. You are now assuming a role of a review initiator/author:

1. Locate and click the **Share with Others** button at the top-right corner of the Acrobat window. It looks like this with the dropdown after you clicked the button:

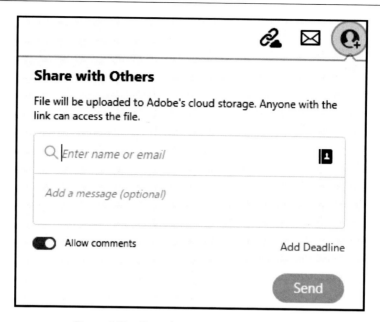

Figure 6.19 – Shared review process initial step

2. Type or select a reviewer's email and instructions on expected feedback.

3. Clicking **Add Deadline** allows you to set a time after which feedback will no longer be accepted.

4. Click the **Send** button.

5. A brief **Invitation sent. Your file is now shared.** alert will appear, which means that the `.pdf` document is now available on Adobe Cloud for others to see and work with it. There is a **SHARED** label and thumbnails for each reviewer on the left of commenting bar. Many of the commenting tools available in the classic desktop version of Acrobat (discussed earlier in this chapter) are now removed. Any comments made from this point are identified using your Adobe ID.

6. Participants will receive a "`your name (email) has shared filename.pdf. You can also comment on it. Due on [date selected in Add Deadline]`" email alert, followed by an **Open** button to access **Adobe Cloud**.

7. You are now a participant reviewer, so click the **Open** button to join the browser-based review.

As a participant, you are working with a **browser version of Acrobat online**. This session does not require having Acrobat installed on the system. All feedback is done in a browser window that hardly resembles the Acrobat workspace. Tools and panes appear on the sides of the screen. They are limited and do not match classic desktop Acrobat. Is this a bit confusing? Yes—it is a work in progress. Hopefully, all this will settle soon, and we will get a unified interface for all environments.

Page markup tools are reduced to one: **Draw Freehand** with choices of color and line weight. Here is a screenshot of what is available:

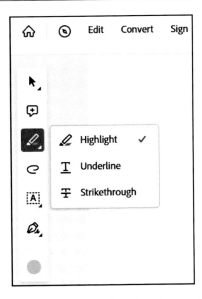

Figure 6.20 – Browser-based markup tools

Take time to explore these options. **Shared files cannot be modified**. You will need to create a copy of the original, which may lose interactive features, such as links in the TOC. A few editing tools are offered. You will need a good internet connection, as you will experience response delays when using the tools.

If the `.pdf` file already has some comments, they will appear in the **Comments** column on the right. Many editors can work on the document at the same time and see all markup as it is added to the document. To organize what you see in the panel, a filter may be applied just like in a desktop Acrobat version.

The **Bookmarks** and **Pages** panes are available and are also located in the right area of the browser screen.

If you lose your internet connection while working in a browser version of Acrobat online, a copy of the `.pdf` file will become available offline, and you can continue working on your desktop application. A title bar will alert you that the document was opened from Adobe Cloud storage, and a **SHARED** button will appear on a toolbar with limited commenting tools, as in this screenshot:

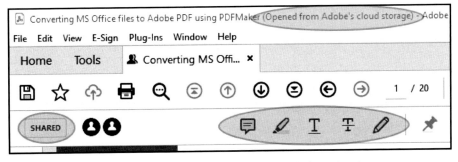

Figure 6.21 – Shared .pdf markup tools in desktop Acrobat

It is very likely that this set of options for review will be updated soon to reflect our growing need for collaborative workflows with everyone continuously connected online.

We will next learn how to ensure that users who use Acrobat Reader can join the review process.

Including Acrobat Reader users in a review process

Since many users are still working on a desktop (or laptop) version of Acrobat when reviewing a .pdf document, their access to features depends on which application they use: Acrobat, Acrobat Pro, or a free version Acrobat Reader.

In free Acrobat Reader, the commenting features are available only in a .pdf file with commenting enabled. This requires an extra preparatory step using a full version of Acrobat, before sending files for review.

To ensure that editors working with a free Acrobat Reader have the ability to participate in a review, you need to activate **Enable Document for Commenting**. Here are the steps:

1. Open a .pdf file that will be distributed to free Acrobat Reader users.

2. Select these options from the top menu: **File | Save As Other | Reader Extended PDF | Enable Commenting and Measuring**.

3. An alert will appear, reminding you that the copy of the file will be altered:

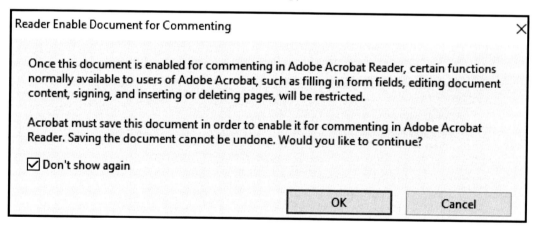

Figure 6.22 – Browser-based markup tools while working offline

4. Save the file with a name that hints that it is an extended .pdf file for Acrobat Reader users.

Your publication is now ready for markup by anyone who is included in the review process.

Summary

We have covered a lot of ground in this chapter. I hope that sorting out the multitude of options offered in the commenting area of Acrobat helps you to use the tools effectively and to choose the best review process for your projects and organization.

Writers and editors should receive good training on the proper use of the Acrobat **Replace Text**, **Insert Text**, and **Strikethrough Text** commenting tools in order to eliminate duplication of effort in text markup editing cycles and to minimize the potential for errors when re-typing corrections.

The desktop version of Acrobat comments allows auto-edit supported in InDesign and FrameMaker, which speeds up the production bottleneck for graphic designers and authors, but the feature cannot be used in browser-based comments.

In the next chapter, we will cover the process of creating interactive `.pdf` forms. We will learn the details of collecting information in a highly structured way that gives you, the author, great control over what is submitted and how.

7

Creating and Modifying PDF Forms

Forms are a highly structured method for gathering data. The owner of a form may request very specific information and collect it in a very precise format appropriate for a purpose. Forms can be distributed to a clearly defined group with a stated deadline for response or posted online for use whenever needed. Forms have been around for a very long time, initially used mainly by legal professionals faced with writing and signing repetitive statements, contracts, by-laws, and so on.

In our world, filling out digital forms is a daily task – for example, replying to a request to place cookies on our devices involves providing data through a form. Organization of feedback submitted through forms allows us to process countless pieces of information, which can be analyzed individually or as patterns. The possibilities are endless, and so are form types.

Beyond paper forms, which are still in use, digital forms have become the norm. Digital forms are created in three major formats – **HTML**, coded for interaction directly in browsers; **XML Forms Architecture** (**XFA**), which is a hybrid of a PDF-like presentation to an end user but internally coded in XML for use in databases; and **PDF AcroForm**, a native Acrobat format used during the creation, filling out, and submitting processes.

In this chapter, we will focus on native PDF forms, often referred to by programmers as **AcroForms**. We will step through the process of creating a form page background, adding interactive fields, and setting their properties, and finally, we will take some steps to make the form compliant with accessibility standards.

The following topics will be covered in this chapter:

- Creating an interactive PDF form with accessible form fields
- Validating and calculating data
- Adding action buttons
- Collecting data from filled-out PDF forms

Let's start at the very beginning of the process, where a .pdf page background is created and then transformed into an interactive form.

Creating an interactive PDF form

PDF forms fall into two categories, consistent with all .pdf files: flat or interactive. We discussed the differences between the two categories as applied to general documents in *Chapter 3, Converting Microsoft Office Files to Adobe PDF Using PDFMaker*. Here, we will focus on a unique functionality of PDF forms:

- **Flat forms** must be filled out manually, in the same way as paper forms. Often, they are printed, filled out with ink pen by hand, scanned, and submitted via email. Acrobat users familiar with the **Comment** tools can manually fill out a flat form using the **Text** tools from a toolbar. Submitting form data this way prevents efficiency and the other possibilities offered by using interactive fields, both for those who provide the data and those who collect it. It also does nothing to achieve a paperless office but instead generates an even greater need for paper and ink usage.
- **Interactive forms**, on the other hand, provide fields where data can be entered, formatted, validated, and enforced if needed, and finally, submitted and collected by the form owner. At the end of the process, gathered data can be organized and interpreted, possibly using scripts. All this can be done using Acrobat.

Take time to understand the reason why you need a form. Is it a purchase order, requisition, or feedback from clients? What will you do with the collected information? Will you immediately use it to respond, as in a requisition or permission request, or does data need to be merged and presented as a report? Will you need one or multiple signatures to approve or certify the form? What is its shelf life – in other words, how often will a form need to be updated or changed? Think about the design of the entire cycle needed to accomplish a purpose.

In the next section, we will create a new form, going through all the typical steps in this process.

Understanding the data collection process

The following chart presents the process involved in making forms useful. First, you will note that the work begins in an authoring application where a form page layout is created. Once a page is designed, it is exported or printed to a `.pdf` file. Even though Acrobat has tools for creating lines, boxes, and text, they should be used for touch-ups or fixes only. To create a good layout, possibly including organizational branding elements, it is best to use MS Word or InDesign.

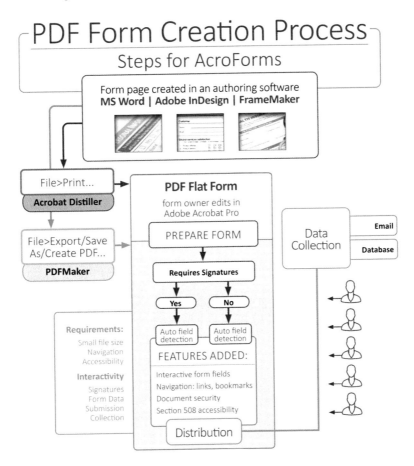

Figure 7.1 – The steps to create, enhance, distribute, and collect data using an interactive PDF form

The new page becomes a background of the .pdf form. Acrobat Pro uses it as a guide to place interactive fields. A well-designed background in a form will prevent extensive visual formatting of the data fields so that you can focus on their functions.

Acrobat Pro begins with the auto-detection of fields. It takes quite a lot of time to add and edit fields and features to make the form functional. When it is done, the content should be protected with a password. Finally, the form is either posted online or distributed to those who provide the required data. The end goal is to collect all the information in the most efficient manner. It may be as simple as receiving an email with a filled-out form, or it may involve writing a script to merge data into a database.

> **Important note**
> Do not use Photoshop to create a background for forms, since bitmap text will not be accessible and the file size will be excessively large.

The following are some guidelines to help you during the design and layout stage of creating a new form.

Form layout guidelines

If your responsibility involves the creation and management of forms in a large organization, you can visit the **Business Forms Management Association** (**BFMA**) (`https://www.bfma.org/`) website, where best practices and guidelines in delivering forms and management services are discussed, especially if you need to consider roles and operations.

Here, we will consider just a few general tips important when authoring a form background. These should be incorporated during the design and layout stage:

- **Each field must have a unique name**; thus, if you have multiple fields with similar information, identify each one with a unique text label. For example, if your form collects email addresses from a buyer and a seller, each field should be labeled as **Buyer Email** and **Seller Email** rather than just **Email**.

- The organization logo and a form title should be positioned at the top area of a page, numbers identifying a form are usually positioned in the lower-left area, and in multipage forms, page numbering is expected in the bottom-right region.

- Fields collecting information related to user identity should be placed in a logical group, organized in such a way that the tabbing order across these fields represents a naturally expected order when filling out the form.

  For example, when filling out a form, it is expected that the **First name** field is followed by the **Last name** field, followed by the **Email** field. It is *not* natural to type `First name`, `Email`, and then `Last name`. Positioning these fields to the left/right or top/bottom in relation to one another creates a logical tabbing order.

- The background of forms should be simple, with decorative elements used mainly to communicate the separation of groups. Use plenty of white space.

- The font size for text should be rather large. The recommended range is 10 to 24 points.

- Rich ornamentation, drop shadows, and background graphics generally should be avoided, especially on field text labels. Simple is better, especially in complex forms.

- Field boxes should never overlap; the same applies to underlined field areas.

- White is the best choice for a background color for both form text and field values.

- Checkbox or radio button symbols should be distinct and consistent, placed to the left of the field labels and surrounded by plenty of white space for clear meaning.

- Instructions and language should be written for a third-grade reading level, in consideration that, for some people who will be filling out a form, English is a second language.

- Buttons that are expected to complete the process of filling out a form should be placed at the end of the form content, often at the bottom of a page. This applies to fields such as **Signatures**, **Reset**, **Submit**, or **Print**.

Auto field detection greatly speeds up adding interactivity. Page elements with underlines, textboxes, and tables with borders are recognized as form field areas and are automatically converted to text fields.

> **Important note**
>
> When planning a `.pdf` form layout, give thought to page size, orientation, and dimensions. We tend to stick to 8.5" by 11", a standard letter size in the USA, but if your form will not be printed and will be filled out mostly on screen, landscape orientation or a square size may be more appropriate.
>
> The default setting for field text size is **Auto**. This is not the best setting, as it will result in a font size change based on the amount of data entered in each field. To prevent that, set a consistent, fixed font size for all fields. You can also choose a font family different than Helvetica, also set as a default.
>
> Page elements that are interpreted by Acrobat as checkboxes are circles, squares, or diamonds with strokes/borders. Circles next to numbers are recognized as radio buttons, and the word *signature* is auto-detected as a signature field.

Here is an example of a form page background created in InDesign:

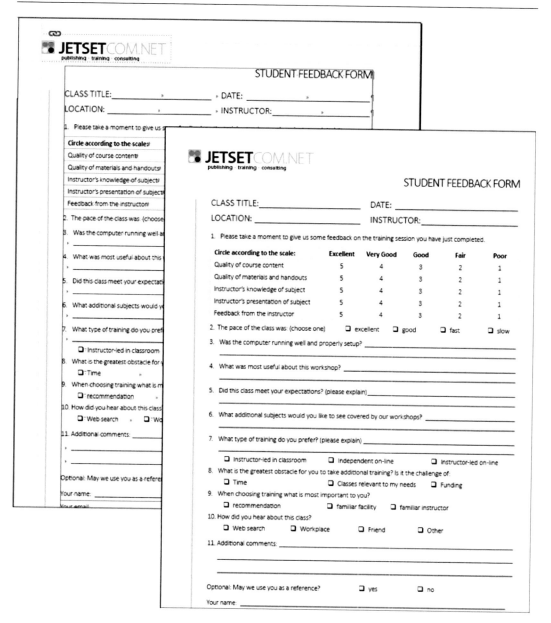

Figure 7.2 – The first step in form creation – a flat .pdf page

Now that we know how to create a flat form page, we will enhance it by adding interactive form fields.

Interactive form fields and properties

To add interactivity to a form, open the **Prepare Form** tool. If a `.pdf` document does not have any fields yet, a screen opens that allows you to select a source of background:

- **Single File** is typically a file that was open when you clicked the tool, but you can change that by clicking the **Change File** option.

- **Scanner** opens the same options that we discussed in *Chapter 2, Creating and Enhancing PDF Files from Scans*.

- **Create New** allows you to work with a blank page. For very simple and short forms, this can be a good choice. If you choose this option, you will need to use both the **Prepare Form** and **Edit PDF** toolbars.

We will work with an existing file that is open in Adobe Acrobat Pro:

1. Open a `.pdf` flat form already created in an authoring application. I used a *student feedback* form created in InDesign.

2. Click on the **Prepare Form** tool, and then click **Start**. Ignore the **This document requires signatures** checkbox.

> **Important note**
> Clicking the **This document requires signatures** checkbox alters the content of toolbar tools available in **Form Editing** mode. It prepares a form for **Adobe Sign**.

3. The page is now open and ready for edits in **Form Editing** mode. Rectangles with labels are active fields that Acrobat detected. A toolbar is displayed at the top of the screen, and on the right, a formatting panel is available:

Figure 7.3 – Form field tools in editing mode

The screen tips appearing when you hover over each tool will help identify functions available after a tool is selected, consistent with other Acrobat toolbars. Here is a brief overview of each tool:

- The **Selection** tool allows you to select, move, and resize existing form fields that are active while the form is in editing mode.

- The **Edit text & images** tool (*added to the form toolbar in 2022 – if you don't see it, you may need to update your Acrobat version*) is the same tool that appears in the **Edit PDF** toolbar. It allows you to select text and delete, format, or replace it with new text. It is also used to select an image so that you can move, resize, or delete it.

- The **Text field** tool creates fields to allow a form user to enter data as text – for example, a name, address, or phone number. A text field is the most common and flexible field type, offering many variations set up in field properties.

- The **Checkbox** tool allows you to create fields where *the user can select as many or as few choices as needed*. Each field is independent of the other and represents a unique value.

- The **Radio button** tool allows you to create many choices within a group where *the user can select only one item from the group*. In a form, multiple groups are allowed, and each one has a unique name. Each field within a group represents a unique and exclusive value. Selecting it deselects another one in the same group. Radio buttons are used often to respond to **yes** or **no** questions.

- The **List box** tool allows you to present choices as a list within a field area. List boxes can include a property that lets a user *select multiple items* using *Shift + click* or *Ctrl /Cmd + click* on the list choices.

- The **Dropdown list box** tool creates fields that allow a user to select from a drop-down menu. One item can be selected, or based on settings, a value can be typed in. Using this field type saves physical space on a page. Many choices can be available but only one is displayed. The most common application is the selection of one of 50 states in the USA, given as choices in an address block.

- The **Button** tool creates a field that initiates an action when clicked on a user's computer. Acrobat offers an extensive list of actions, such as opening a file, printing, or submitting form data to a web server, that can be added to a button. The buttons can appear as images or labeled rectangles. Mouse actions by a user can trigger visual changes such as rollovers.

> **Important note**
> **Action buttons** are not related to **radio buttons**. Action buttons trigger an embedded action, such as printing a document. Radio buttons allow a user to choose form data.

- The **Date** tool creates a text field populated with a widget, allowing users to select a date rather than typing it.

- The **Digital signature** tool defines the area on a page where a digital signature is placed when a user clicks a field to sign a `.pdf` document.

- The **Barcode** tool is used to create an area with a pattern of stripes or dots, based on input from specific fields. Barcodes are interpreted by a decoding device, such as a scanner. Acrobat users need additional software to make this feature functional.

Important note

To recognize which mode of form editing you are in, look at prominent buttons on the right of the **Prepare Form** top toolbar. If it displays a **Preview** button, you are in editing mode and all interactive field areas are represented as black, active rectangles (*Figure 7.4*). As you slide your mouse, they are detected and change in appearance and color. When you click **Preview** to test the fields, the toolbar displays the **Edit** button, and field borders are no longer visible or active. To stop editing the form altogether, click the **Close** button to close the **Prepare Form** toolbar or select a different tool panel on the right.

We have reviewed the **Prepare Form** toolbar tools. Now, we will look at the page area of the document displaying the active fields that Acrobat detected. If you are in **Preview** mode, switch to **Edit** mode. Your form should look like the following screenshot:

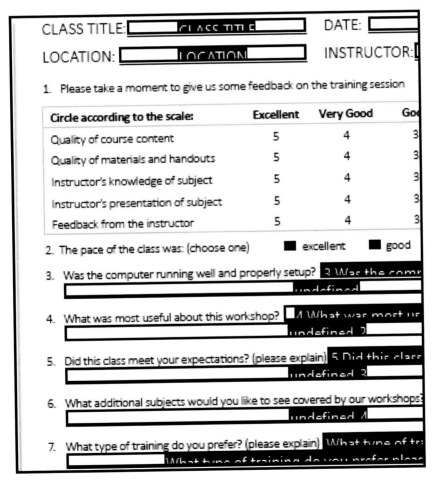

Figure 7.4 – Form fields in Form Editing mode

As a result of the auto-detection of field areas, each field was given a name based on the text to the left of the underlined area. Acrobat uses that text as a hint. Clearly, in our example, all fields need editing, and the names need to be simplified.

> **Important note**
>
> Although Acrobat accepts any set of characters as field names, avoid symbols or wildcards (*, ?, !, #, and so on) and be aware of case sensitivity; **Last Name**, **last name**, and **last NAME** are three different field names.
>
> Use descriptive short names, without spaces; use camel case for easier readability and always stay consistent, especially if your form needs to use **JavaScript**.

All fields have a unique set of properties selected or entered in the **Form Field Properties** dialog box. These settings determine the following:

- Field formatting

- How the form field information relates to other form fields

- Limitations imposed on what a user can enter in a form field, referred to as *validation*

- Operations to perform calculations

- Trigger custom scripts

To access the dialog box, double-click on an existing field or click the **All Properties** link after a new field is created. Properties can be set for any field and vary depending on the form field type.

Properties are organized in a series of tabs. All form field types consistently have these three tabs – **General**, **Appearance**, and **Actions**. Other fields have tabs unique to specific types of form fields. Most form fields have an **Options** tab, but the options available will vary based on the type of form field.

The **FIELDS** formatting panel on the right of the screen gives you controls for arranging fields on a page, such as aligning and distributing. It also contains menus for setting additional operations, such as managing form data and setting a tabbing order. The following screenshot shows the menu locations in the panel.

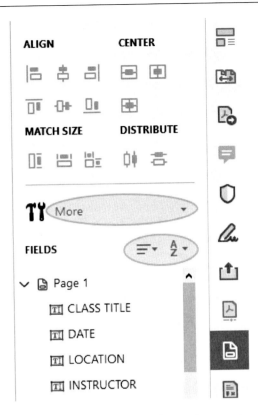

Figure 7.5 – The form fields formatting panel

We will now explore the richness of settings available in the field properties tabs. The best way to do it is to create a simple form in authoring software, convert it to .pdf, use the **Prepare Form** tool, and then take time to either edit fields that Acrobat added to a page or place new fields on the page, using different field tools.

When working on your own, you can also open an interactive form that is already completed and compare settings in each field as you continue reading. As we consider countless combinations of field options, the unique properties of each field type will be discussed. Toward the end of this tour, the process of validating and calculating data in a form will be explained. Let's begin.

Adding form fields and setting up properties

The most flexible field in a form is a **text field**. It provides a rich formatting environment for typed-in data. Here are the steps for placing a new text field and setting up its properties:

1. Click to select a **Text Field** tool, and then click or click-drag the area matching the dimensions of the lines of the form background:

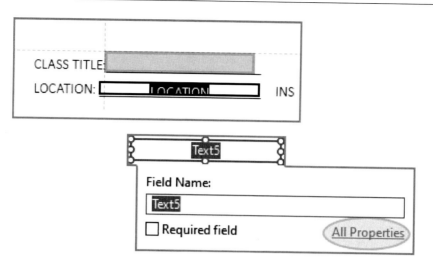

Figure 7.6 – The steps to place a new text field on a page

2.   Click **All Properties** to open the **Text Field Properties** dialog box:

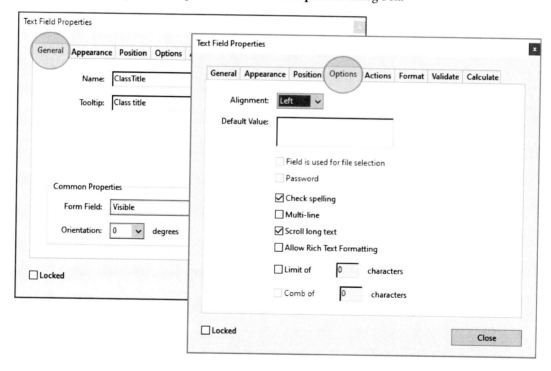

Figure 7.7 – The Text Field Properties dialog box tabs

Choices in settings and combinations of those choices offer limitless possibilities to customize form input formatting and collect specific types of data. The following subsections provide an overview of the meaning of the choices in the **Text Field Properties** dialog box. Text and other field types share properties, contained in the same tabs. Thus, you may want to bookmark this part of the chapter as a reference.

The following list of properties is long but will help you choose specific settings, which will result in precisely gathering the information that you need.

Text field tabs and properties

The following are the **Text Field Properties** tabs and their respective properties:

- The **General** tab for all types of form fields starts with basic settings. It should always be completed first if you create a new field to ensure that you work with one field only. Here are the settings contained in this tab:

  - **Name** sets the unique name of the selected form field. **Tooltip** contains text expanding the meaning of the field name and is a required form accessibility feature. Tooltips appear when a mouse hovers over a form field.

  - The **Form Field** property sets whether the field is displayed, either on screen or in print. This is helpful when a form includes action buttons that should be easy to see on screen, but not on a printed page. Imagine presentation slides with navigation arrows, or forms with **Submit** and **Print** buttons.

  - **Orientation** rotates the form field by **0**, **90**, **180**, or **270** degrees.

  - The **Read Only** checkbox prevents the field content from being changed when it is displayed.

  - The **Required** checkbox enforces a selected field to be filled in. If a required field is blank on the **Submit** function, an error message appears, and the field with missing required data is highlighted.

  - The **Locked** checkbox prevents accidental changes to a field. When selected for editing, the properties dialog box grays all the fields, making them no longer editable; the field cannot be moved or resized until you unlock it.

- The **Appearance** tab properties determine the visual formatting of a field on a page:

  - **Border Color** opens a color picker and a color swatch where the field border can be set. Choosing **No Color** leaves the field without a frame.

  - **Line Thickness** specifies the width of the border, with choices for **Thin**, **Medium**, or **Thick**.

  - **Fill Color** opens a color picker, where a color swatch for the background of a field can be selected. **No Color** makes the field transparent. A **Fill Color** choice other than **No Color** makes a field opaque and will block any images behind it.

- **Line Style** choices for the frame expand border settings to **Solid**, **Dashed**, **Beveled**, **Inset**, or **Underline**.

- **Font Size** sets the size of user-entered text or the selection symbol for radio buttons and checkboxes. The choices include the **Auto, Preset,** or **Typed** values. The **Auto** setting causes the font size to change to fit text in a field, resulting in different font sizes in different-sized fields. To prevent that, always use a specific font size.

- **Text Color** opens a color picker, where a color swatch for the text or symbol can be set.

- **Font** lists available system fonts. This option is not available for non-text fields.

- The **Position** tab lets you control the location of fields on a page where a high degree of accuracy is necessary and there are many fields – think tax forms. Position or size can be set to an accuracy of up to 10,000th of an inch. You can move fields to a specific position on a page.

- The **Options** tab provides formatting for user input, which can be alphabetic, numeric, or both:

  - **Field is used for file selection** allows you to include a file path as a field's value if a file is included with a form at the time of submission. This option is available only when **Scroll Long Text** is selected.

  - **Password** sets field text to be displayed as a series of asterisks (*). This is available only if **Check Spelling** is deselected.

  - **Alignment** aligns the text left, right, or center within a field.

  - **Default Value** sets the text that appears in a field until the user overwrites it. The default value is entered by typing in the text, which can be just one letter that hints at a word.

  - **Multi-line** allows you to have something longer than a single-line text entry, such as comments or feedback. This value is frequently combined with **Limits of characters** to prevent abuses.

  - **Scroll Long Text** builds a scrollbar on the right side of a field when input text extends beyond the boundaries of the field. This setting should be combined with **Multi-line**.

  - **Allow Rich Text Formatting** allows users to format text using keyboard shortcuts, *Ctrl / Cmd + B* for bold and *Ctrl /Cmd + I* for italic. This is helpful where additional formatting is important to the meaning of the text, especially when it is very long.

  - **Limit of Characters** sets a limit on the number of characters that can be entered in a field, as specified.

  - **Check Spelling** checks the text entered by a user for spelling errors.

  - **Comb Of Characters** spreads text entered by a user across the width of a text field. Characters entered are separated by lines of color, selected in the **Appearance** border color. This option is not available if any other checkboxes are selected.

- The **Actions** properties specify any actions associated with the form field. For example, you can select **Go to a page view, Reset a form,** or **Print file**:

  - **Select Trigger** specifies the user action that initiates an action on a mouse key position – mouse up, mouse down, mouse enter, mouse exit, on focus, or on blur.

  - **Select Action** specifies what happens when a user triggers the selected action.

  - **Add** opens a window, where specific selections of affected fields can be made, types of operations chosen, and so on. Options change based on an action selected in the dropdown.

  - The **Actions** window displays a list of defined triggers and actions.

  - The **Edit** button opens the same window used to set up the action initially.

  - The **Delete** button removes the selected action or trigger-action pair.

- The **Format** tab is available only for the text and drop-down form fields. The available options vary based on a choice in the **Select Format Category** drop-down menu:

  - When a format is selected, the bottom area of the dialog box displays a live preview of results for chosen settings.

- The **Validate** tab options are also available, only for the text and drop-down box fields. Validation properties limit entries to specified ranges, values, or characters, enforcing input of the desired data:

  - The **Field Value Is Not Validated** validation is turned off.

  - **Field Value Is In Range**, a numeric range, is set for field values entered either as a number or a percentage.

  - **Run Custom Validation Script**: If JavaScript is created and placed in this field, it will run a specific validation function.

- The **Calculate** tab, available in text field and dropdown box, allows setting options to perform automatic mathematical operations using selected field entries and display the result:

  - **Value Is Not Calculated** is a default setting when the field entry is straight-typed text.

  - **Value Is The** makes calculations possible.

  - Pop-up menu options include **Sum** to add the values entered in the selected fields, **Product** to multiply them, **Average, Minimum,** and **Maximum**.

  - **Pick** opens a list of the existing fields in the form that you select to add or deselect to remove from the calculation.

- **Simplified Field Notation** depends on JavaScript with field names and arithmetic symbols. The **Edit** button opens a dialog box where scripts can be written, edited, and added.

- **Custom Calculation Script** allows you to see any custom scripts added for calculations. The **Edit** button opens a dialog box where new JavaScript can be written, edited, and added.

Now that we have explored all the tabs in the **Text Field Properties** dialog box, we will move on to learn about other field types and their unique properties and functions.

Check box field properties

The **Check box** field presents users with yes-or-no selections for individual items. If the form contains multiple checkboxes, **the user can select as many or as few of these as needed**. This type of field is used when a few choices are displayed on the page and all or none can be selected.

For example, a presenter may offer participants a form where checkboxes represent class files, handouts, and 1 hour of tutoring time. An attendee can select one or all checkboxes, based on what they need. Each choice is independent of another, and one or all choices can be selected.

Settings for the **General**, **Appearance**, **Position**, and **Actions** tabs in this field are the same as **Text Field Properties**, so for more details, refer to the list of tabs in the *Text field tabs and properties* section.

We will now add a new checkbox to our form:

1. Select the **Check box** field tool, click or click-drag on the page, and then click the **All Properties** link.

2. In the **General** tab, enter a field name and tooltip

3. Click the **Options** tab that contains properties unique to the **Check Box** field, as shown in this screenshot:

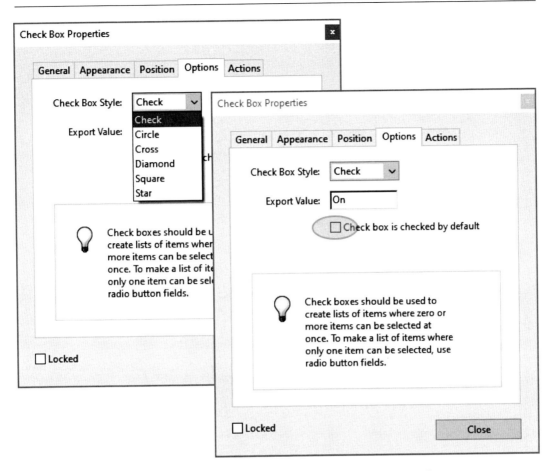

Figure 7.8 – The Check Box Properties dialog – the Options tab

- **Check Box Style** options are self-explanatory, with one reminder that I repeat during training sessions – don't mess with conventions; our world is complicated enough. What does this mean? If your readers have worked with checkboxes for decades, and a check symbol always meant a selected option when filling out a form, why would you confuse them and give them a circle, which normally appears in radio buttons? You can do what you want – Acrobat gives you plenty of choices and it is a free country – but consistent visuals make for fewer errors as a result of confusion.

  You will read the same reminder again very soon.

- The **Export Value** field defines a value that represents the item on export when filled it. Any character or number can be used.

- The **Check box is checked by default** checkbox will display on the form as selected unless the user deselects it.

Radio button field properties

The **Radio button** field creates a group of choices from which *only one item from the group* can be selected. Imagine asking for feedback on a presentation you made. Was the pace of the class good? Too fast? Too slow? Radio button choices on the form will allow only one selection of the three, unlike a checkbox that allows all or one choice for handouts, as shown in our earlier example.

All radio buttons must have the same name to work together as a **group**. If there are many choices exclusive of one another and you need to use page space efficiently, using a drop-down list field may work better. This will be discussed later in this section.

The **General**, **Appearance**, **Position**, and **Actions** tabs are same as **Text Field Properties**, so for more details on these, refer to the list of tabs in the *Text field tabs and properties* section.

We will now explore settings unique to radio buttons:

1. To create a **Radio button** selection group, select the tool and click or click-drag on a page.

2. You will see two fields and an alert, as shown in the following screenshot:

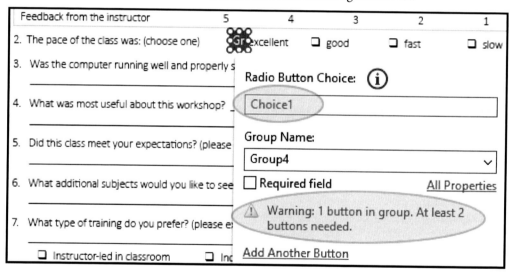

Figure 7.9 – A new radio button group in the process of creating

The **Warning:** is simply a reminder that you cannot use a radio button field alone. You must create a group of at least two fields. Now, click the **All Properties** link.

3. In the **General** tab, enter Pace as the name of the group. A shared name for the fields makes a group. This is unlike all other fields that must have a unique name.

4. Select the **Options** tab that contains properties unique to the **Radio Button** field. The following screenshot shows the tab's drop-down options and a value field. An expanded description will follow:

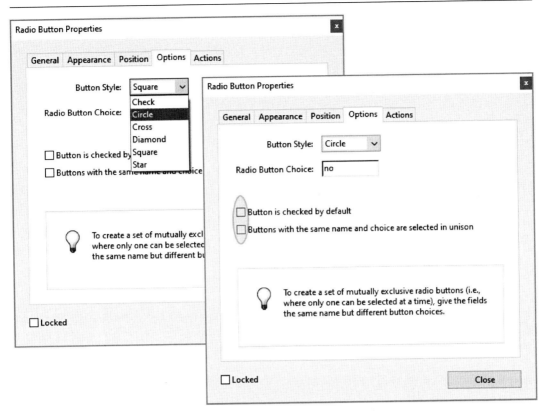

Figure 7.10 – Radio Button Properties dialog box – the Options tab

- **Button Style**: The choices are self-explanatory again, with one reminder that I repeat during training sessions: don't mess with conventions; our world is complicated enough. What does this mean? If your readers have worked with radio buttons for decades, and a **circle symbol** always meant a single choice within a group when filling out a form, why would you switch and give them a check, which normally appears in checkboxes? You can do what you want – Acrobat gives you plenty of choices – but consistent visuals make for fewer errors as a result of confusion.

- The **Radio Button Choice** field defines a unique value that identifies it from other buttons in the group and represents the selected item when it is exported. I entered good in my example.

- If **Check box is checked by default** is checked, the field will display as selected on the form until a user deselects it.

- When the **Buttons with the same name and content are selected in unison** option is checked, a user can select multiple related radio buttons with a single click. For example, a radio button that has the same field name and choice value as another can be clicked, and both radio buttons will be selected.

5. To make the group functional, copy and paste the radio button field that you just created (using the *Ctrl /Option + click-drag* shortcut), and in the **Options** tab, change the **Radio button choice:** value. I entered `fast`.

6. Click **Preview** in the top toolbar to test the two buttons. When you click one, the other is deselected. A user can only choose one feedback option in the **Pace** group.

Let's move on to some more settings for more form field types.

List box field properties

In the **list box** field properties, the **Options** tab offers choices unique to this field type. List boxes can include a setting that allows users to select multiple items on the list with *Shift + click* or *Ctrl /Cmd + click*. This field is useful if choices represented by checkboxes would take up too much space on a form page. In a small area, you can place many choices available to a user that are accessed by a scroll bar.

The **General**, **Appearance**, **Position**, and **Actions** tabs are the same as **Text Field Properties**, so for more details on these, refer to the list of tabs in the *Text field tabs and properties* section.

An example of where you would use this type of field is a list of training classes. If a student wants to select only one class, a single value selection would suffice, but if they want to take more classes, you can set up the field for multiple classes. The dimensions of the field dictate how many options are visible to a user. It is a good idea to display at least three or four entries. A scroll-down bar appears automatically if all choices don't fit the field size. Here are the steps to create it:

1. Create a new field using the **List Box** tool. Simply click-drag an area on a page next to a relevant label and open the properties by clicking the **All Properties** link.

2. In the **General** tab, enter `Classes` for the field name and `Select training classes here` in **Tooltip:**.

3. Enter the first value, `InDesign`, in the **Item:** field.

4. Enter `INDD` in the **Export Value:** field.

> **Important note**
>
> An export value is used in lists when you need to use symbols or acronyms/abbreviations in your database when a form is submitted, but you want a user to see the full term displayed as a choice. An export value is not visible when a form is filled out.

5. Click the **Add** button. The field text does not clear automatically, so be sure you delete it after the entry appears in the **Item List:** window.

6. Click in the **Item:** field again, delete text if there are any remnants left, and enter the next choice, `Photoshop`, with `PS` in the **Export Value:** field, and then click **Add**.

7.   Enter the following items as listed here:

- For Illustrator, enter AI in the **Export Value:** field

- For Acrobat, enter Acro in the **Export Value:** field

- For InCopy, enter IC in the **Export Value:** field

- For FrameMaker, enter FM in the **Export Value:** field

- For Captivate, enter CT in the **Export Value:** field

- For Premiere Pro, enter PPO in the **Export Value:** field

You can see all entries now appearing in a random order, as shown on the left side of the screenshot, or alphabetically, as shown on the right side:

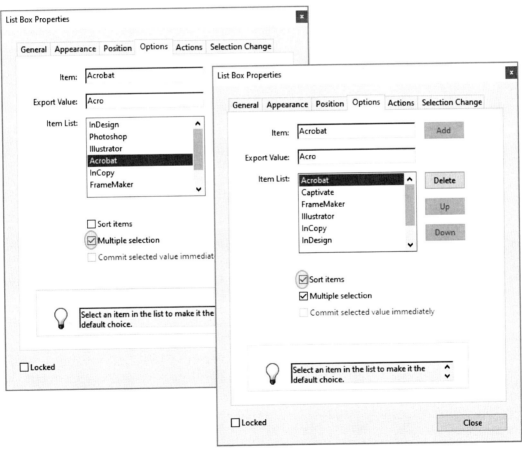

Figure 7.11 – List Box Properties dialog box – the Options tab

8.   Click the **Multiple Selection** checkbox. This will enable a user to choose more than one class.

9. Click the **Sort Items** checkbox to arrange the items alphabetically. If you need to add another value and move it up or down, use the buttons on the right. To move values, **Sort Items** must be unchecked.

10. To test results, click the **Preview** button on the toolbar at the top.

Nice, isn't it? Now, you know the method of adding selection fields. Next, we will examine a field type very similar in settings but different in its presentation on a page. Only one choice appears in the field, with more available in a dropdown after a click.

Dropdown list field properties

The **dropdown list** tool creates fields that allow a user to choose one item from a drop-down menu or to type in a custom value. Using this field creates great efficiency of space on a page. Many options can be arranged neatly and out of sight until a user is ready to make a selection. A perfect example of that is a list of the 50 states in the USA. As an example, we will create a list of 16 southern states in the USA.

The **General**, **Appearance**, **Position**, and **Actions** tabs are the same as **Text Field Properties**, so for more details on these, refer to the list of tabs under the previous *Text field tabs and properties* section.

Follow these steps to create a drop-down list of states:

1. Select the **Dropdown list** tool from the top toolbar and click-drag an area on a page next to the field label.

2. Click the **All Properties** link.

3. In the **General** tab, enter State for the field name and Select state in **Tooltip:**.

4. Select the **Options** tab to enter choices that will appear in the dropdown.

5. Enter the first value, Florida, in the **Item:** field.

6. Enter FL in the **Export Value:** field.

7. Click the **Add** button. The **Item List:** window will display the entered value. You should see Florida.

8. Delete the text from the **Item:** field if it shows in the **Item List:** window (the same odd field behavior as mentioned when discussing the list box field).

9. Enter another value, Pennsylvania, and in the **Export Value:** field, add PA, and then click **Add**. Pennsylvania now should appear in the **Item List:** window.

10. Complete the **Item List:** by continuing to add the remaining choices in the **Item:** field, accepting each entry by clicking the **Add** button. Here is the list of entries:

    • For Virginia, enter VA in the **Export Value:** field

    • For South Carolina, enter SC in the **Export Value:** field

    • For Tennessee, enter TN in the **Export Value:** field

- For North Carolina, enter NC in the **Export Value:** field

- For Georgia, enter GA in the **Export Value:** field

- For Alabama, enter AL in the **Export Value:** field

- For Arkansas, enter AR in the **Export Value:** field

- For Delaware, enter DL in the **Export Value:** field

- For District of Columbia, enter DC in the **Export Value:** field

- For Kentucky, enter KY in the **Export Value:** field

- For Louisiana, enter LA in the **Export Value:** field

- For Maryland, enter MD in the **Export Value:** field

- For Texas, enter TX in the **Export Value:** field

- For West Virginia, enter VA in the **Export Value:** field

You can see all entries now appearing in random order, as shown on the left side of this screenshot:

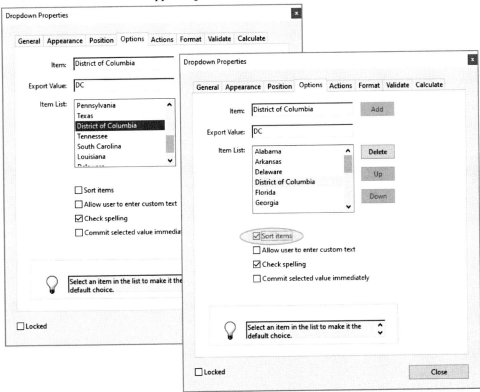

Figure 7.12 – Dropdown Properties dialog box – the Options tab

11. The **Allow user to enter custom text** checkbox expands the choices to a typed-in value, such as a location in a different country.

12. Click **Sort Items** to arrange them alphabetically. If you need to add another value and move it up or down, use the buttons on the right. To move values, **Sort Items** must be unchecked.

13. To preview results, click the **Preview** button on the toolbar at the top.

Working nicely? Click **Edit** on the toolbar at the top to return to **Form Editing** mode.

Next, we will create a button and make it functional by adding an action.

Button field properties and actions

The **Button** tool creates a field that initiates an action on a user's computer when clicked. **Actions** include opening a file, printing, or submitting form data, either via email or directly to a server using a script.

The buttons can be set up using images, or text formatted using button properties. Positioning a mouse and clicking allows you to add focus or rollovers, and visual changes to help a user predict what will happen on click.

It is worth repeating that action buttons are different from radio buttons, which represent data choices made by a user.

The **General**, **Appearance**, **Position**, and **Actions** tabs are the same as **Text Field Properties**, so for more details on these, refer to the list of tabs under the previous *Text field tabs and properties* section.

Options in the **Button Properties** dialog box allow you to make buttons pretty in addition to functional. Choices in the **Layout:** dropdown activate the dialog box choices for selecting text **Label only**, **Icon graphic**, or a combination of both, with icons and a text label position on the button.

It is a good practice to create backgrounds for buttons in the authoring software. Color can be matched to other graphical elements, and button position in relation to other fields can be set ahead of time, so you can focus on functionality when working with .pdf.

In our example, we do not have a background, so we will cover all steps to create a button entirely in Acrobat. Here, the steps are to ultimately create a green **Print** button (see *Figure 7.13*):

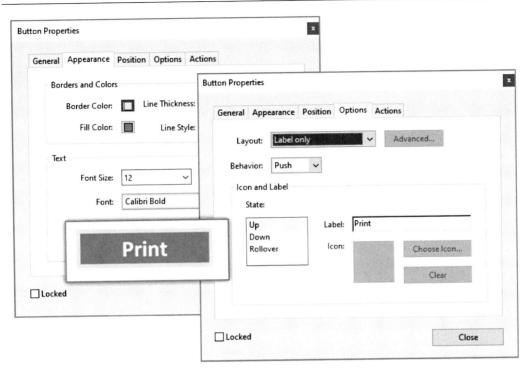

Figure 7.13 – Button Properties dialog box – the Print button

1. From the top toolbar, select the **Button** tool and click-drag on the page.

2. Click **All Properties** to open the dialog box.

3. In the **General** tab, type Print in the **Name:** field and Click to print form in **Tooltip:**.

4. In the **Common Properties** group at the bottom of the box, select **Visible but doesn't print** for the **Form Field:** field.

5. Select the **Appearance** tab and choose these options for the respective fields: **Light Green** for **Border Color:**, **Green** for **Fill Color:**, **12** for **Font Size:**, **White** for **Text Color:**, and **Calibri Bold** for **Font:**.

6. Select the **Options** tab, choose **Label Only** for **Layout:**, and in the **Label:** field, type Print, as shown in the screenshot.

7. Select the **Actions** tab, choose **Execute a menu item** from the **Select Action:** dropdown, and then click the **Add…** button.

8. This is where the magic of the buttons happens. There are all kinds of choices for preset actions. All you need to do is choose one. Click the **File | Print** options, and then click **OK**.

    The **Actions** window in the properties box contains a confirmation that you included an action in your button. Ready to test it?

9. Click **Preview** in the top toolbar, and then click your brand-new, shiny **Print** button. The **Print** dialog box should open, and you can proceed either to close it or print the file.

    Note in the print preview window that the button itself will not print. We chose that option in the **General** tab. Neat, isn't it? There's no need to waste ink.

We are moving along in our exploration of different field types. A few more need to be discussed – date field, digital signature, and barcode, so let's go.

Date field properties

The **date** tool creates a preset version of a text field with the **Format** tab options preselected. It creates a widget, allowing users to select a date rather than type it. It's very easy to use; just don't forget a unique name and a tooltip for the field, since the dialog box opens on a **Format** tab rather than a **General** tab.

The **General**, **Appearance**, **Position**, and **Actions** tabs are the same as **Text Field Properties**, so for more details on these, refer to the list of tabs under the previous *Text field tabs and properties* section.

Digital signature field properties

The **digital signature** tool defines the space to electronically sign a `.pdf` document with a digital signature. It opens a discussion on an entire industry of document security, signing, and so on, which we will cover in *Chapter 8, Adding Digital Signatures and Security Settings*.

For now, we will cover the mechanics of creating the field. This is very consistent with everything we've done previously. Here are the steps:

1. Select the **Digital Signature** field tool and click-drag on a page. Typically, the bottom of the page content is a good location. You can even have the signature area defined as part of the page layout. You will get a field outline with a red tab, as shown here:

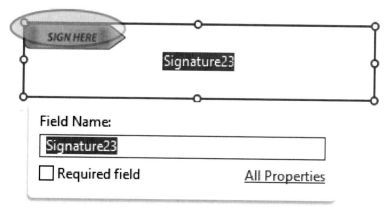

Figure 7.14 – The Signature field in the making

2. Click **All Properties** to open the dialog box. The **General, Appearance, Position**, and **Actions** tabs are the same as **Text Field Properties**, so for more details on these tabs, refer to the list of tabs in the *Text field tabs and properties* section.

3. Complete the settings in the **General** and **Appearance** tabs according to the needs of the form.

4. Click the **Signed** tab. Options here specify what happens when a user who signs the form clicks the field. See the screenshot here:

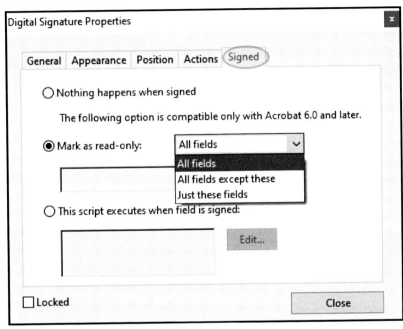

Figure 7.15 – Digital Signature Properties dialog box

Here is the meaning of the choices:

- **Nothing happens when signed** means that only a digital signature is placed, and nothing happens to the content of the form. The signature itself will provide security to the document as intended. More on this is covered in *Chapter 8, Adding Digital Signatures and Security Settings*.

- **Mark as read-only:** This sets all fields selected in the dropdown as uneditable after signing.

- **This script executes when field is signed:** This allows you to insert precise instructions using JavaScript.

Barcode field properties

The **barcode** tool encodes the input from selected fields and displays it as a visual pattern that can be interpreted by a decoding device, such as a scanner. Incorporating barcodes into forms requires more extensive licensing and setup than the scope of this chapter.

The software needed to work with barcodes in forms and address enterprise-level workflows is **Acrobat Capture** and **LiveCycle Barcoded Forms decoder**, sold by Adobe Inc. In Acrobat, you will get an alert, as shown in this screenshot, if you do not have specific licensing in addition to those applications:

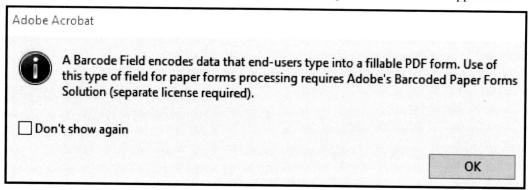

Figure 7.16 – A barcode license alert

We will leave it at that for barcodes.

We have reviewed all form tools, field types, and some of their properties, but didn't come close to exploring all the possible combinations of settings. This is where experience comes in. Do take time to play. Like with everything, over time, patterns emerge and obscure setting details become new tricks. I certainly have enjoyed setting up more and more ambitious forms over many years.

We will now move on and discuss options to help you ensure that a form is easy to fill out and helps users to enter accurate information. We will set up validation of form data parameters.

Validating form input data

Validation of input assures that information entered fits certain criteria. For example, if items on a **Requisition** form must be under a certain dollar value, a field setting can enforce that. Here is how it is done:

1. Create a text field and complete the name, tooltip, and settings in the **Appearance** tab:

2. In the **Format** tab, under **Select format category:**, choose **Number** (other options will only allow validation using a custom script). For reference, see the following screenshot:

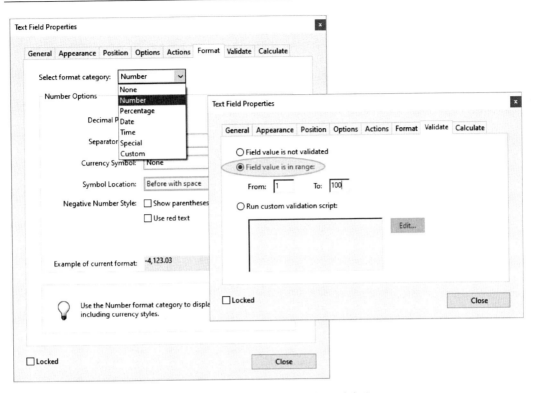

Figure 7.17 – Setting up field value validation

3. Select the **Validate** tab and click **Field Value is in the range**, as shown in the preceding screenshot.

4. Enter 1 in the **From:** field and 100 in the **To:** field.

5. Click **Close** and test the validation in **Preview** mode by entering any number over 100 in the field. You will see an alert like this one:

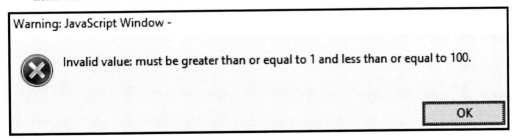

Figure 7.18 – A failed data entry value alert

Validation of input forces a user to enter the correct information. Custom validation scripts give form designers the power to define very precisely what type of input they will accept. This is how you achieve precision and accuracy when collecting form data.

Next, we will automate input by setting up a calculation formula in a field so that forms that collect numeric data can provide ready results – think purchase orders or attendance numbers.

Creating a calculated form field

Automatic calculations speed up the filling out and accuracy of entry for specific types of forms, such as purchase orders, requisitions, polls, and the number of participants. Totals, subtotals, sales tax, shipping charges, and other fields should be set up to fill in automatically as a calculated value. They work with values entered in other fields, so you will need a form with the most interactive fields for data already in place. We used a purchase order as an example. The **Price** and **Quantity** fields have already been created and formatted as numbers.

Calculated fields are text fields formatted as numbers. We will work with the **Item Total** column data, where each cell will be a row total.

Here are the steps to set up calculations:

1. Create a text field **Text field** and complete the name, tooltip, and settings in the **Appearance** tab.

2. Select the **Calculate** tab and choose **product (x)** in the **Value is the** dropdown. Here is a screenshot:

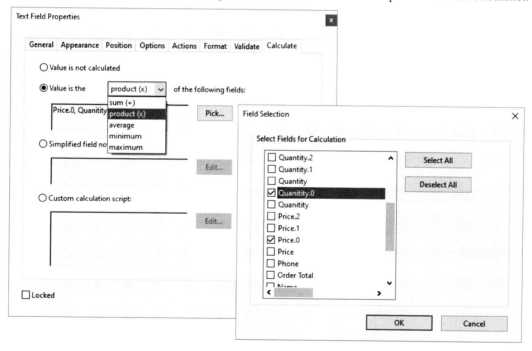

Figure 7.19 – Setting up a calculated field in the Calculate tab

3. Click the **Pick…** button to open the **Field Selection** dialog box.

4. Select fields corresponding to the **Total** field that you are setting up. In our example, the calculation is set up for the `Total.0` field, so the chosen fields are `Quantity.0` and `Price.0`. Click **OK** to close.

5. You can see your chosen fields in the top window of the **Calculate** dialog box. If this is correct, you can close **Text Field Properties** and test your work.

6. Go to **Preview** mode and enter a number in the **Price Each** and **Quantity** fields.

7. The **Item Total** field is automatically calculated. You may need to refine the formatting of data, such as text alignment, separator style, and currency symbol, which you know how to do.

8. To finish setting up calculations for totals in all rows of the *purchase order* form, simply repeat *steps 2* to *5*, being mindful that cells in each row have different field names. Be sure to pick corresponding fields for calculations.

9. When finished setting up, test the form in **Preview** mode.

Having fun yet? This is another example of how extensive formatting of interactive fields can be. No wonder some manuals on creating forms are more than 1,000 pages long… Yes, you read it correctly – over 1,000 pages! The combinations are endless.

This brings us to a final check on our form. We must ensure that the fields are easily accessed by all users, including those who cannot see. These users do not use a mouse but depend on the *Tab* key. We will set up the correct tabbing order next.

Form tabbing order

For any user, interacting with a form online is a personal experience. Some prefer using a mouse to enter each field before typing text, others prefer using the *Tab* key, and most use a hybrid method. I usually *tab* from field to field for text and click on fields for selections.

It is very important that the order of tabbing follows the logic of the form. As a user, you would not expect to enter your first name in a field, followed by email, and then followed by the last name. There is a certain pattern that is expected. This is just an example of why setting up a proper tab order matters to everyone. For accessibility, *tabbing* is crucial. Visual users can quickly recover; a person depending on logic can take much longer to find the proper context.

Here is how to address this issue:

1. In **Form Editing** mode, locate the **FIELDS** menu in the formatting panel. Here is a screenshot:

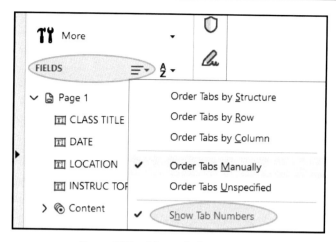

Figure 7.20 – A barcode license alert

2. Click on the **FIELDS** menu to get a submenu related to tabs.

3. Select **Order Tabs Manually**, as checked in the previous screenshot.

4. Select **Show Tab Numbers**.

Each form field on the page now displays the number representing the order in which a user tapping on the *Tab* key will enter each field. This feature makes it easy to identify problems. If you need to adjust the order, use the panel below the **FIELDS** menu.

Let's examine the following screenshot:

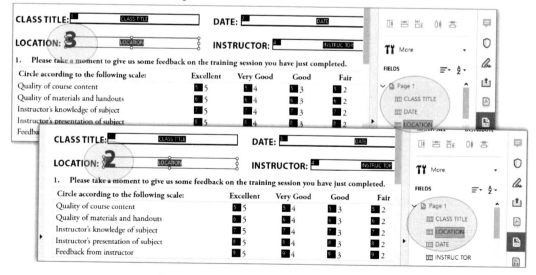

Figure 7.21 – Adjusting a form tabbing order

Screenshot numbers when printed are very small, but you should have no difficulty seeing them on your monitor. Compare the position of the field in the formatting panel in the highlighted areas. Then, compare the field **Tab** number on the page. Changing the position of the field in the formatting panel changes the tab number, thus the tabbing order. The location of the field in the layout did not change.

To adjust tabbing order of the entire form, simply move fields in the formatting panel while watching the numbers on the page. Test the logic of the tabbing order frequently by tapping the *Tab* key in **Preview** mode and observing whether the progression from field to field makes sense. This is not difficult but a tedious process, a bit like moving accessibility tags. Once you have done it a few times, it's not hard.

> **Important note**
> Do put the task of setting the tab order on your work checklist. Perform a check after creating and editing the form, when all fields are in place. It is very easy to forget this step when designing interactive forms.

Your form is now designed; the fields are formatted and contain the desired settings. The next step is to set up a process to collect the information that users will send your way. This is what we will learn next.

Collecting data from filled-out PDF forms

This section involves setting up the final step of the information-gathering process. The form is still in your hands, the form designer expert. You have tested all the fields, corrected errors, and made sure calculations, validations, format numbering, and the tabbing order all work.

We will now create a **Submit** button and make decisions about how to collect the information when a user fills out our form and is ready to send it.

Follow the steps in creating a button in the *Button field properties and actions* section; alternatively, here's a little cheat – simply copy and paste the **Print** button and position it on a page. I usually keep all buttons close together at the bottom of the form.

Since you have a duplicate field, first, you need to change the **Name** field value, tooltip, and label of the field. Following that, we will spend some time on **Actions**. Here are the steps if you copy and paste and update the button:

1. Copy and paste the **Print** button. Use *Ctrl /Option + click-drag*, holding the *Ctrl /Option* key until you release the mouse. You now have two **Print** buttons.

2. Double-click on one to open the properties dialog box and update the following:

    -   In the **General** tab, update the **Name** field to Submit and **Tooltip:** to Click to submit
        form.

    -   There's no need to make changes in the **Appearance** tab, as these options are already set as
        a result of copying and pasting the field. Nice payback!

    -   Update the **Label:** field to Submit Form in the **Options** tab. The button label on the form
        page should now replace Print and display the new function.

3. Go to the **Actions** tab, where we will now set up the details of submitting the form data.

4. First, delete the current action. Click in the **Actions** window on the **Mouse Up** entry and click
    the *Delete* key.

5. From the **Select Action** dropdown, click the **Submit a form** choice then **Add...** button. A
    dialog box opens with settings to facilitate the best format and process for collecting data.
    Here is a screenshot:

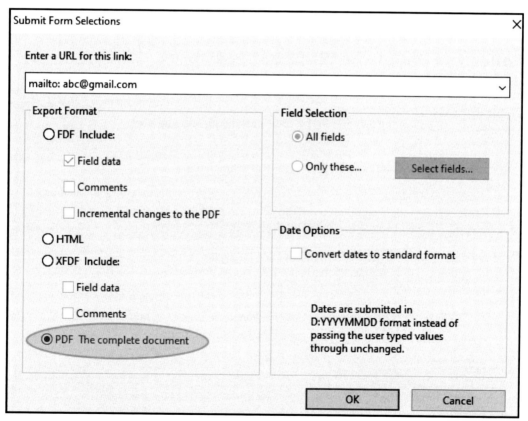

Figure 7.22 – Selecting the form data submission format and process

6. We will submit our data as a complete `.pdf` document sent via email.

7. In the **Enter a URL for this link:** field, enter your email, following the `mailto:` command. The command tells Acrobat to launch the user's email application.

8. Click the choice for **PDF The complete document**. This selection will attach the filled-out `.pdf` form to the email. The form will include all data that the user provided and saved in the file.

9. Click **OK** and close the **Button Properties** dialog box.

10. Go to **Preview** mode and test your form. Fill it out and then click on the **Submit** button. Your email software should launch with the form attached.

Good job! The form is almost finished. The final task is preventing unauthorized changes to the content of the form before it is ready for deployment. We will discuss the protection of the integrity of `.pdf` documents, including forms, in the next chapter.

Designing an interactive form is a very extensive topic, and we just could not address every option. My attempt was to introduce the meaning behind field settings and patterns so that you can explore them on your own – or take a class.

Summary

Working with forms is challenging but very satisfying. In this chapter, we touched on the principles of form design and layout and stepped through the process of automatically detecting field areas. The **Prepare Form** tool is only a starting point for the setup. We looked at all tools and settings available for each field. We tested the validation and calculation of input in fields and finally set up a process to collect the form data using submit action button to email the form to the form owner.

This is a good start to working with forms. It is an industry, so learning will be a long process if this is your main career task.

In the next chapter, we will learn how to ensure the integrity of `.pdf` documents, such as our form, by adding password protection, set up a digital identity, and create and validate electronic signatures.

8

Adding Digital Signatures and Security Settings

PDFs have evolved from simple read-only pages to documents rich with features that include interactive forms, multimedia, scripts, attachments, and much more. The exciting possibilities unfortunately make the files vulnerable to malicious code that can steal data, damage your computer, or waste resources.

Security lets you protect computers and entire networks against these threats by either blocking potentially damaging actions or selectively permitting those only from trusted files and locations. As everyone adopted the use of .pdf format as a common digital page, concern for the privacy of the content of many types of documents, such as personal taxes or confidential correspondence, also became an issue.

Security concerns can be addressed in two general categories: software active on users' systems or other devices, and .pdf document content security.

Application security is meant to protect Acrobat and Reader against vulnerabilities, malicious attacks, and other risks. Options in **Preferences** allow you to customize the application and prepare it for potential attacks. Large corporate or government networks depend on specific tools available in their interface to predict threats and prevent them from taking over their systems. This often means limiting user access to outside content, often requiring a thorough safety scan before use. To accomplish all this, much more is needed than Acrobat, but in our discussion, it is helpful to understand the scope and the context in which desktop users function.

Content security is focused on features to protect the integrity of a .pdf document. Settings saved in the file can enforce the privacy of the information contained, prevent unauthorized changes, restrict printing to protect intellectual property, and so on.

Digital security has become an enormous industry, and the tools it depends on need to be regularly updated to keep a step ahead of threats. Not a great world, but… there it is.

In this chapter, we will explore options that every user of Acrobat Pro should be aware of. We will not discuss general security policies and features implemented at an organizational level, though it is important to understand the verification process. Additionally, we will not discuss in this chapter document signatures or related options, covered already in *Chapter 1, Understanding Different Adobe Acrobat Versions and Services*.

I will do my best to stay away from industrial jargon for security terminology and will attempt to explain those concepts in human terms. The process is complicated enough.

The following topics will be considered in this chapter:

- PDF document password protection settings

- Creating a digital ID and a signature

- Signing a document

- Understanding the validation process

- Certifying a document

We will begin with learning how to protect the integrity of a `.pdf` publication by applying password protection settings.

PDF document password protection settings

When a publication is ready for distribution or being posted on the World Wide Web, we need to protect the content from unauthorized changes, copying, and—in some cases—printing. Printing of purchased `.pdf` publications is often restricted to enforce copyright protection. Forms especially need to be protected from altering field settings and data manipulation. The easiest way to assure that only authorized users can alter content is to set up password protection. Here are the steps:

1. Open a `.pdf` document that you would like to work with.

2. From the top menu, select the **File | Properties...** options.

3. Click the **Security** tab at the top and review the current **Document Restrictions Summary** list in the lower part of the dialog box. There are none—all operations are allowed, which means that the file is not protected yet.

4. Click the **Security Method:** dropdown and choose **Password Security** to open a dialog box where you can set protections to your file, from authorization to view content to minimal restriction of removing pages. Here are the dialog boxes that you will work with:

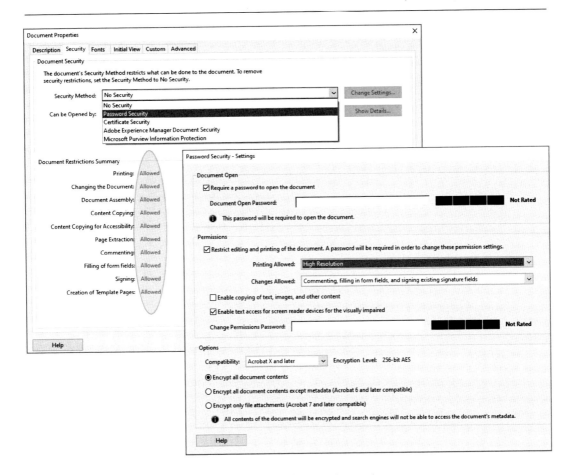

Figure 8.1 – Password protection settings

5. Password fields are grayed out until you click a checkbox that makes options active. Choose **Require a password to open the document** if you need to protect the privacy of a document's content. This setting will prevent previews in file browsers to show, and when someone attempts to read that file, it will open only to those who have the password. You may immediately think of some documents that will need this type of protection: personal taxes, medical records, confidential messages, and so on.

    If the document you work with does not need this level of protection but is meant to be read by everyone, you can move on to the next checkbox in the **Permissions** group.

6. Click the **Restrict editing and printing of the document** checkbox and read the alert line that follows. You need to have a password in mind. That's all. Two dropdowns now become available:

   • **Printing Allowed:** with choices for **None, Low Resolution (150 dpi)**, and **High Resolution**—these options are meant to protect intellectual property from unauthorized reproduction. Ads, photos, and others are not useful at 150 **dots per inch** (**dpi**). Books' and journals' settings may not allow printing at all. For the example document that you are working with, select **High Resolution**. We will not limit the printing of the document if it does not infringe on restrictions to the distribution of intellectual property rights.

   • The **Changes Allowed:** dropdown is where you allow users to provide form data but restrict any content changes. Select **Commenting, filling in form fields, and signing existing signature fields**. Available fields in a form can be filled out, but labels, backgrounds, positions, or settings are only editable by those with a password. If a document is not a form, only commenting and signing will be allowed.

7. The **Enable text access for screen reader devices for the visually impaired** checkbox should always stay on. Unchecking it means that a screen reader (used by visually impaired users) will not be able to read any of the text aloud for those users, making the form inaccessible.

8. **Change Permissions password:**—the time has come; type it in… it is your little secret. Just be sure you remember it. Memory failing? You probably have a long list of passwords, so don't forget to add this one to the list.

9. Click **OK** to close this dialog box. An alert pops up: read it if you want or click **OK** to move on. Now, it is time to confirm the **Permissions** password and test your memory in the process. If you typed it correctly, another alert pops up, reminding you to save the file. Until then, file passwords are not functioning. Click **OK**, then one more time **OK** to close the large dialog box.

10. Save your file; I use *Ctrl + S* as a shortcut.

11. You will now see the **Security Settings** pane on the left of the screen with a small padlock icon. When you click the icon, the pane reveals that the file is password protected. Here is a screenshot:

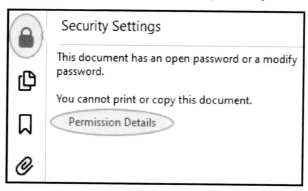

Figure 8.2 – Security Settings pane in a protected file

12. Click **Permission Details** to open a dialog box with a detailed **Document Restrictions Summary** list. The list of allowed operations is now updated and reflects the settings applied to the document.

Protecting your publication using a password is the simplest form of ensuring that no unauthorized changes are made to the `.pdf` content. There is a warning that there may be other applications that don't respect this security. The protection is based on encryption contained exclusively within the file that remembers the password. This means that the forgotten password cannot be retrieved.

In the next section, we will expand the discussion to understand how a digital identity is created, allowing you to sign and certify documents and validate signed documents you receive from others. This process will involve encrypted files external to a `.pdf` publication.

We will next learn what a digital ID is, how it is verified, and how to create one on your system so that Acrobat knows who you are, as a signer.

Creating a digital ID and a signature

Acrobat becomes aware of who you are at the time of software installation. Your operating system provides basic login information such as **Name for Author name** for commenting and account information and spells out other details, such as which functions you can access based on your software license.

For signatures, one more piece of information is necessary, and that is your **digital ID**. Typically, it contains your name, email, the name of the organization, a serial number, and an expiration date. It is a lot like your passport or grocery store card with a photo. Close enough comparison? Essentially, you are setting up a way for Acrobat to identify who is certifying or signing the document.

Things get even more fun when you realize that you can create multiple identities since Acrobat recognizes that we function in a complex world and perform many tasks in different roles.

Digital IDs rely on two keys: **private** and **public**. To sign your document, you use a **private key**. On the other hand, to allow others to confirm that it is really you, you give them a **public key**, also referred to as a **public certificate**. Those who want to validate your signature will use the digital public certificate, a bit like banking institutions compare your ink signature kept in their records to ensure the authenticity of your signed checks or contracts.

Here is how it works, more or less:

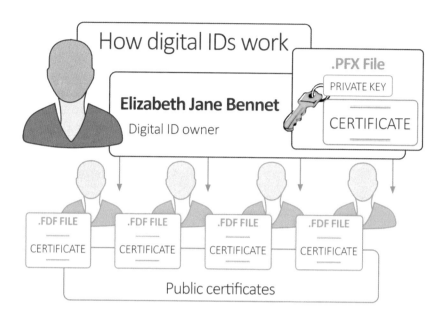

Figure 8.3 – How digital ID private key and public certificates work

To illustrate the process, let me introduce you to Elizabeth Jane Bennet, a young woman who owns a classic bookstore, *Window Nook, Inc.*. Elizabeth employs four people and wants to ensure that final copies of book purchase requests, payroll, vacation days agreements, and other internal documents are preserved as signed `.pdf` files. She decided that the volume and the level of protection these documents need are sufficient for her to manage the security herself. She is ready to implement what she learned in a class she recently attended.

Elizabeth begins to work with digital signatures and creates her own digital ID. Her private key and public certificate are contained in a single file that is stored in her system. When she needs to sign any documents, Acrobat finds and refers to that file. It confirms her identity after she typed a password that only she knows, and it matches the private key-encrypted information.

When her signed document leaves her system, the recipients open it, and if they never had any prior contact with Elizabeth, the signature would show as invalid. However, they know who she is, call or email her, and request her public certificate file. When she replies, the file is copied to a proper folder on the recipient's system, Acrobat finds it, compares the certificate information with the signature in the document, and if these match, it **validates** the signature. From now on, Elizabeth may send signed documents to these recipients, and all her signatures will be validated. No one who receives her certificate has access to her password since it is contained in her private key, which stays only on her system.

This is a very simple explanation of the process. Of course, in technical terms, there are policies, trusted digital signing certificates, globally recognized legal requirements, updates…and so on. Well, that's why we have security experts and the entire industry to support them.

Business transactions require third-party validation by a **certificate authority** (**CA**), an organization that manages all aspects of certifying identities, signatures, and their legal compliance. IT departments depend on access to services provided by a long list of internationally recognized security organizations. Trusted certificates used by Adobe are edited and updated in the **Preferences | Trust Manager** settings.

A complete list of companies approved by Adobe as CAs or trusted **service providers** (**SPs**) is available for reference on the Adobe website under the **Adobe Approved Trust List** (**AATL**). As third-party SPs, these organizations are recognized globally. They issue a confirmation of authenticity for digitally signed documents as legally binding, in a similar way to a credit card company confirming to a vendor that a buyer is legitimately using a credit card and the bank will pay the charges. The trust list is downloaded and accessed by Acrobat and Reader when a signed document is first opened or created. The setting allows for an automatic update of the list every 30 days.

In the next section, we will go through the steps of setting up a digital identity that we will use to sign and certify our document. The process of verifying authenticity that we will use is adequate for a small group of users, such as in a small business or department, somewhat like the bookstore owned by Elizabeth J. Bennet described earlier. Using this method is limited to those who know one another personally. If you work for a large organization, your ID and the entire certification and validation process are likely set up already. All you need to do is use it. However, knowing how it all works on a smaller scale is interesting, and you may find it very useful in your office.

Let's create a new digital ID next.

Creating a digital ID

Creating a new digital ID takes quite a few steps. They are not complicated, but they involve a lot of similar dialog boxes. Let's explore the process on your system:

1. Select **Edit** and then **Preferences** from the top menu.

2. Click **Signatures** on the left list of options in the dialog box.

3. Click the **More** button in the **Identities & Trusted Certificates** group. You will see the first of many dialog boxes where you will provide information about yourself. This part works as a wizard, where you can go back if anything needs to be changed. The screenshot gives you a preview of the steps:

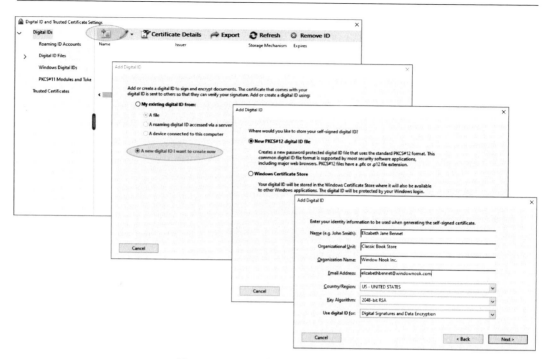

Figure 8.4 – New digital ID wizard steps

4. Click the **Add** button (the first option on the left, represented as +) as highlighted on the first screen in *Figure 8.4*.

5. Select **A new digital ID I want to create now**, then click **Next**.

6. Accept the next default setting for the location of the digital ID, and click **Next**.

7. Complete the fields with the information requested on the next screen. You can use data from our example and then click **Next**.

8. Finally, type the password. Be sure you remember it as it will be tied to this identity. The same password will be used in signatures representing it. I used books100 for our example.

9. Click **Finish**. A new identity is added to the list (the screen opened in *step 2*). See the following screenshot:

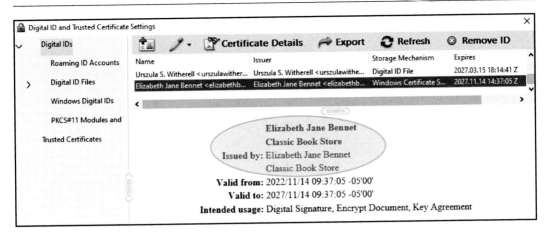

Figure 8.5 – A new digital ID added to the list of users

Important note

Acrobat allows you to create multiple identities. Why? It reflects different types of documents that you may sign. You may need to sign personal income taxes, or you may be replying as an owner of your business or as a parent of schoolchildren signing permission slips. Each identity can have a different signature attached to it.

If you forget your password used in signed documents, it is not possible to retrieve it. Be sure you have good methods for keeping your passwords safe and accessible to you.

A new file containing both the certificate and the key (see *Figure 8.3*) is created in a folder where the Acrobat application will look when validating an identity and a signature. Usually, it looks like this:

`...\AppData\Roaming\Adobe\Acrobat\DC\Security\ElizabethJaneBennet.pfx`

The `.pfx` file is encrypted and contains both the **private key** and the **certificate**. You can copy and paste it in the corresponding location (as you see in the preceding code) if you change your computer or need to have the same identity set up on a desktop and laptop.

If you want to share your certificate with others who need to validate your signature, you will only export a certificate component of the `.pfx` file. The public certificate is exported to `.fdf` format. Here are the steps to share the **public certificate** with others:

1. If you are still in the dialog box with identities (opened from **Preferences | Signatures | More**), select the identity from the list of identities that you want to create a public certificate from.

2. Click **Export**. An **Export Options** dialog box opens:

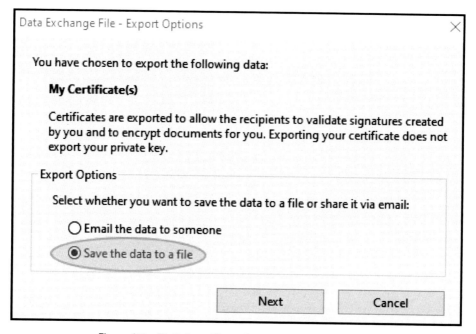

Figure 8.6 – Digital certificate Export Options dialog box

3. Select **Save the data to a file** and click **Next**.

4. Save the file to a folder. Acrobat uses this file to keep certificate information but not personal keys with a password. Notice the file extension is .fdf (**Forms Data Format**), the same when exporting comments or interactive form data.

5. Exit the **Digital ID and Trusted Certificate Settings** dialog box, but do not close **Preferences**. We will use another option from this group of **More...** buttons.

Your identity is set up and saved as a .pfx file. You can share a portion of this information with others through a public certificate that is saved as a .fdf file. Acrobat now knows who you are—well, sort of... It does not know you as a person or your family. Only your certificate numbers.

Let's now go through the process of creating a digital signature.

Creating a digital signature

We already created a digital identity that will represent itself at signing with a digital signature.

A **digital signature**, just like a wet signature in the physical world, provides a unique mark identifying the user who placed it. There are many ways Adobe addresses the need to sign .pdf documents. We are still focused on the process available in the desktop Acrobat in a context of a group of people who know one another.

Here are the steps to create a digital signature representing the digital ID created earlier:

1. The **Preferences | Signatures** dialog box should be still open.

2. Click the **More...** button on top in the **Digital Signatures** group.

3. A **Creation and Appearance Preferences** dialog box appears with choices allowing you to control what information is displayed when a signature is placed.

4. Checked items should include the following:

   - **Show reasons**

   - **Show location and contact information**

   - **Include the signature's revocation status**

   Compare *Figure 8.7* to see how these are entered when signing.

5. In the **Appearances** group, click the **New** button on the right. A large dialog box opens again and it is waiting for your selections. Here is a screenshot showing information after it has been typed in:

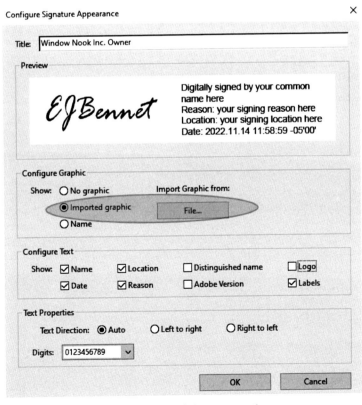

Figure 8.7 – Digital signature settings

6. The image that represents the **EJBennet wet signature** is based on a .pdf file selected from the **Imported graphic | File...** option. A signature such as this can be either a .pdf file created from a scan, typed using a decorative font, or an image from any file format that Acrobat can import.

7. Deselect the **Logo** checkbox to remove the Acrobat logo.

8. Click **OK** to accept the settings. You are now back in the **Creation and Appearance Preferences** dialog box. The **Appearances** window at the bottom (shown in *Figure 8.8*) shows the new signature as an option to use when signing a document.

If you need more than one signature, you will have to simply repeat *steps 1-7*, but change relevant information, such as title, password, and so on:

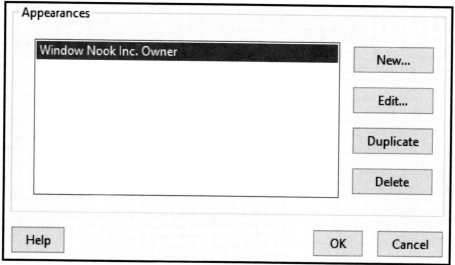

Figure 8.8 – Digital signature appearance listed as available

9. Click **OK** to close the dialog box and click **OK** again to exit **Preferences**.

We have completed two necessary tasks to start a paperless process of signing documents. We created a digital identity and a digital signature that will be placed on documents to certify their validity.

In the next section, we will look at how a signature is placed on a document page.

Signing a document

In the context of our example, signing documents within a group where people know one another depends on an interactive signature field. Field(s) can be prepared ahead of time before a document is filled out, or a signature area can be drawn at the time of signing and the position will be determined by the signer.

Placing a signature field on a page

Creating a field that will accept a digital signature allows you, the document owner, to specify the signature location. Most often, it is placed in interactive forms using the **Prepare Form** tool. Specific steps and the meaning of choices were discussed in the *Digital signature field properties* section of *Chapter 7*. The process of placing the field on a page was shown in *Figure 7.13 – Signature field in the making.*

First, let's create a new signature field. Here are the steps:

1. Select the **Prepare Form** tool. If a document selection page appears, the **This document requires signatures** option should not be checked. Click the **Start** button.

> **Important note**
>
> A document selection page appears only when a document is not a .pdf form and the **Prepare Form** tool is used for the first time. A signature field should be placed after all other form fields are already in place, since the signature settings refer to specific field names in the form if the **Mark as read-only** option is selected in the **Sign** tab of the **Digital Signature Properties** dialog box.
>
> Protected documents, such as contracts, must have predefined signature field(s) with permission settings allowing their use.

2. Select the **Signature** field tool, then click-drag an area on the page and complete setting up the field options.
3. Accept the settings by clicking the **Close** button, and then close the **Prepare Form** tool.

We will now use the field, the same way a signer would if the field were **predefined**. We will sign the document by clicking the field just created:

4. Click on the **Signature** field. A dialog box opens where you can choose your identity. I selected **Elizabeth Jane Bennet**.
5. Since you already have an ID to use and the signature was created earlier, simply click **Continue**.
6. Another dialog box appears where you can refine your signature information and provide a password to confirm that you are authorized to use this mark in the current document. Here is what you will work with:

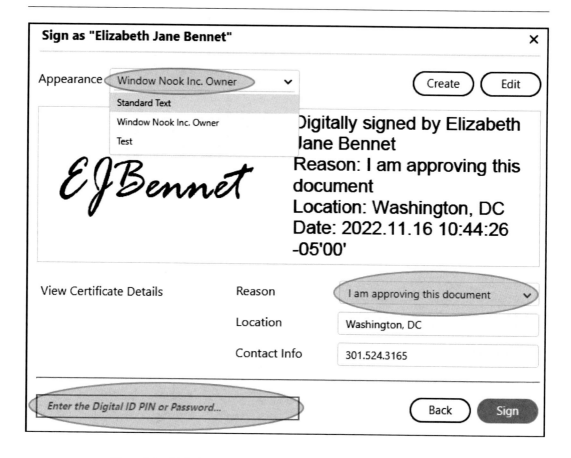

Figure 8.9 – Digital signature appearance selections and password area

7. Select from the **Appearance** dropdown how the signature should display. I chose `Window Nook Inc. Owner`, created earlier in this chapter.

8. Select a reason from the **Reason** dropdown.

9. Type your password, then click **Sign**. You are prompted to save the `.pdf` file as a new file. This is an important step in providing a backup of a document. If you sign one and forget the password, there is no going back—you cannot retrieve it—especially because we are using the self-signing process, not involving third-party organizations for verification.

10. Give the file a new name and click **Save**. I usually suffix the word `_Signed` to a filename to easily recognize it before opening.

    Your document is signed successfully—the signature mark shows the choices you made when creating it. The entire document is now certified, and all the protection rules are in place.

We will now step through a process of adding a signature on a page of a document where there is no predefined signature field set up.

Creating a signature area by a signer

Signing a document that is a flat .pdf file with no interactive fields is still not uncommon. Placing a digitally valid signature on those pages requires creating a signature area at the time of signing. The placement and size are determined by the document signer if the document is not protected.

Let's explore this process:

1. Open a new .pdf document. Any will work.

2. From the **Tools** tab, select **Certificates** from the **Forms & Signatures** group.

3. We will now work with the top toolbar that opened. Here is a screenshot:

Figure 8.10 – Certificates tools

4. Select the **Digitally Sign** tool from the top toolbar and accept an alert if it appears (Alert content: *Using your mouse, click and drag the area where you would like the signature to appear...*).

5. Click-drag the signature area to create a field.

6. The same dialog box appears as displayed in *Figure 8.9*.

7. Complete the signing selection tasks as in *steps 4-7* when signing a form field.

In this instance, you used your existing digital ID to confirm who you are by placing a password-protected signature in an area defined at the time of placing the signature, rather than having it predefined.

We know now how to proceed to the point of digitally signing documents using accepted verification standards contained in the marks of a signature, but what if things don't go smoothly?

In the next section, we will review how the validation process happens and what needs to be done to address any issues.

Understanding the validation process

Not all .pdf documents need to be signed. Those that need signatures usually involve contracts, purchases, permits, and so on. Let's see how the process of validation happens. Without validation, all the prior work to ensure security is not very meaningful.

When a signed document is received, validation of the signature(s) confirms the identity of the signer and the authenticity of the content signed. Once set up, validation takes place automatically. There are two aspects of validation:

- Confirmation that the **signer's certificate** exists in the list of trusted identities. In our example, this would be the local hard drive `Security` folder for Acrobat. It also validates that the certificate is not expired and that it fits the requirements of the Acrobat or Reader configuration.

- Verification of **document integrity** and confirmation that the signed content was not changed after it was signed. If the content does change, the verification confirms the limits imposed by the signer or alerts the owner about changes to the document. This may change the document status. If content, such as comments, was added after a document was signed, the **Signatures** pane will list changes and provide a link that you can click to view the signed version.

To help you sort this out, we will work with the **Signatures** pane next:

1. Proceed with the next steps if your signed document is still open, or locate one and open it.

2. From the top menu, select **View | Show/Hide | Navigation Panes | Signatures**.

3. Our document is signed, the signature is valid, and the details are listed in the panel. Here is a screenshot:

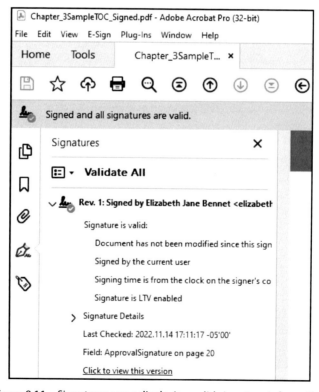

Figure 8.11 – Signatures pane displaying valid signature information

All files certifying the authenticity of the signature are in place—Acrobat finds them and gives us a green check for a valid signature.

See what happens if the certificate file is missing. Here is a screenshot:

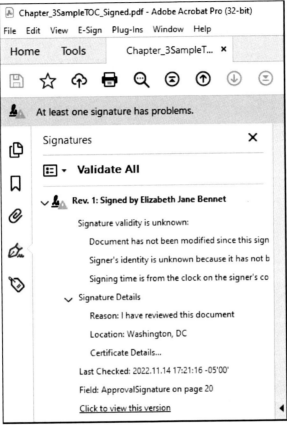

Figure 8.12 – Signatures pane displaying invalid signature information

Since Acrobat cannot find the certificate file, it alerts you about that. Now, it is up to you to resolve it. Most likely, it will be a phone call requesting the `.fdf` certificate file that the signer can export, the same way we did in the paragraphs preceding *Figure 8.3*.

When you receive the certificate and copy it to the location where Acrobat finds it, you still need to take a few steps to accept it and make it functional. Here are the steps:

1. Open the **Signature** pane if it is not open yet and from the top-left pane drop-down menu, select **Validate Signature**.

2. You will receive a **Signature Validation Status** alert stating **Signature validity is UNKNOWN**.

3. Click the **Signature Properties…** button, then the **Show Signer's Certificate…** button.

4. Another dialog box opens with a set of tabs at the top in the main area. Select **Trust**:

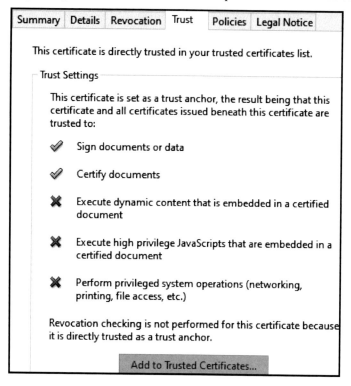

Figure 8.13 – Confirmation of trust policies dialog box

5. Red **X** symbols tell you that the certificate is not trusted in any of the categories listed. We will change that now. Click **Add to Trusted Certificates...**.

6. Accept the alert. Yet another dialog box opens where you can check the components of the .pdf document for which this certificate may be trusted.

7. Check **Use this certificate as a trusted root**.

8. The next options checked should be **If a signature validation succeeds trust: Signed document or data** and **Certified documents**.

9. Click **OK** twice, then click the **Validate Signature** button. Your screen may blink on this action—you are ready to close this dialog box.

    The new certificate was successfully added as trusted, and the digital signature in the .pdf file depending on its data is now validated.

10. The symbol in the **Signatures** pane has changed from orange to green, indicating that the signature is valid, and the certificate is accepted.

11. Close the dialog box.

Digital signatures may still exist on your system even if the certificate is missing. However, they cannot be used. When you type the password, an alert will display that it is invalid.

Signatures typically appear at the end of the process when a document is managed or filled out. If the process of providing the final document is extensive and there is a need for landmarks in authenticity, Acrobat allows you to certify a document before it will be signed. We will take time now to understand the purpose of certification and how it compares with signing.

Certifying a document

Certifying a .pdf document confirms the integrity of its content. Let's use an example of a real estate contract, with many clauses and disclosures. To ensure that the content of the contract itself is not modified, the document should be **certified**. However, the purpose of the contract is to have two or more parties agree on the terms spelled out. This is where signatures come in. Signatures validate signers' identity and confirm that the person(s) agrees with the content even with legal consequences. If pages or content are modified or removed, the document is no longer certified.

The following diagram illustrates the process:

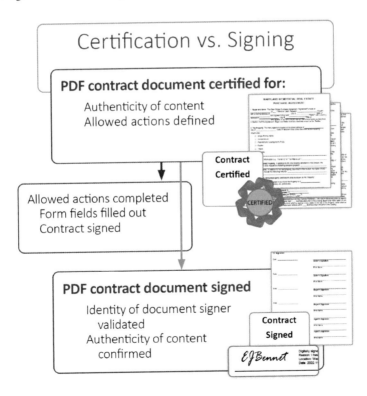

Figure 8.14 – Certification versus signing of a PDF

> **Important note**
> You can apply a certifying signature only if the PDF doesn't already contain any other signatures.

What does certifying a document mean in the real world? It is timing. Certified documents can be signed if that is a permitted action specified when the file was certified, but documents that are signed can no longer be certified. Let's explore this aspect of the security process and certify a document step by step:

1. Open a .pdf document that does not have any security or password protections set.

2. From **Tools**, open the **Certificates** tool.

3. From the top toolbar, select the **Certify (Invisible Signature)** tool.

4. Read the alert, since it spells out the terms of certification, including steps that need to be taken prior to certifying, such as creating a digital ID. Since we already did all this, click **OK**.

5. A **Sign with Digital ID** dialog box opens, where you can choose an identity that you want to use from the list.

6. A dialog box opens where you can make selections for **Reason** and **Permitted Actions After Certifying**. See the screenshot:

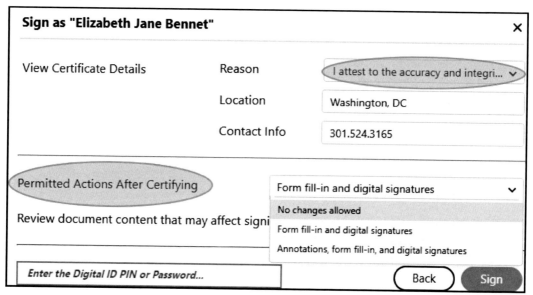

Figure 8.15 – Certifying a document and choosing permitted actions

If a .pdf document is to be signed later, it will only be possible if **Permitted Actions After Certifying** is selected to allow digital signatures, two of the three choices in the dropdown.

7. Enter the password. Our example is `books100`.

8. Save the file with a new name. I usually add `_Certified` to quickly recognize it in a folder.

9. The **Signature** panel displays the details of a valid certification including actions allowed.

Certifying signatures can be visible or invisible. We selected an **Invisible Signature** certification method that does not leave any visible mark on the document page. A **Visible Signature** certification would simply add a visible mark on a page, like the signature area we placed earlier.

Does your organization need all the components of document security that we discussed so far? You decide… I tried to describe this process in as human terms as possible, assuming that people working in a small business or a department are not likely to be document security experts. If you are concerned with the privacy, integrity, and security of the documents, as in an accounting or law office, this level of security is likely not sufficient and may need to expand significantly. In fact, you may need to employ expert services specializing in document and workflow security to have it all set up.

Summary

In this chapter, we have covered information related to security and document integrity when working with `.pdf` files. We learned how to protect a document with a password, and reviewed the cycles at the heart of the certification of documents and validation of signatures and signers' identities. We created a new identity and a new signature and learned how you should use them. These are rather complex topics that only introduce the issues. Hopefully, a simplified presentation takes the mystery out of the concept.

In the next chapter, we will have plain fun. The title alone—*Designing Multimedia Presentations*—makes me think of playing with options in Acrobat that make you look good as a professional presenter. My favorite job!

9

Designing Multimedia Presentations

Multimedia presentations have evolved into a highly sophisticated combination of video, animation, dynamic text, live photos, captions, and so on. Presentations can be destined for very large screens, such as the ones dominating Times Square in New York City, iPhones, and everything in between in terms of the size of the viewing area and delivery digital format. And let's not forget that audio is often a crucial part of the presentation.

Our expectations for multimedia in PDF must be adjusted to a more realistic level. Acrobat's path as a presentation delivery format began as static images of pages exported by a layout application. We were excited to show our clients actual fonts and color images on a screen rather than using expensive ink or laser toner on paper. With exciting updates in new versions of Acrobat came the euphoria of being able to do anything. The world of rollovers, animations, pop-up video players, and embedded movies came all-inclusive within a `.pdf` file.

Playtime was fun, but it became apparent rather quickly that all this exciting content could be used only very conservatively, for two major reasons. The first is the very steep learning curve for a typical Acrobat user to actually produce video, animation, and audio content of satisfactory quality to be included in a `.pdf` file as a presentation.

The second reason is the reality of output, where formats, operating systems, and hardware are changing at warp speed. Add to that a very uneven timing of updates by an increasing number of casual users and the need for additional software components to make it all work (such as QuickTime, Flash, or Windows Media Player), and it becomes clear that there are limits to the practical application of the dynamic content in a `.pdf` file. When things don't work, people move on. We do not try to figure out why the video is not playing or an animation alert pops up. We simply move on.

In our current world, most interaction with multimedia happens on a smartphone or tablet. PDFs are not a good vehicle for that, and Acrobat simply does not support the rich media that we may expect it to. This leaves us with classic multimedia presentations delivered to a large screen using a desktop computer or a laptop. Enriched with multimedia, these files may become a branding display at a conference or a welcome running information board. This is the context of our discussion in this chapter, which is meant to simply introduce possibilities, rather than explain ever-changing technical specifications.

We will explore options that you can include in two sources: InDesign and PowerPoint – documents created in InDesign by graphic designers due to its broad range of expert typographic features, and layout controls and those that serve as a backup to PowerPoint slides, which often do not preserve visual integrity when transferred from one computer to another.

PDF documents designed as presentations can include audio, video, interactive, and 3D elements. This chapter will only present the tools available in Acrobat for viewing and editing after a file has been exported to `.pdf`.

The following topics will be covered in this chapter:

- Adding video, audio, and 3D elements using rich media tools
- Adding navigation action buttons and page transitions
- Setting playback options for interactive elements
- Preferences for running slideshows
- PowerPoint slides conversion to PDF

Let's start with a `.pdf` presentation sourced from an InDesign layout. We are inviting our audience to visit London. The publication was created entirely in InDesign and exported to `.pdf`. All multimedia components will be added in Acrobat.

Adobe InDesign allows us to add multimedia content during the authoring stages. Since not everyone using Acrobat has InDesign, our project did not include any multimedia upon export to `.pdf`. However, the background for the buttons and the area for the video were deliberately designed during the layout stage.

In the next section, we will enhance the presentation by adding buttons, video, and audio. Later, we will adjust the document and Acrobat properties to make it a running slideshow.

Adding multimedia using Rich Media tools

Adding multimedia to a PDF publication is done by using toolbar tools under the **rich media** tool. In this section, we will enhance a presentation created in InDesign and exported to `.pdf` by adding navigation buttons, a video, and sound. Let's start with buttons that will take us places.

Adding navigation buttons

Navigation buttons in PDFs need both a background and interactivity through action. Both components can be created in Acrobat. However, to have more precise control over color and position in the layout, it is better to create the background for buttons during authoring. The click action will be added to the visual area of the button. Here are the steps:

1. Locate **Rich Media** on the **Tools** page, add it to the column of panels on the right, and click it to open its top toolbar. Tool names are self-explanatory, each one providing a unique function – a lot like all the previous tools we used.

2. We will add **actions** over the button backgrounds created in the layout software. Button actions will provide dynamic navigation to the document. Note that visuals are already in place, so we will choose visual properties settings for our buttons that do not obscure what we already have.

3. Keep in mind that *page 1* does not need navigation to the previous or first page, and the last page does not need navigation to the next or last page.

4. Select the **Add Button** tool and click-drag to create a small square that covers the **next page** symbol, as shown in the following screenshot:

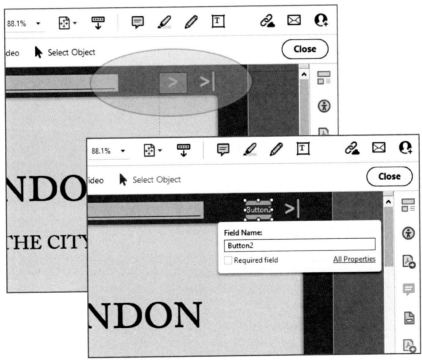

Figure 9.1 – Adding multimedia buttons over a button background

5. Click the **All Properties** link to open a dialog box for **Buttons**.

6. Fill the fields with the following:

   - In the **General** tab: **Name**: `NextPage`.

   - In the **Tooltip**: `Click here to go to the next page`.

   - In **Common Properties | Form Field**, select **Visible but doesn't print**.

   - In the **Appearance** tab | **Border Color**: **No Color** and **Fill Color**: **No Color**.

   - Skip the **Position** and **Options** tabs.

   - Select the **Actions** tab. This is where we will add magic.

7. In the **Actions** tab from the dropdown for **Select Action**, choose `Execute a menu item`.

8. Click **Add**.

9. From **Menu Item** choices, select **View>Page Navigation>Next Page**. See the following screenshot for reference, which displays many more actions that we will use later.

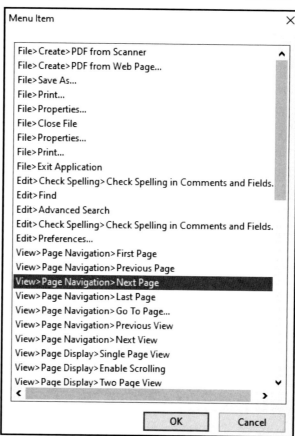

Figure 9.2 – The actions menu items

10. Click **OK**. Now, you can see the action in the **Button Properties** dialog box in the **Actions** window.

11. Now, click **Close**.

Additional settings for button appearance and options were covered in *Chapter 7, Creating and Modifying PDF Forms (Desktop Only)*, in the *Button field properties and actions* section.

We will now test the button to make sure it functions properly:

1. Close the **Rich Media** tool. Nothing new appears on the page, but when you hover over the next page symbol, you will see a link pointer.

2. Click the symbol, and you will see the next page of the presentation. The button works but only on the page where we placed it. When you click the similar symbol on the new page, nothing happens. We will eventually fix this.

We will now add three more button actions to our navigation area. We need the **Last Page**, **Previous Page**, and **First Page** buttons.

Here are the steps for **Last Page**:

1. Return to *page 1* where the first button was created.

2. Open the **Rich Media** toolbar and click the **Select Object** tool.

3. *Ctrl + click* and *drag* (*Option + click* and *drag* on macOS) the existing button to create a duplicate, and position it over the **Last Page** symbol. The button size and most of your settings are already in place. You only need to modify settings in the **General** and **Actions** tabs.

4. *Double-click* the new button field to open the **Button Properties** dialog box, and change the fields as follows:

   • In the **General** tab: **Name**: Last Page. *This should be the first step for all duplicated buttons. Failing to rename a field will copy edits to other existing buttons with the same name.*

   • **Tooltip**: Click here to go to the last page.

   • In the **Actions** tab in the **Actions** window, click **Execute a menu item** and then click the **Edit** button, as you can see in the following screenshot:

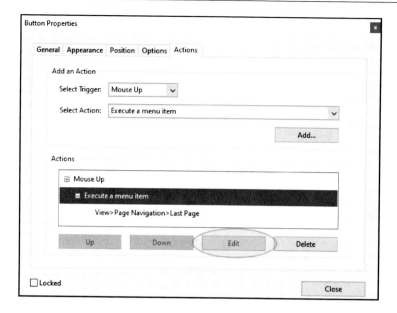

Figure 9.3 – Editing actions

5.   Choose the **View>Page Navigation>Last Page** action.

6.   Click **OK**. Now, you can see the updated action in the **Button Properties** dialog box in the **Actions** window.

7.   Click **Close** to accept changes.

Test the **LastPage** button the same way you did with the **NextPage** button (close the **Rich Media** toolbar, use a hand grabber tool, and click the **LastPage** button). Ideally, you should now be on the very last page, where the two symbols for **FirstPage** and **Previous Page** are ready.

To complete the functionality of the remaining buttons, work on the second page of the document and continue adding the clickable area and changing actions to the **PreviousPage** and **FirstPage** buttons.

Once you have successfully created four navigation buttons, you will find that they only work on the pages where we placed them. Don't worry, you do not need to repeat the entire process on each page. The beauty of computers is that once you create something, it can be reused over and over.

We will now duplicate the buttons across pages. Duplication puts the buttons in exactly the same position on each specified page. First, we will use the fields on page 1:

1.   On page 1, open the **Rich Media** toolbar if it is closed, and then select both the **Next Page** and **Last Page** buttons using the **Select Object** tool.

2.   *Right-click* inside one of the buttons.

3.   From the menu, select **Duplicate Across Pages…**.

4. In the dialog box, click **From:** and type 2 in the field, and then type 7 in the **To:** field.

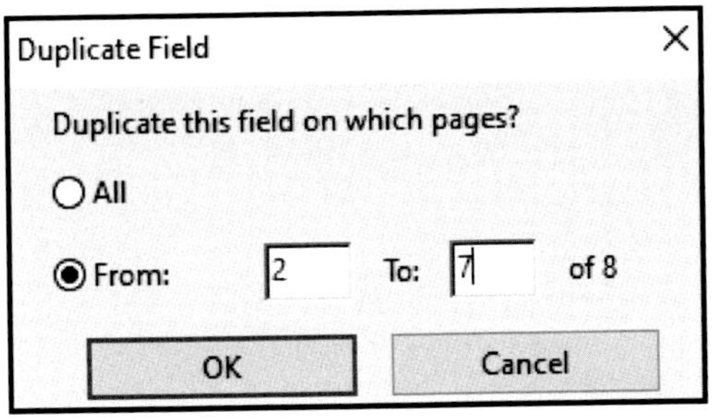

Figure 9.4 – Specifying the pages for duplicated fields

5. Remember that you already have buttons on *page 1*, so we only need copies on pages without button actions, and the last page does not need **Last** and **Next** page buttons.

6. Scroll through *pages 2 to 7*; you will see two buttons positioned precisely in the same location as on the *page 1*, over the visible symbols for page navigation as in *Figure 9.1*.

7. Use the same process to duplicate both the **Previous Page** and **First Page** buttons from *page 2*.

8. Now, close the **Rich Media** toolbar and test your buttons. Do they work? Isn't it exciting?!

So, this is what we accomplished here. We used existing button backgrounds to create action areas using the **Add Button** tool. We refined each one to perform the desired action, and then we populated all pages with needed buttons using the **Duplicate Across Pages…** function. This part of the multimedia is done. Next, we will place a video in our presentation.

Adding a video to a presentation

Adding a video to a .pdf file has become tricky, due to a confusing array of video formats and curiously irregular support by vendors providing media players. Add to that Window, macOS, and mobile OS platform differences and you can see why you will need to think through how to incorporate a video into a .pdf file. We will not cover technical specifications here, as there is plenty of that online.

Having said that, let's explore how to do it if you want to. On the last page, there is an empty box where we will position the video. Here are the steps to do this:

1. If closed, open the **Rich Media** toolbar, and select the **Add Video** tool.

2. Click-drag the area of the box. When you release the mouse button, a dialog box opens, as you can see in the following screenshot.

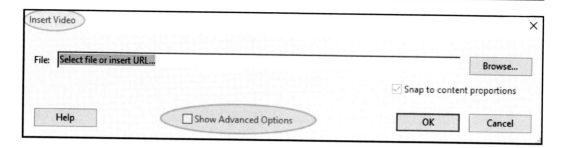

Figure 9.5 – The insert multimedia dialog box

3. Click the **Browse… (Choose…** on macOS) button and locate the movie file.

4. Select it and click **Open** to place it.

5. The **Snap To Content Proportions** checkbox, which is checked by default, ensures the playback area keeps the height and width proportions of the video.

6. Click the **Show Advanced Options** checkbox. If you don't, you can get it back later by double-clicking the movie box. Here are the choices:

    -   The **Launch Settings** options allow you to specify when a movie begins to play:

        -   **Enable When:** The The content is clicked choice allows the presenter to control when the video starts playing.

        -   **Enable When:** The The page containing the content is opened option is for self-running presentations. Selecting this choice starts playing the video automatically. Controlling the launch of media happens by setting the page transition **Auto Flip** time to a value that allows a long enough time to play the entire video. We will discuss these options a little later in this chapter in the *Preferences for running slideshows* section.

        -   **Disable When:** These choices allow for either manual or automatic control to stop the video playback.

        -   **Playback Style:** These options control whether the video should be played on a page or in a floating window.

    -   The **Poster Image** group gives you choices for an image showing when the video is not playing. It may be the first frame from a movie, or you can use any file created beforehand.

    -   The **Controls** tab expands controls only if they are built into the video during video editing. They will appear in the dropdown. Acrobat does not add any video controls.

    -   The **Video** tab displays internal video settings if any are included as options that Acrobat supports.

> **Important note**
>
> Acrobat supports the following movie formats: `.mov`, `.mp4`, `.m4v`, `.3gp`, and `3g2`.
>
> A more predictable way to add multimedia to your PDF presentation is to enter a URL referring to a video file or streaming media. Three types of URLs can be used: RTMP, HTTP, and HTTPS. On HTTP and HTTPS servers, H.264-compliant MOV and MP4 files are supported.
>
> When video (and audio) files are embedded, they cause the PDF to swell in size. Streamed media, on the other hand, requires a server/internet connection to view the media.
>
> Flash movies (`FLV` and `F4V` files) are no longer supported and cannot be embedded in both Acrobat and PDFMaker.

It is worth repeating that even though we stepped through the process of placing a movie in a `.pdf` file, *only a desktop or laptop version of Acrobat* will actually play it. Mobile devices do not support videos embedded in a `.pdf` file.

In the next section, we will enhance our presentation with audio.

Adding audio to a presentation

Audio added to a presentation will make it more pleasant and engaging, particularly if it is music. In other cases, it may serve as an accessibility tool or a language learning aid that is used to read the content of the publication.

Here is how to include sound in our slide:

1. Open the **Rich Media** toolbar if it is closed.

2. Select the **Add Sound** tool and *click-drag* on a page. If you want the audio to begin playing at the beginning of the presentation, place it on the first page.

3. Click the **Browse...** (**Choose...** on macOS) button and locate the audio file.

4. In the **Launch Settings** dialog box, you have the following options:

    *   **Enable When:** These choices allow you to start playback when the audio is clicked or immediately when a page is open.

    *   **Disable When:** The **Disable Content is selected from the context menu** option will play the entire audio file to the end of the presentation, or will stop when a presenter right-clicks the content and manually selects **Disable Content**.

5. The **Poster Image** group allows you to place a small graphic on the page, rather than leaving it as a default white rectangle with a black border. I used a small arrow on a round button. You can find plenty of button images available, either in MS Office or online. They just need to be in a file format that Acrobat supports. Click **Create poster from file** and then **Browse....**

6. Select an image you want to use as an audio button. Click **Open**, and then click **OK** to close the big dialog box.

7. Adjust the size of the audio box on the page if you need to and test the audio.

8. Close the **Rich Media** toolbar, select the hand grabber tool, and click the audio to begin playback.

Isn't that nice? You can now enjoy music while watching the slide. You would follow the same steps if you used the audio file as a voice recording. Decide how applicable it is to your project.

> **Important note**
>
> Embedding audio or video is not the same as attaching multimedia files to a .pdf file. Embedded files are meant to be played as content; attachments are files included to be retrieved from the .pdf document and used independently.

In the next section, we will explore placing a 3D object, a product of many hours of labor by engineers, architects, and designers. Once finished and exported to the final format, Acrobat or reader become a presentation medium for those projects.

Placing 3D objects

Content created in 3D modeling software such as 3D CAD or other brands can be also embedded in a .pdf file, a lot like video or audio. Files exported with data to offer different views allow a user to display a wireframe only, parts of a model that are hidden, parts covered or removed, and objects rotated and manipulated, creating an experience that is very similar to handling a real object without the need for CAD application on the viewer's computer.

Acrobat supports the **U3D** format very well. U3D stands for **Universal 3D**, a compressed file format for 3D computer graphics. It contains structure data for wireframe or mesh, light, shade, and motion.

> **Important note**
>
> **3D PDF** documents with U3D-embedded objects can be viewed in Acrobat Reader *version 7* and above. The format has been around since August 2005. Initially, it was developed with the goal of becoming a standard for 3D graphics exchange. This did not fully materialize, and now Acrobat 3D creates U3D by converting a supported 3D file type of the modeling software for use in PDF publications.

A display of 3D objects is controlled through the **Model Tree** pane. Components of a 3D model are exported from the application that created the model. I will work with an existing .u3d file. Here is a method to embed a 3D model in Acrobat:

1. Open the **Rich Media** toolbar, if closed.

2. Select the **Add 3D** tool.

3. *Click-drag* to create an area on a document page.

4. A dialog box opens, like the one you saw when adding a video and audio. Click **Browse…** (or **Choose…** on macOS):

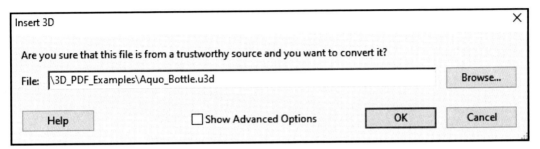

Figure 9.6 – Inserting a 3D object

5. Locate the .u3d file, select it, and click the **Open** button.

6. Click the **Show Advanced Options** checkbox.

7. The **Launch Settings** tab options allow you to control when the 3D model becomes active and what poster is displayed when it is static:

    *   **Enabled:** When clicked or the page containing it is open

    *   **Disabled:** When it becomes a static image again

    *   **Poster Image**: The **Retrieve poster from default view** option is the default setting, but you can change it to a different one from a file that you can select

8. The **3D** tab allows you to set **Default Display Settings**. I will leave the settings unchanged and explore them after the model is placed on a page. Click **OK**.

9. The **Click to activate…** alert appears. When you click on it, a toolbar appears, allowing you to manipulate the model and see different views.

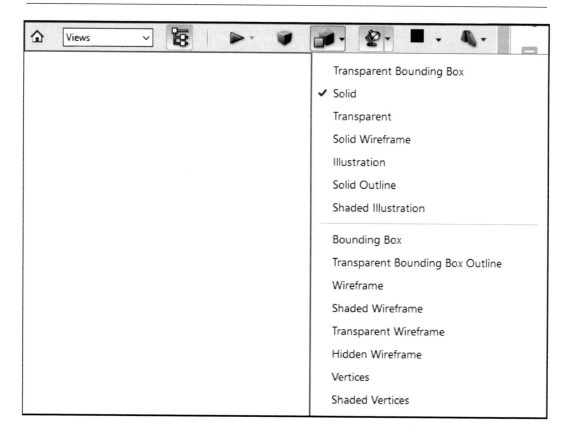

Figure 9.7 – The 3D object toolbar and views

To see additional information about the 3D model, you can work with the **Model Tree** pane. To explore it, follow these steps:

1. From the top Acrobat menu, select **View | Show/Hide | Navigation Panes | Model Tree**.

2. A pane opens, populated with information exported from the 3D modeling software. Options in the menu contain viewing choices and data export format selections. With a mouse, you can now rotate, move, magnify, and perform many other operations to see the details of an object. Selecting wireframe views lets you see the inside of the object; transparent views create an illusion of a glass-like surface. Clicking the **Model Tree** pane content displays views saved at the time of exporting the model. Here is one example:

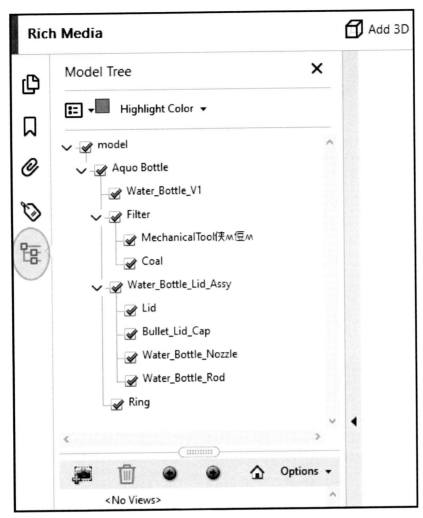

Figure 9.8 – The 3D object structure displayed in the Model Tree pane

That's all for exploring a 3D object. If you are an engineer, it's likely you will use a 3D PDF file as a source of data to be read and evaluated in a final example of a finished product that will possibly be produced in the physical world. If you are not an engineer, I hope you enjoyed the presentation. Should you ever need to open a 3D PDF file, this exercise is meant to make it easier to navigate through the options.

Let's now return to our multimedia slide presentation and set the options for its delivery.

Preferences for running slideshows

We will now explore Acrobat's settings for presentations delivered by a human presenter and auto-running slideshows. We have already set up the navigation action buttons. Now, we will look at the presentation in **Full Screen Mode**:

1.   From the top menu, select **View** | **Full Screen Mode**, or use the *Ctrl/Cmd + L* keyboard shortcut.

     Pages of the document fill the entire screen and the software interface disappears. If your show has begun and pages are turning too fast or too slow, you can control the slide auto-advance time settings.

2.   Tap the *Esc* keyboard key to exit **Full Screen Mode**.

3.   From the top menu, select **Edit** | **Preferences** | **Full Screen** (**Acrobat Pro** | **Preferences** | **Full Screen** on macOS) to open settings that can be applied to an entire document. Here is a screenshot:

Figure 9.9 – Full Screen Mode presentation preferences

Note the **Advance every** 3 **seconds** option. This sets the amount of time for a viewer to look at a page before it turns to the next page. This value should be always set to allow sufficient time to read the content. The **Full Screen Transitions** options allow you to select default page transitions for the entire slide. Select one then click **OK** to exit **Preferences**.

For individual pages with more information, global settings can be adjusted in the **Pages** pane. We will do this next:

1. Open the **Pages** pane on the left of the screen.

2. Select **Page 1-3 thumbnails** and click the **Options** menu.

3. Select **Page Transitions…**; a dialog box opens with settings that can be applied to selected pages. The **Page Transition** group gives you effects while pages are turning. I selected `Glitter` but left additional dropdowns refining the direction and speed of the effect unchanged.

4. The **Auto Flip** setting allows you to override a value you have just set as a default for all pages in **Edit | Preferences (Acrobat Pro | Preferences…** on macOS). Ours was **3** seconds, not giving us much time to linger on the photos and captions, so we will change the number to `10`. This is how we can set a different duration for different slides in a presentation.

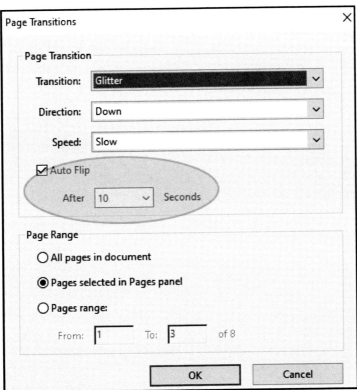

Figure 9.10 – The Page Transitions settings from the Pages pane menu

5. Click **OK** to accept changes. We will now test the new settings.

6. Pressing *Ctrl/Cmd + L* keys opens the document in **Full Screen Mode**. Watch the new slide settings in place. Both the timing and transition effect are applied to pages 1–3.

   You can apply different transitions and **Auto Flip** values to all pages in the document, or you can make them change every so often. You can also tweak one page or a group of pages. Looking good, doesn't it? If you want to pause or speed up the slide progress, simply hold the mouse or tap the up or down arrow keys.

We learned how to add buttons, video, audio, and 3D objects, and how to control the timing and transitions of each slide.

There is one more topic that we need to address, and that is the conversion of PowerPoint presentations to PDF slides. We will explore this next.

PowerPoint slides conversion to PDF

MS PowerPoint is a great tool for creating presentations and slides. It is built to be both an authoring tool, and when a project is completed, it is an output format to a screen in **Slideshow** mode. It is very generous with animations and timing controls, effects, transitions, and many other eye-catching treatments.

However, as an authoring tool for content and the final output for presentations, PowerPoint application settings affect the display of slides during a presentation. This means that if fonts are missing, a computer system's default settings change, or other such issues, the presentation may become unusable, not to say the presenter may also appear incompetent. Ouch!

Therefore, you may want to create a .pdf version of your slides simply as a backup. Acrobat does not preserve all the details of animations, but with page transitions and a stable page layout, it will display the same on any system. All it needs is the free Acrobat Reader. This is something to consider if you present a lot of slideshows in different locations. Secure agencies may even require you to preview presented content, in which case the .pdf format is the safest bet for preserving the layout.

A starting point in creating a .pdf backup of your slides is to work with **PDFMaker**. A detailed discussion on the topic of PDFMaker was covered in *Chapter 3, Converting Microsoft Office Files to Adobe PDF Using PDFMaker*.

This section will focus on how to use it in the context of converting PowerPoint slides to a .pdf file.

PDFMaker in PowerPoint (Windows only)

We will now go through the steps to effectively convert our PowerPoint slide to a .pdf file. We want to preserve interactive features of the presentation that were already built in PowerPoint:

1. Open a presentation in **PowerPoint** and click on the **Acrobat** ribbon to see the options.

2. Select **Preferences** to open **PDFMaker Settings**. Here is a screenshot of the dialog box:

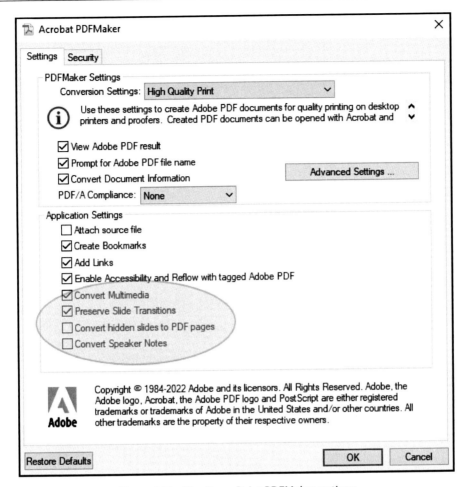

Figure 9.11 – The PowerPoint PDFMaker options

3. Note the highlighted checkboxes unique to PowerPoint. The corresponding content parts and settings applied during authoring will be preserved.

4. Click **OK**, and then click **Create PDF** on the Acrobat ribbon. To preserve multimedia and slide transitions, **do not print a PowerPoint to** `.pdf`.

> **Important note**
>
> Printing to the Adobe PDF printer will create a flat `.pdf` file. All interactivity and features requested in the **PDFMaker** settings will be lost.
>
> PDFMaker is no longer supported on macOS. A method currently recommended by macOS publishers for creating `.pdf` documents in *MS Office for Mac* is printing to Adobe PDF, but it does not preserve any interactive components discussed here.

5. When your file opens in Acrobat, tap *Ctrl/Cmd + L* to open it in **Full Screen Mode**.

6. Test your presentation now in `.pdf` format. It is more static than a PowerPoint slide but safe for any presenting environment. Transitions are preserved; you can refine them in Acrobat following the steps we discussed earlier when creating a presentation sourced from InDesign.

This concludes our exploration of multimedia options available to Acrobat users. How you combine all these will depend on your project.

Summary

In this chapter, we learned what multimedia is available in PDFs and what the practical limits are. We added navigation buttons, video, and audio. We explored 3D PDF tools for viewing content exported from 3D modeling software. We also refined the transitions between pages in a finished presentation and adjusted the settings for an auto-running slideshow. Finally, we created a `.pdf` version of a PowerPoint presentation that will serve as a backup if the use of a PowerPoint file is not possible, or when you simply need an archive.

The next chapter is exciting. We will learn how Adobe InDesign and Acrobat work together. Many features are so closely integrated that you may want to expand your own tool set for authoring publications, such as commenting, accessibility, interactivity, and color. If you already are an InDesign user, you will find many details that will help you in the production process.

10

Integration with Adobe InDesign

When Acrobat and PDF were first introduced, Macs used by graphic designers did not talk to Windows software used by most clients in typical business offices. This gap made it really complicated to share and present files. Using fonts was a real challenge, as they had to be converted from one operating system to another, always with disappointing results.

We have come a long way. Adobe layout applications now have an extensive set of options for converting source documents to PDF. All aspects of a final publication are catered for – interaction through links, bookmarks, animations, and accessibility refinements. Tools for collaborative editorial review make the entire process of producing a `.pdf` document streamlined and unified.

In this chapter, you will discover how the integration of options in InDesign and Acrobat allows you to create a fully featured accessible `.pdf` document. We will also review how both applications are taking you into the future of live collaborative reviews, delivered by editors working on any operating system and any device. We will focus on two areas of integration – accessibility and editorial reviews.

The following topics will be considered in this chapter:

- Accessibility design and workflow
- Formatting consideration when creating a layout in InDesign
- Adding alternate text descriptions to images
- Managing content structure in the **Articles** panel
- Mapping InDesign text styles to PDF tags
- Automating the creation of bookmarks
- Preserving interactive and accessibility features when exporting to PDF
- Document reviews and collaboration in InDesign

> **Important note**
> Information and most of the examples in this chapter assume that you have experience working with InDesign. Our focus here is on the active use of tools, workspace, and functions, rather than having to explain them.

In the next section, we will explore the process of using tools and functions in InDesign to create an accessible document.

Technical requirements

This chapter is aimed at current and potential Adobe InDesign users with a working knowledge of the application. If you would like to recreate the steps listed in the examples used here, you will need Adobe InDesign, Bridge, and Acrobat installed. If you use Creative Cloud, you will also likely have Photoshop and Illustrator already installed. These apps are also helpful but not required to understand the topics discussed.

All functions in InDesign and Bridge are the same for Windows and Mac users. Alternate keys are listed for each operating system.

Accessibility design and workflow

In this section, we will focus on Adobe InDesign's set of controls to produce publications that are fully accessible when exported to `.pdf`. Authors and graphic designers who understand accessibility can take advantage of the following functions:

- **Parent pages** for page layout elements that should be treated as background or navigation
- Paragraph, character, and object styles
- Tables formatted using Table and Cell styles
- Threading stories across pages in multi-article journals or newsletters
- The **Articles** panel to control the content of a tag structure and the reading order in Acrobat
- Anchoring images and image groups for precise positioning within text
- Adding alternate text to images and charts using metadata and/or object styles
- Paragraph style settings to control the creation of corresponding accessibility tags when exported
- Hyperlinks, cross-references, bookmarks, and text anchors
- A generated table of contents, index, and other lists
- Extensive **Export to PDF** options that specifically address accessibility requirements
- Automatic conversion of numbered and bulleted lists

Proper use of all these tools will eliminate the need for remediation of inaccessible `.pdf` files in Acrobat. General issues related to accessibility are discussed in *Chapter 5, Remediation for Accessibility in PDF Publications*. First, let's review some principles of accessible layout that graphic designers should keep in mind.

Formatting considerations when creating layout in InDesign

Requirements for accessibility do not demand document design alterations; however, a simple, legible layout is always the best way to make a publication easy to read and easy to convert to a logical document structure as a PDF.

Here are some guidelines to follow:

- **Simplify page layout** and learn how to use all properties for each element. For example, do not create a color background box, place a textbox on top, and then place other elements on top of that if they can all become a single story, placed in a frame and formatted using properties. Here is an example:

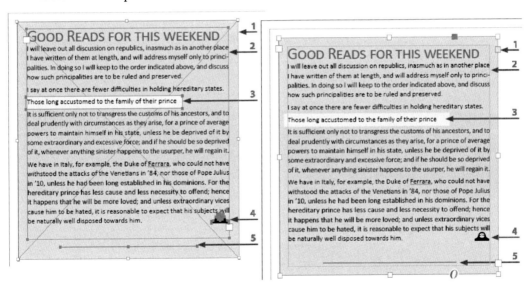

Figure 10.1 – A streamlined layout using frame and text properties

The desired layout, which looked the same when printed, was accomplished in two ways:

- **On the left**: By placing multiple objects on a page
- **On the right**: By placing one text frame and using formatting properties for both frame and text

Let's take a minute to compare this example that illustrates different approaches taken by designers when creating a page layout. Elements and corresponding properties are numbered for reference.

	Layout on the left using multiple objects	Layout on the right using frame and text formatting properties
1	An **unassigned** content frame with a blue fill used as a background	A **text** frame with text content and a blue fill
2	Another smaller **text** frame provides an illusion of margin for the text in the frame	Text frame **inset spacing** provides a margin for the text in the frame
3	An **unassigned** frame with yellow fill was used as a highlight	The **Paragraph Borders and Shading...** text formatting property is applied as a highlight
4	A small **graphic** is used as dingbat (the end of the story symbol)	The *Webdings* **glyph** font (a special character) is entered at the end of paragraph text
5	A red **stroke** ends the text in the sidebar	The **Paragraph Rules...** formatting property is applied to show the ending of the text in the sidebar

Table 10.1 – Comparing different layout methods in Figure 10.1

The preceding comparison also demonstrates how proper production methods separate content from formatting, making a document more flexible when exported to other formats:

- **Use styles consistently** whenever they apply. Styles save settings for formatting and your desired export options, giving you very precise control at the paragraph, character, or object level to specify how a `.pdf` document will be created.

- **Create proper lists,** both bulleted and numbered. Manually numbered paragraphs are not tagged correctly for accessibility.

- **Use tables for data only**, and use proper formatting to define table headers, body, or footers. Be sure to use table styles.

- In long documents, **generate a table of contents** and an **index**; do not type entries manually.

- Use the **Articles** panel to control the structure of the document when exported to `.pdf`.

- Explore many ways you can **add image descriptions** as **alt-text**, and choose the most efficient method.

- Work with Adobe Bridge to add or edit **metadata** for alt-text or captions.

- **Preserve settings** when exporting to `.pdf`. InDesign uses this last step to create tags, structure, place the document title, and define language.

- Finally, if needed, **edit default tags** to refine the definition of the `.pdf` content, using a list of accessibility tags, which we will discuss in *Chapter 13, Acrobat Pro Tools, Shortcuts, References, and Mac Notes*.

The preceding guidelines can also serve as a checklist before a `.pdf` document is created and sent off as a final.

We have learned which features should be used to maximize formatting options when creating a page layout. Next, we will explore placing images as anchored objects so that they are placed in the correct position in a document structure when exported to `.pdf`.

Anchoring images and frames

Accessibility by its very nature is dependent on text. Characters, words, and sentences are read by a screen reader, conveying to a visually impaired person the information that they are interested in.

I always keep this in mind when working on page layout. Text in InDesign is contained in text frames that can be threaded/linked, such as a long story that fills many pages, or can be independently placed on a page, such as short text.

The most common process of placing images in InDesign resembles placing a *Post-It* note on a page. It is very flexible, easy, and independent – exactly what layout artists love about InDesign. However, since each image frame is just an independent item on a page and accessibility is text in a story, we must connect the two layout element types. Welcome to frame anchoring.

Anchored frames most often contain images, but they can also contain text. Anchoring allows designers to place an anchor that attaches a frame to a specific location in a paragraph text. When text is edited and flows from column to column or page to page, frames that are anchored follow. **Anchored frame properties** control how a frame relates to text and provide settings for automatic positioning in page layout.

> **Important note**
>
> *MS Word* users almost always anchor images in text; *InDesign* users rarely do. Therefore, it is good to understand this process as an optional layout approach in InDesign. In the context of accessibility, it is necessary to use anchoring of images conveying information as a primary method. It allows precise positioning of images/figures during the authoring stage, with results appearing in the **Tags** pane document structure in Acrobat.
>
> Background images that are tagged as `Artifact` do not need to be anchored.

Let's explore the anchoring of images in text and the settings associated with it. Please take time to look at the details of the screenshot from the InDesign layout page:

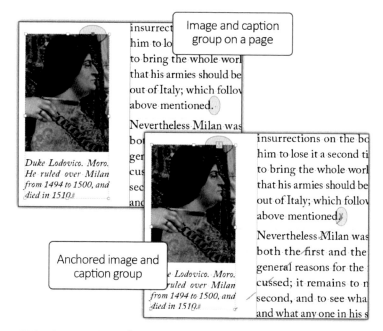

Figure 10.2 – A comparison of two methods for placing images in an InDesign layout

The image area under **Image and caption group on a page** is a typical method for positioning graphics in InDesign. The blue highlight in this group shows a graphic frame on a page, and the paragraph text simply ends with a period and space.

The image area under **Anchored image and caption group** has different symbols in the corresponding region of image and text. A small anchor highlighted in the top-right corner of the image and a dotted line connecting the bottom-right corner of the image/caption group, with a text anchor ending the paragraph text, are all clues that this image group is anchored.

We will next examine the settings that make anchoring suitable for layout and for accessibility. You will be working with InDesign, of course. We will put Acrobat aside for now.

Here are the steps to anchor an image (*image* refers to **image frame**; in this context, it also refers to any frame, including a text frame such as a pull quote, or a group of frames, as shown in *Figure 10.2*):

1. Open InDesign and open a file with text and graphics. A simple publication will work best.

2. Allow enough white space between a column of text and the edge of the page. If you want to create a new document, here are the page settings (I work with picas, a much more convenient unit of measure when working with paper and page dimensions):

   - **Letter page size**: 51p0 by 66p0 (8.5" by 11")

   - **Number of pages**: 12 and facing pages checked

- **Columns**: 2 and **Column Gutter**: 1p6 (0.25")
- **Margins**:
  - **Top**: 7p6 (1.25")
  - **Bottom**: 6p0 (1")
  - **Inside**: 6p0 (1")
  - **Outside**: 15p0 (2.5")

3. Use the **Type** tool to create two text frames following the dimensions of the column guides, and then thread the frames using frame ports.

4. If you do not see text threads after threading the frames, select from the top menu the **View | Extras | Show Text Threads** option. Threads appear only when at least one of the frames in a story is selected with a **Selection** tool.

5. Next, place your text. You can use **File | Place…**, although I use the *Ctrl + D* or *Cmd + D* shortcut. The text should be longer than one page. Here is what you should see once it fills the pages:

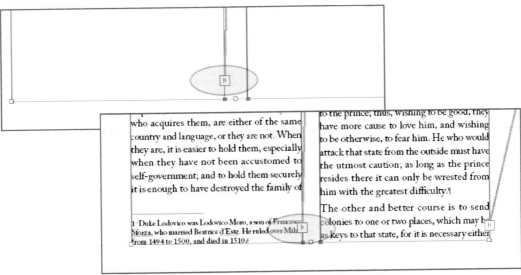

who acquires them, are either of the same country and language, or they are not. When they are, it is easier to hold them, especially when they have not been accustomed to self-government; and to hold them securely it is enough to have destroyed the family of

1 Duke Lodovico was Lodovico Moro, a son of Francesco Sforza, who married Beatrice d'Este. He ruled over Milan from 1494 to 1500, and died in 1510.

to the prince; thus, wishing to be good, they have more cause to love him, and wishing to be otherwise, to fear him. He who would attack that state from the outside must have the utmost caution; as long as the prince resides there it can only be wrested from him with the greatest difficulty.¶

The other and better course is to send colonies to one or two places, which may be as keys to that state, for it is necessary either

Figure 10.3 – Threaded text frames before and after placing text. The frame port is highlighted

6. Deselect everything. I use *Ctrl + Shift + A* or *Cmd + Shift + A*.

7. Now, place an image. I use *Ctrl + D/Cmd + D* again, or you can go to **File | Place…** from the top menu, locate and select an image, and click **Open**.

8. Click-drag to create a frame that fits within the dimensions of the white space in the margin area on the left.

9. Your image is placed on a page; it is independent of the text. If a column is resized and text reflows, the image is stationary and does not move.

We will now anchor the image to a paragraph text:

1. Select the image frame with a **Selection** tool and cut it. I use *Ctrl + X/Cmd + X*.

2. Change tools in the **Tools** panel. Select the **Type** tool, and then click at the end of a paragraph in the column. You should see a blinking insertion point.

3. Now, paste the image using the *Ctrl + V/Cmd + V* shortcut or **Edit | Paste**.

4. Your image is now anchored in the text. It is probably looking messy, sitting on top of the text in the column. Select it with the **Selection** tool again, and you will see a small anchor in the top-right corner of the image and another anchor inside the text. If your text anchor is not displayed in the text, go to the top menu and select **Type | Show Hidden Characters**. Both symbols look like this:

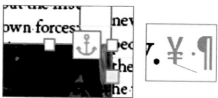

Figure 10.4 – Symbols showing that a frame is anchored in the text

We will adjust the position of the image so that it does not obscure text using **anchored object properties**. Later, we will create a style to preserve these settings.

5. With the **Selection** tool click on the anchored frame to select it. Be sure you are working with the frame containing the image and not the image itself, or the content inside the frame. *Anchoring properties are only assigned to frames.*

6. With your frame still selected, choose **Object | Anchored Object | Options…** from the top menu.

7. This is where the magic of positioning anchored frames is found. The dialog box looks as shown here:

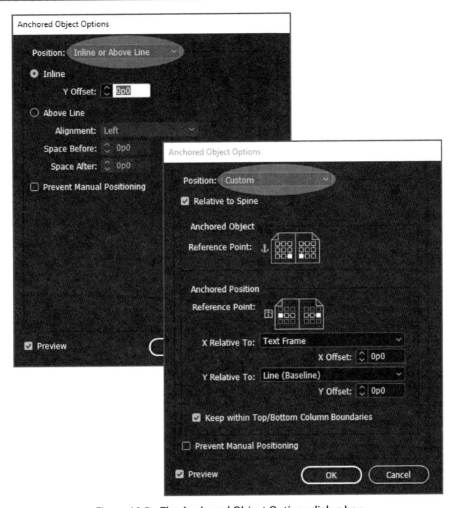

Figure 10.5 – The Anchored Object Options dialog box

We will now review the most important settings that will be applied to different types of images:

- **Position**: **Inline or Above Line**:

  - **Inline** places a frame at the text baseline and treats it as if it were a character. Paragraph text alignment and leading will move the image along with all other text. This setting works well for icons or small graphics. Text leading should be adjusted if it is lower than the frame's height; otherwise, the frame will obscure text in adjacent lines.

  - **Above Line** places an image at the text baseline and pushes the text of the line above to the top of the image, creating space to fit the image height. The result is similar to the **Text Wrap | Jump Object** property for independent images. An anchored image will move with the text.

- This method works well with images and charts that have a width close to the text column width. It is helpful to create a paragraph formatted with a unique paragraph style to control alignment and space before and after the image. The frame can be moved up or down a little, but the position within a column depends on paragraph alignment and other settings, such as indents.

- **Prevent Manual Positioning** forces designers to work with a dialog box numeric value, preventing overrides if a template is used. I prefer visual feedback when adjusting the frame position on a page; therefore, there is no need to check this option.

- **Position**: Selecting **Custom** from the dropdown creates an entirely different positioning environment. Instead of a rigid spot inside a paragraph, this set of options allows you to keep a text anchor in the body of the text but position the frame anywhere on the page, while keeping it connected in relation to the text:

  - **Relative to Spine** refines the position further in layouts with spreads/facing pages. If an image is placed on the outside edge of a spread, it will automatically adjust its position from the left edge to the right edge, based on the corresponding page.

  - I usually take my time before I finalize the settings. Start with defaults, then click **OK** to close the dialog box, manually position the frame, and return to the dialog box to see how the numeric values have changed.

When done with anchoring and setting position using one image, I test the same values using a few more images. If images automatically move to the correct position, I am ready to create an **object style** to preserve the settings and apply them easily to all related images in the story. We will do that in the next section.

Creating and using object styles

Styles are a very powerful tool in InDesign to preserve and consistently apply multiple properties to different elements used in a layout. The most common are text styles, which we will discuss in detail later. For now, we will focus on **object styles**, a way to preserve rich formatting for frames. Our focus, of course, will be anchored frames.

When a new frame is created, it typically has default settings for stroke weight, color, fill color, effects, and so on. The default for graphic frames is **Fill: None** and **Stroke: black 1 pt** – not very exciting. Object styles allow you to change multiple frame settings with one click. If changes are required toward the end of document production, and frames are using object styles, making adjustments to settings will be applied to all frames that use the same style. Imagine edits for 50 images – a choice of one change to a style applied to 50 images or a change repeated 50 times without using an object style. There's no need to elaborate on what I would rather work with.

In the following steps, we will create an object style appropriate for anchored frames:

1. Select the anchored image that you worked with. Add a stroke color and weight; I chose green for my example and a **Stroke** weight of 0 . 5 pt. Anchored properties should be applied and tested to make sure that they work well. Keeping the image frame selected opens the **Object Styles** panel. You can find it on the top menu under **Window | Styles | Object Styles**.

    The default object style highlighted in the panel is usually **[Basic Graphics Frame]**+ or **[None]**+.

    The plus symbol (+) means that the selected frame has formatting overrides; in other words, it was changed from the initial default settings. If you hover over the style label in the panel, you will see the type of overrides applied to the frame.

2. From the panel menu, select **New Object Style…**, as shown in the following screenshot:

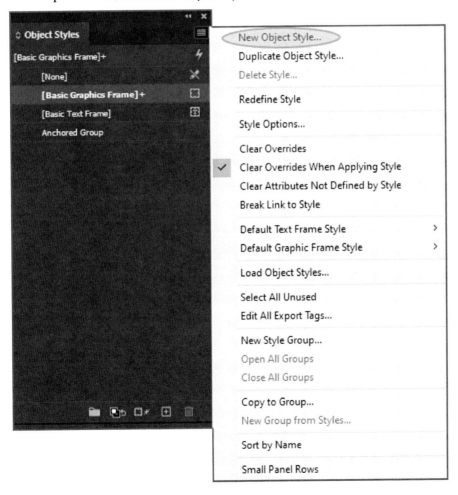

Figure 10.6 – Object style menu options

A large dialog box is now open, with numerous tabs and checkboxes on the left and corresponding settings visible after you click on a tab. If a checkbox is selected, it means that the property is included in the formatting definition; if you see a minus, that property is excluded from the style definition. To see relevant properties, you must click on the tab/label, not only a checkbox, as you can see in our example with the active **Anchored Object Options** tab. Here is a screenshot:

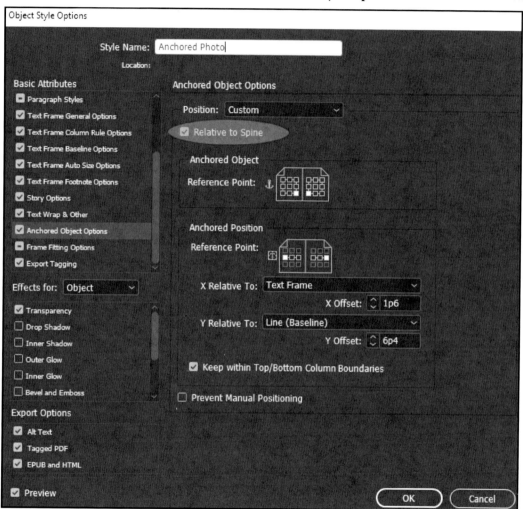

Figure 10.7 – The Object Style Options dialog box

3. Please look closely at the settings in *Figure 10.7*; they reflect all the settings that we have applied to our frame, including stroke color and weight. All we need to do is give the style a name. Type in the top field under **Style Name:** Anchored Photo.

> **Important note**
> The most efficient way to create a new style is to apply all the formatting manually to one element of a layout. When satisfied with the results, select the object (or text), choose the **New Style…** menu from the relevant panel, and give the style a name. All properties applied to the selected object or text will be saved as a new style.

4. Click the **General** tab and click the **Apply Style to Selection** checkbox so that the object that you started with and is the source of formatting also uses the style you just created. This is not a default setting; it needs to be selected.

5. Test the style by placing a new image on a page, anchoring it in the text, and then clicking the new object style. The image frame should quickly move to a proper position saved in the style and receive the stroke settings we entered.

    All new photos can now get the same settings very quickly. Great job!

We have learned how to anchor frames in text and create a style to easily apply anchoring settings to image frames. Next, we will learn how to add alternative text (alt-text) tags.

Adding an alternate text description to images

Adding alt-text tags to images in InDesign during authoring eliminates the need for fixes in Acrobat when a document becomes a `.pdf` publication. There are three methods to do it:

- Select a frame containing an image, and from **Object | Object Export Options**, open a dialog box where you can type the alternate text

- Select a frame containing an image, and from **Object | Object Export Options**, open a dialog box where you can choose metadata for the `alt-text` source

- Add the setting to choose metadata for the `alt-text` source in the object style used for anchored frames

We will learn how to use all these methods, as you may encounter different scenarios. Let's start with the first one.

Typing alternate text manually for each image frame

Here are the steps to add **alt-text** tags if you only occasionally use some images and volume is not a concern:

1. Select the image frame and click **Object | Object Export Options** to open a dialog box where you can type the alternate text. Be sure that the frame is selected, not the content (grayed-out options in the dialog box mean you selected the image content). Here is the screenshot:

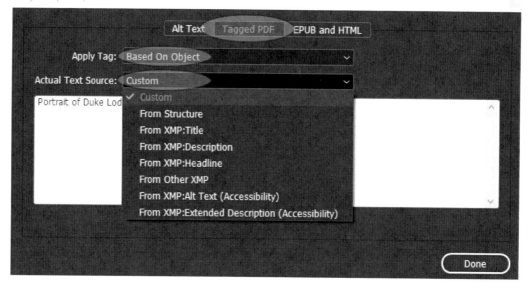

Figure 10.8 – Adding an alternate text description to an image frame manually

2.   Click the **Tagged PDF** tab at the top of the dialog box.

3.   Choose **Based on Object** from the first dropdown.

4.   Choose **Custom** from the lower dropdown.

5.   Type the alternate text and click **Done** to accept the update.

This method is simple enough and works well if the publication is one of a kind and does not have a lot of images, such as a memo, short white paper, or invitation to an event. It can also give you the advantage of expanding the description of an image and the context in which it is used, helping a non-visual reader to understand more fully the meaning of the image in a unique context of a story.

However, if you take, for example, a newsletter or a report where dozens of images are repeated in each issue that is published every few months, a page with a board of directors, or a page with seals and logos, you will need a better way to work.

We will now improve our method of adding **alt-text** by taking advantage of metadata saved with image files. Here is the process.

Adding alternate text from the metadata description

Most image files exist outside an InDesign layout. They usually contain a lot of information about them as metadata. Examples of metadata include file properties such as file format, date of creation, color mode, creator, and copyright.

Some metadata fields in images allow us to provide a description of content. They have been recently expanded. XMP:Alt Text (Accessibility) and XMP:Extendeed Description (Accessibility) are new metadata added specifically for accessibility. If they are not yet available in the images you work with, use the XMP:Description field.

All metadata can be viewed and edited from the **File | File Info...** menu in the application that created/edited it, such as Photoshop, Illustrator, a file browser, or Adobe Bridge.

Since we are discussing tools in InDesign, we will expand our range to **Adobe Bridge**, an application that connects many functions across Adobe software and likely is already installed on your system.

If you have not used *Adobe Bridge* yet, you may be selling yourself short. It is a great tool to preview, organize, and edit files all at once rather than one by one. This applies also to viewing and editing metadata. This is what we will do next.

We will open Adobe Bridge and add XMP:Description to an image, and then we will use it to automate the process of creating alt-text tags in InDesign before exporting the document to .pdf. Here is a simplified chart of how this would work:

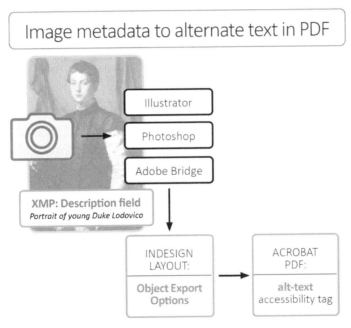

Figure 10.9 – The process of adding an alt-text tag from metadata

This chart approximates the cycle where a photo is taken and then edited in **Photoshop**, where editable metadata fields are filled in. The image is placed in an **InDesign** layout, and when a publication is finished, it is exported to .pdf, forwarding the selected metadata connected to the image – in this case, the information to create **alt-text** tags, which can be viewed in **Acrobat**.

Images, of course, can be sourced from many devices, or they can be created entirely within an application such as Illustrator. Metadata descriptions can be added at any time, both before and after placing an image in a page layout. To process many images, it is easier and much more efficient to work with Adobe Bridge. Let's now go through the steps shown in the following screenshot:

1. Open **Adobe Bridge**. If InDesign is open, select **File | Browse in Bridge…** from the top menu.

2. Locate an image that you used in the InDesign layout and click it in Bridge to select it. If your screen displays the **Essentials** workspace, you will see the panels and metadata arranged somewhat like the screenshot here:

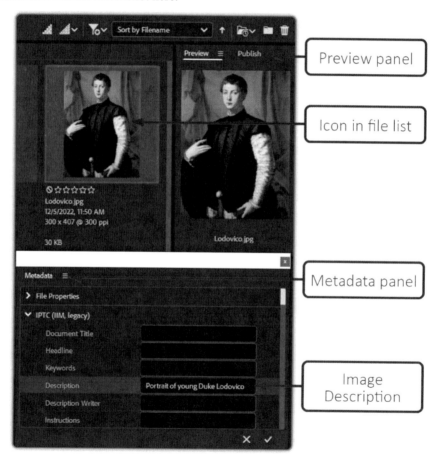

Figure 10.10 – Adding image description metadata in Adobe Bridge

3. Click in the **Description** field of the **Metadata** panel and type the text. In our example, it is `Portrait of young Duke Lodovico`. To accept the change, click the checkbox at the bottom of the panel. The file is updated and saved with the added metadata. You can now use it in InDesign.

4. Switch back to the InDesign document. Be sure to update the image link in the **Links** panel.

5. Select the image if deselected, and choose **Object | Object Export Options...** from the top menu.

6. In the dialog box that opens, click on the **Tagged PDF** tab, and then from the **Actual Text Source:** dropdown, select **From XMP:Description**. The text of the description appears in the dialog box window. It is not editable here; it is placed directly from the metadata field we updated using Adobe Bridge. Pretty neat, isn't it?

For this process to work dependably, all images used in the layout need to be processed the same way. This means that filling in information in the XMP:Description metadata should be a step in the production process that is followed consistently. The advantages are obvious in terms of description accuracy, the ability to automatically create captions, and the use of settings to create alt-text tags when exporting to .pdf.

But wait – this is not all. Here is one more thing we can do to automate adding alt-text tags. Let's revisit the object style settings for the style we created earlier.

Adding alternate text from metadata using object styles

Now that we have the necessary metadata and we have already created an *anchored photos* object style specifically to apply to images that will be exported as meaningful content, we can combine settings to fully take advantage of automation when creating alt-text tags in InDesign.

Here are the steps:

1. In InDesign, select the image that we updated by adding description metadata.

2. Open the **Object Styles** panel and click the **anchored photo** to apply the style.

3. Double-click the style label to open the dialog box.

4. Click the **Tagged PDF** option in the list on the left.

5. Select **Based on Object** from the **Apply Tag:** dropdown.

6. Select **From XMP:Description** from the **Actual Text Source:** dropdown.

7. Click **OK**. You are now finished setting up the process of adding alternate text to images when exporting to .pdf using an object style.

We have covered three methods of adding alternate text to images, with the most advanced using metadata and object style settings. If a designer consistently uses images with metadata and properly sets up object styles, the accessibility requirements for images will be completely satisfied.

You have seen the power of object style; we will now learn how to create a document text structure and control which images are tagged as meaningful content and included in a .pdf document structure. It is all done in the **Articles** panel in InDesign.

Managing content structure in the Articles panel

When the **Articles** panel was added to the toolset in InDesign, it changed the way documents were authored with accessibility in mind. We have a way to control the logic of how text and images are organized and presented in the **Tags** pane in Acrobat. To understand how the **Articles** panel works, we need to also review the concept of an InDesign story.

A **story** in InDesign is text continuously flowing in a single text frame or in many frames that are threaded/linked. Take a look at the following screenshot:

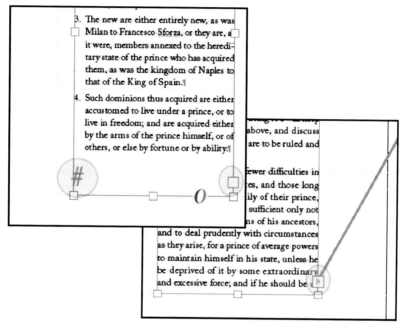

Figure 10.11 – An InDesign story placed in text frames

If text fits entirely inside one frame, the outport highlighted at the bottom-right area of the left frame will be empty, and the **End of the Story** symbol will display, as highlighted in the bottom-left corner of the frame. Contrast this with the lower frame, where there is too much text to fit the frame; therefore, it flows to the next linked frame. The outport symbol in the bottom-right corner of the frame has a tiny triangle and a thread line attached to it. This is a different story that flows across many frames or pages. InDesign makes it very easy to separate stories the way a journal separates articles. A story can be as long as a publication or as short as a caption.

Now, we are ready to work with the **Articles** panel, where *story* means the same as *article*. As InDesign documents have stories, the **Article** panel will have many articles. The process is simple; with a **Selection** tool, click a frame that you want to become part of the document content structure in .pdf and add it to the panel.

Here are the steps:

1. Open an InDesign document that is almost ready for export to .pdf. It should have text and graphics in place. If you are using our example file, recall that some images were anchored in the paragraph text.

2. From the top menu, select **Window | Articles** to open the panel. If this is the first time the panel is used in a document created from the **File | New** function, rather than one based on a template, it will be empty, only displaying instructions, as shown on the left side of the screenshot here:

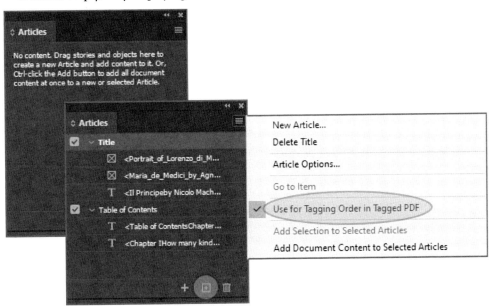

Figure 10.12 – The InDesign Articles panel

3. With a **Selection** tool, click on a story text frame and then click the plus (+) symbol, as highlighted in the screenshot (you can also use the **New Article…** menu option). Another dialog box will open, as shown here:

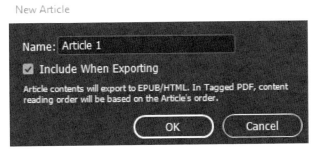

Figure 10.13 – Adding a new article to the panel

4.   Now, you can identify the story by typing in the **Name:** field a label reflecting the content of the story. *Figure 10.12* displays two stories placed in the panel – **Title** and **Table of Contents**.

Each story needs to be placed individually and given a name.

5.   Images that are not anchored, such as in the opening pages' backgrounds, need to be also added to the panel individually. The process is the same as adding stories, or you can click-drag an image and drop it in the panel. You can position it inside an existing article by moving the label up or down inside the panel. You can also create a new article for images only. This can work for multiple images on a page, such as a gallery.

Here is how the **Articles** panel manages images:

- Anchored images are automatically included in the article, and the anchoring position sets the position in the document structure when exported to .pdf. This works well for very long documents, such as books or reports with images, or charts that need to be close to the related text, but a story needs to be placed across many pages. As the text reflows, so do images.

- Images that are not anchored can be placed inside the panel at the beginning or end of a story/article. This works well for very short stories, such as in a newsletter where images are on the same page as the related text.

- Images that are not anchored and not placed in the **Articles** panel are ignored and tagged as artifacts when exported to .pdf.

6.   Be sure to check the panel menu's **Use for Tagging order in Tagged PDF** option; otherwise, the content of the panel will be ignored by InDesign. It is not selected by default.

Organizing content in the **Articles** panel is now done. You will see the results in the **Tags** pane in Acrobat. We will now move on to working with text styles, specifically paragraph and character styles that will give us control over how accessibility tags are assigned when exported to .pdf.

Mapping InDesign text styles to PDF tags

Paragraph and character styles were introduced with the very first version of Adobe InDesign back in the previous millennium, in the year 1999 – a long time ago! The styles then served mostly as a tool to apply consistent physical formatting to headings and body text. Font style, size, and color, along with paragraph alignment, spacing, and some more detailed options for hyphenation, keep options, and so on were the main concerns for designers. Grouping paragraphs with a style label made formatting and editing long documents so much easier. When a style was adjusted, so was all the text formatted using the same style.

When digital communication became standard, styles increasingly became important in mapping the meaning of printed paragraph text to an online coded text equivalent. For example, the **Head 1** style would become an **H1** tag when exported to .pdf or .html. This is how the functionality of styles expanded to address accessibility in InDesign. Over time, more attention was given to the details of automatic tagging of content when exporting a `.indd` file to `.pdf`. The process now is greatly streamlined. The conversion engine assigns accessibility tags to text in document pages and displays the results in the **Acrobat Tags** pane document structure that digital screen readers use. Tags give the `.pdf` content a **logical reading order** that is managed during the authoring stage of document production through the use of styles.

In addition to placing stories in the **Articles** panel, as discussed earlier, organizing logical reading order through tagging is accomplished by **mapping the InDesign text styles** to specific `.pdf` accessibility tags. Defaults assign only a limited number of predefined options. Since authors decide what text should be a top-level heading or a subhead, what a caption is, or what a body paragraph is, they are also in the best position to tag content using styles. A well-designed style sheet makes this task easy and transparent, once it is adopted as a standard practice. Although it requires planning and disciplined use of styles, the results are well worth it.

The **Articles** panel controls a document structure by organizing a logical order of stories in a page layout. In Acrobat, you will see the `<Art>` tags with a label corresponding to an article name. Anchoring images, paragraph styles, and the proper formatting of text completes the rest of the structure within articles by assigning appropriate tags. Some of them are assigned automatically, and some you can define using styles.

In this segment, we will learn how to recognize correct style mapping, how to define tags for export to `.pdf`, and finally, how to assign tags to elements that should be treated as background.

InDesign assigns the following tags automatically for correctly formatted content:

- Figures use `<Figure>`, although `alt-text` needs to be added by an author
- Body text level paragraph tags are represented by `<P>`
- Lists, both numbered and bulleted, are formatted using the **Bullets and Numbering…** option in the paragraph settings
- Tables include the entire table structure, where `<Table>` is the top tag, `<TR>` tags are assigned for each table row, and `<TH>` and `<TD>` are created at the cell level
- Generated lists and entries include table of content tags (`<TOC>` and `<TOCI>`) and `<Index>` tags
- Links for hyperlinks, footnotes, and index entries are represented by `<Link>`

Headings and **artifact** tags need to be added by an author, based on content. Let's start with headings.

Headings provide both visual and logical structure to a publication. Large bold text immediately is interpreted as a heading, whereas small text in a long paragraph is not. This is for those who can see. For a screen reader – that is, readers who cannot see – a tag serves as a way to mark text as prominent or not. In terms of importance, the `<H1>` tag is at the top while the `<H6>` tag is at the bottom.

Headings need to follow consistent nesting. This means that a top-level heading tagged <H1> can be followed by text, tables, and figures, but the next heading must be either the same level, <H1>, or one step lower, <H2>. A <H1> heading followed by a <H3> heading will fail the accessibility test. <H2> can be followed by <H1> or <H3> but not by <H4>… I think you get the idea.

Let's now do some hands-on work with a sample heading in a document. We are still using InDesign:

1.   From the **Tools** panel, select the **Type** tool and place an insertion point in a heading.

2.   Open the **Paragraph Styles** panel. Our example file highlights the **Subhead1** style name in the panel.

3.   Double-click the name label to open the style options. Here is a screenshot:

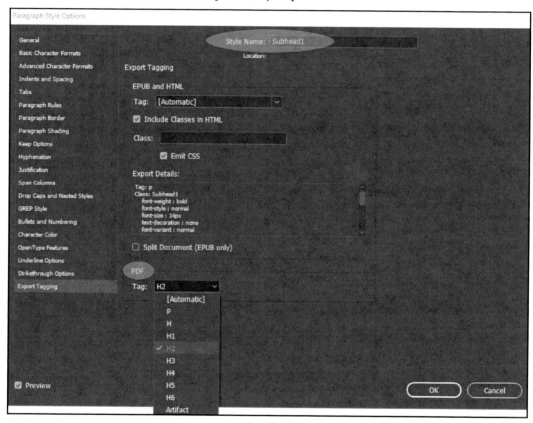

Figure 10.14 – Mapping paragraph styles to accessibility tags

4.   Click the **Export Tagging** option to access a dropdown, where you can choose which tag should be associated with the text formatted using this paragraph style, highlighted at the top.

5.   Click the tag to assign it and then click **OK** to save changes. It's that simple.

Now, you just need to make sure that each paragraph in the publication is formatted using a specific style and that each one includes the proper `.pdf` **Export Tagging** setting. Styles that are not updated will use a default `<P>` tag.

> **Important note**
> **Parent page** (formerly **master page**) layout elements are always tagged as **Background/Artifact**.

We have learned how to use layout methods and formatting options to prepare page content for accessibility. We will now add bookmarks that make navigation in long documents possible when a reader with visual impairments cannot use a mouse, depending solely on a keyboard, although, in fact, all of us benefit from bookmarks.

Automating the creation of bookmarks

Bookmarks in Acrobat open in the **Bookmarks** pane. They work a bit like a table of contents, but instead of being placed on a document page, they are located in a pane. Bookmarks can be added in Acrobat; however, the most efficient way to add them, especially in long documents, is to use InDesign functions. There are two ways to create them in InDesign:

- The automatic way, using settings to generate a **table of contents**
- The manual way, using the InDesign **Bookmarks** panel

We will explore both methods next. Here are the steps for the first method, the automatic one.

Creating bookmarks using a generated table of contents

We will generate a table of contents that builds entries based on headings formatted with paragraph styles. This will also allow us to create bookmarks based on the same headings. Here are the steps:

1. Open an InDesign document that consistently uses styles for headings. I will continue working with the example file used earlier.

2. From the top menu, select **Window | Interactive | Bookmarks** to open the **Bookmarks** panel. It is empty at the moment (see the left area of *Figure 10.16*).

3. Create space for a table of contents. You may need to add a blank, new page. A quick way to do that is to click-drag a parent page to the pages area of the **Pages** panel. When the space for a table of contents is ready, move on to the next step.

4. From the top menu, select **Layout | Table of Contents…** to open a dialog box, where the settings for generating and formatting a table of contents are found. Here is a screenshot:

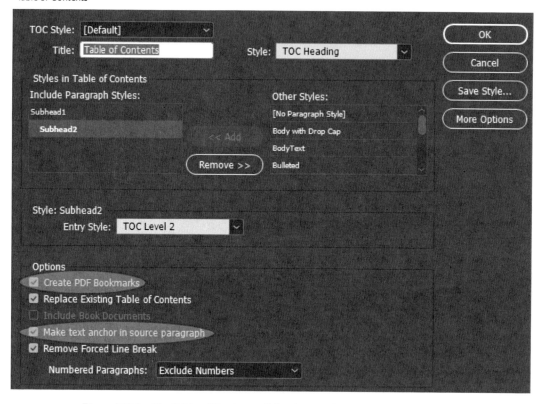

Figure 10.15 – The Table of Contents dialog box settings to create bookmarks

5. Note that this document will have **two levels of TOC entries**. The formatting of text for each level is set up using paragraph styles already created in this document.

    This will also give us **two levels of bookmarks**.

6. In the **Options** area of the dialog box, there are checkboxes that specifically control bookmarks. Select **Create PDF Bookmarks** and **Make text anchor in source paragraph**, as highlighted in *Figure 10.15*.

7. Click **OK**, and wait a moment for InDesign to process your request. For documents that are not very long, this is instantaneous.

8. Your cursor will be now loaded with text. Click to place it on the blank area of the page.

9. Your table of contents was generated following the settings in the dialog box and is now placed on a page. The **Bookmarks** panel is now populated with entries, as seen in the screenshot here:

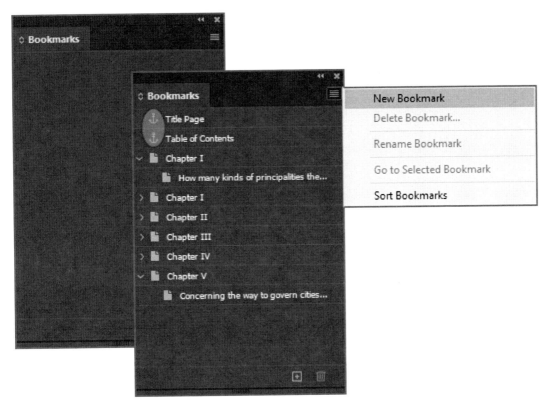

Figure 10.16 – The Bookmarks panel before the table of contents
was generated and after. Two were added manually

Creating bookmarks based on headings when generating a table of contents is very efficient. However, sometimes you may need to create a bookmark for content that is not a heading and is not included in a table of contents. We will manually add two bookmarks using the **Bookmarks** panel next.

Creating bookmarks using the Bookmarks panel

We will now use the second method – manually creating bookmarks using the **Bookmarks** panel. We will add one bookmark for the **Table of Contents** page, since it is not created automatically.

Here are the steps:

1. Click in the blank area of **Bookmarks** panel so that no bookmark is highlighted.

2. Select the *Table of Contents* **heading text** using the **Type** tool.

3. From the panel menu, select **New Bookmark**. It now appears in the panel with a small anchor symbol on the left as highlighted in *Figure 10.16*.

4.   Click and drag the bookmark to the very top of the panel.

5.   If you want to add more bookmarks to your documents, simply repeat *steps 1–3*.

I also added a bookmark to *Title Page*. Instead of selecting the text, I placed an insertion point in the title, clicked (+) at the bottom of the panel, typed `Title Page`, and then moved the bookmark to the top, above **Table of Contents**. You can recognize the two manually added bookmarks; in the panel, they have a small anchor icon, highlighted in blue. See the top two bookmarks in *Figure 10.16*.

We have learned how to organize our workflow in InDesign so that accessibility in exported `.pdf` documents does not need remediation in Acrobat. All bookmarks created in InDesign will provide interactive navigation to the `.pdf` file, but only if the document is exported properly.

In the next segment, we will step through PDF export options that preserve all the functionality and accessibility of the document that we took time to build.

Preserving interactive and accessibility features when exporting to PDF

The process of correctly preparing document files for a final version of a printed or digital page takes a lot of planning, consistent use of formatting options, and finally, a thoughtful send-off. We will focus now on settings that complete all components that an accessible file needs. We will start by adding the necessary metadata. Here are the steps:

1.   From the top menu, select **File | File Info…**.

2.   Type text in the **Document Title:** field, and add **Author:** and **Description:** information.

3.   Type text in the **Keywords:** and **Copyright Notice:** keywords, if applicable.

4.   Click **OK** to save.

Next, we will step through the PDF Export options, appropriate for an accessible `.pdf` document:

1.   From the top menu, select **File | Export…**.

2.   From the **Save as type:** dropdown, select **Adobe PDF (Interactive) (*pdf)** and click **Save**.

> **Important note**
>
> It is critical to use the **Adobe PDF (Interactive)** export settings to preserve the accessibility of the publication. Additional options such as **Adobe PDF (Print) (*pdf)** or using **File | Print** to send it to an Adobe PDF printer create flat `.pdf` files that are meant to be used as printed paper output, not for online distribution.

3.   A dialog box with **Export to Interactive PDF** settings opens. Here is a screenshot:

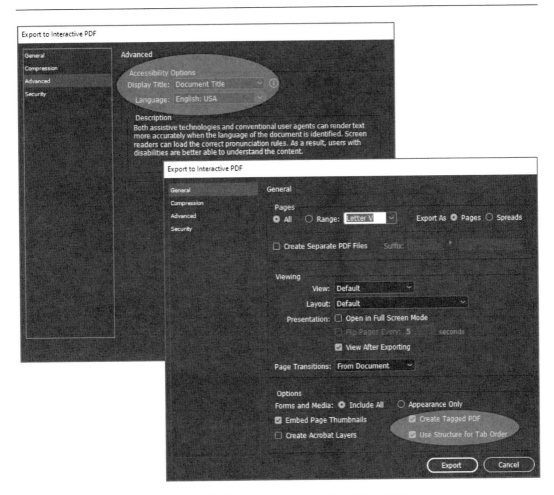

Figure 10.17 – The Export to Interactive PDF settings

4. In the **General** tab, ensure that **Create Tagged PDF** and **Use Structure for Tab Order** are checked, as highlighted in *Figure 10.17*.

5. In the **Advanced** tab, ensure that **Document Title** from the **Display Title:** dropdown is selected and that an option is selected in the **Language:** field (**English** for our project).

6. Click **Export**, and you are on the way to producing a fully accessible .pdf document.

7. Run the accessibility checker in Acrobat to test the file. It should pass. Isn't it amazing?

This was very optimistic of course; it's likely you will need to make some tweaks in the source document. However, tweaks and remediation are very different tasks. Tweaks in an InDesign document remain for every new .pdf version, whereas fixes in Acrobat need to be reapplied after each exported .pdf version. I think I have made my point enough times (and if you are rolling your eyes at this, I hope you are doing so with a smile!).

Well, here is what we have learned so far. We know how to anchor image frames, and how to create object styles to preserve these settings. We have tried different methods to add alternate text to images and organized content in the **Articles** panel for use as a document structure in PDFs. We mapped paragraph styles to accessibility tags that refine logical reading order within articles in the document structure. Finally, we exported our project as an interactive .pdf document that converts InDesign elements to accessibility features in Acrobat.

Creating accessible documents is only one area of integration of InDesign in Acrobat. Another important way that these applications work together is in a continually evolving cycle of providing editorial feedback. We will now explore **creative cloud**-based direct collaboration and review options for editors interacting with graphic designers using InDesign.

Document review and collaboration

In a demanding workflow, graphic designers and editors work together using InDesign and InCopy. Edit changes and tracking of those changes are done collaboratively with great efficiency. However, not all design houses adopt InCopy as part of their publication production tools. Yet, it is always necessary to review all projects, most of the time in a very short turnaround time.

InDesign and Acrobat now provide tools for closer-than-ever collaboration, using both email-based and **shared review** functions. We discussed tools and methods for document reviews in *Chapter 6, Using Acrobat in A Document Review Cycle*. In this section, we will focus on an InDesign approach and how using PDF comments and a shared review allows many editors to add markup and comments directly to a source InDesign file.

> **Important note**
>
> At the time of writing, the auto-edit function is available only in an email-based review. For more information on the overall **shared review** process and how it differs from an **email-based review**, see *Figure 6.7* in *Chapter 6, Using Acrobat in A Document Review Cycle*.

Email-based review comments and markup

Discussing an email-based review here refers essentially to a classic approach where a .pdf file is created by an author and delivered to an editor, either by email, a link to a URL, or made available on a network drive. A reviewer receives a complete publication as a .pdf file with a request to provide feedback, using comment tools found on a desktop version of Acrobat. Considering how many variations there are, I think that it is necessary to narrow the process here.

When the review is completed, the author receives the feedback and imports markup to InDesign using the **PDF Comments** panel. Markup can be accepted or rejected, and the **auto-edit** function automatically changes the text. It is very powerful, and if done correctly, it takes away the duplication of effort and the potential for additional errors when retyping text edits. Commas, typos, and deletions are done based on editorial input, with no need to repeat the process. *Figure 10.18* shows the progress of this review method:

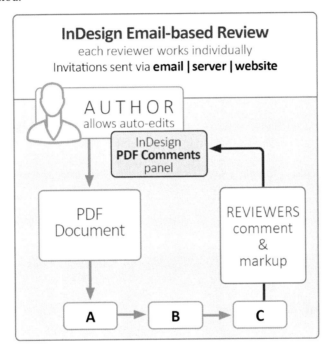

Figure 10.18 – InDesign PDF comments review

It works very well, but like with everything, the optimal outcome comes from applying optimal discipline throughout the process. It is especially important to create tagged PDFs for this review. We will explore the details next.

InDesign allows several methods to accept editorial changes. In this section, we will focus on the main tool for **auto-edits**, the **PDF Comments** panel. Here are the steps to use it:

1. Export your InDesign publication to `.pdf` using the **File | Export…** options from the top menu. (Be sure you are not printing to Adobe PDF.)

2. InDesign gives two types of `.pdf` in the **Save as type:** dropdown. You can select either, but in the dialog box that opens, be sure to select the **Create Tagged PDF** checkbox. Ignoring this little detail will make auto-edits somewhat unpredictable.

3. Open Acrobat and use text editing markup tools to mark replace, delete, and insert a sentence or two. Save the `.pdf` document in Acrobat.

4. Return to InDesign and open the **PDF Comments** panel. If closed from the top menu, select the **Window | Comments | PDF Comments** options. You can also import comments using the **File | Import PDF Comments…** options from the top menu. Here is a screenshot of the panel before and after the comments were imported:

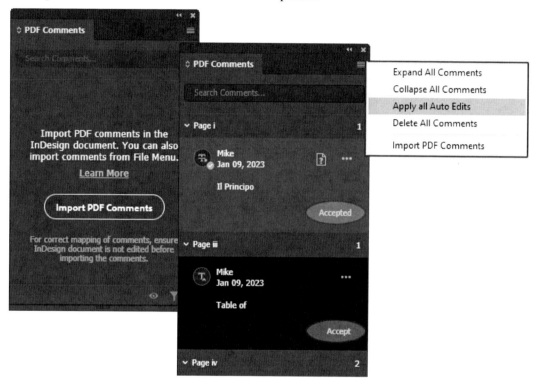

Figure 10.19 – The PDF Comments panel before and after comments are imported

5. Click on any comment. It will take you to a page layout where changes are requested. Clicking the **Accept** option (as highlighted in *Figure 10.19*) will automatically change text marked by the text markup tool in Acrobat. From the panel menu, you can also use **Apply all Auto Edits**.

> **Important note**
> InDesign track changes are a separate set of functions and do not relate to the **PDF Comments** panel options. The menu options from the **Type | Track Changes** options are for edits done entirely in an InDesign/InCopy workflow.

You can see how this workflow helps to streamline the review process. Instead of reading and retyping text edits, the auto-edit function lets an author/designer simply accept changes. However, this method depends on a traditional approach where authors and editors work on desktop systems and the feedback is linear; if editors need to collaborate, the process takes a lot of time and versions. Therefore, a new approach of working independently yet together is very appealing – online collaboration in a shared review.

In the next section, we will consider how immediate feedback can be implemented, allowing all involved reviewers and authors to see the review progress, regardless of what device they use.

Shared review comments and collaboration

We will now explore how an InDesign document ready for editorial marks can be sent for review and then modified based on feedback. A graphic designer can see the feedback immediately as it happens and edit the publication content in InDesign, based on the just-in-time review. To clearly see the difference between the two methods and panels, compare *Figure 10.18* and *Figure 10.20*:

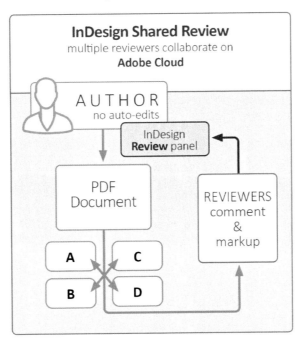

Figure 10.20 – The InDesign shared review workflow

Here are the steps to initiate a review of a document from within InDesign:

1. From the top-right area of the InDesign window, click the **Share** button to open the options and then click **Share for Review…**, as shown in the screenshot here:

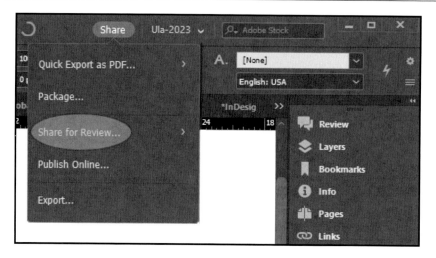

Figure 10.21 – The InDesign Share for Review… menu options

2.   A dialog box opens, where you type the email addresses of those who are invited to participate. Here is a screenshot:

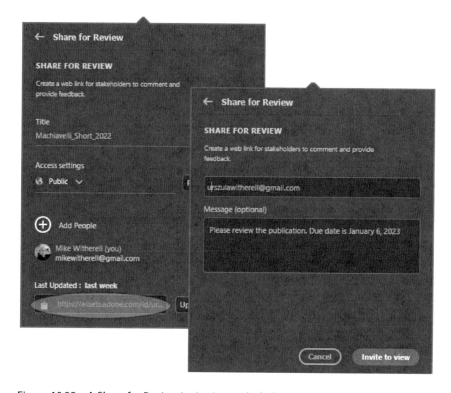

Figure 10.22 – A Share for Review invitation and a link to connect online (highlighted)

3. Click the **Invite to view** button to start the process of connecting to **Creative Cloud** and uploading a `.pdf` file to be edited, using the review service online commenting tools. A reviewer does not need to install Acrobat and can make comments and mark up the file on any device. All that is needed is a connection to the internet.

4. Click the highlighted link to the **Creative Cloud** assets (in the bottom-left corner of *Figure 10.22*) to see the tools and file in a browser version of an Acrobat-like review service. This is the reviewer's workspace.

5. An editor can mark up the document, using the currently available tools for commenting, deleting and replacing text, and making pencil marks. Anyone provided with a link can connect to the same file while the review is in progress and will immediately see the feedback.

6. When commenting is finished, the InDesign file when opened shows all the markup in the **Review** panel and the document layout. Note that this is a different panel than the **PDF Comments** panel used earlier.

7. Select **Window | Comments | Review** to open the **Review** panel where all the comments appear, as shown in this screenshot:

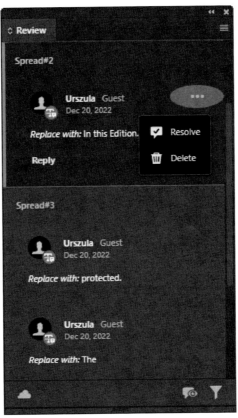

Figure 10.23 – The Review panel with comments from the shared review

8. Click on any comment in the panel to go directly to the markup on the page. Although InDesign document pages display areas of edits, currently there is no way to automatically accept or reject all changes. However, they are very easy to find in the layout.

We have reviewed how InDesign and Acrobat work together, integrating many functions. Many options related to accessibility or commenting are streamlined. You experienced that when producing a publication with accessibility as a goal, using InDesign options and settings. Once a publication is exported to .pdf and edited changes need to be marked and found quickly, there are choices available for the best workflow, depending on the specific needs.

Likely, more upgrades will come, especially in the area of collaboration, as our work becomes less dependent on a physical office location or a specific device.

Summary

This chapter gave us an opportunity to learn how to use Adobe InDesign page layout techniques to create an accessible .pdf document to export. We also briefly reviewed what a shared review is, supplementing information on the Acrobat review process covered in *Chapter 6, Using Acrobat in A Document Review Cycle*. Skills introduced here will give you the flexibility to successfully meet the demands of the constantly changing workflows.

In the next chapter, we will go professional. It is all about professional publishing, where physical paper meets digital tools in Acrobat to produce beautiful, printed publications. I hope you are ready for advanced options in Acrobat.

11
Using Acrobat for Professional Publishing

Publications and books printed on paper require special features that are used by printing devices. Color fidelity, ink intensity and distribution, trim, binding, paper quality, and so on must be considered long before a publication is printed. This should happen during the production process. The quality of photos, fonts, and other elements will define the quality of the output.

Our discussion in previous chapters focused on the interactivity of `.pdf` files. Our main concern was making sure that content looked good on screen and was available to all who want to read it, including those with visual impairments.

This chapter will focus on the visual elements of a `.pdf` file instead of interactivity. We will explore the tools that Acrobat offers to identify, control, and compensate for potential issues when a document is printed on paper. Errors can be very expensive. A digital publication can be easily replaced with a new version, but this is not so easily the case if it is printed. So, we depend on highly skilled and experienced professionals to do the job. As designers and authors, our job is to understand what they need and communicate clearly when unsure.

We will review some tools and options in Acrobat from the perspective of a graphic designer working primarily with Adobe InDesign. Images, fonts, guides, and more are handled very differently in MS Office applications and those files are typically printed with an office printer, not a commercial printing press. However, we will look at the settings that affect the quality of output regardless of what software created the `.pdf` file.

Here are the main topics we will discuss:

- PostScript and paper print requirements
- Customizing PDF output quality by manipulating Adobe Acrobat Distiller settings
- Converting colors and working with Ink Manager
- Working with Preflight and applying the most common fixes

The information presented here does not by any means cover all the options available in Acrobat to control print production. However, many authors do not have a deep background in commercial printing. The chapter introduces and explains, in general terms, some of the issues that may be encountered when sending documents for commercial printing and how Acrobat helps to spot them.

If you are expected to prepare files for a commercial press, you will need to do a lot more homework after reading this chapter. The best resource is your printing vendor. The professionals who will print your publication do not want to waste time and they will be happy to tell you what they need so that you also do not waste your time and money. Do communicate every detail and take good notes. This chapter covers a sample of tools that should give you direction on what to explore more on your own. Let's start sampling.

PostScript and paper print requirements

What is PostScript? It is a programming language created by Adobe Systems. **PostScript** is a language for printing devices to define areas of wet ink/toner on a physical paper, affecting the quality of the printed output. The currently used version, PostScript 3, was updated in 1997. It has been around for a long time.

PostScript's early adoption for printing was in the Apple LaserWriter desktop printer, and very quickly, the language was adopted by larger printing devices and finally huge printing presses. Designers provided the final output printed to a .ps file.

As new creative effects were added to authoring applications, PostScript-based workflows were replaced by **Adobe PDF Print Engine** (**APPE**). The changes addressed printing problems, especially those related to the transparency used in elements of the page layout. Today, most digital and commercial printing is done directly from a PDF using advanced **Raster Imaging Processors** (**RIPs**) managed by printing company staff.

A RIP is software used in commercial presses that converts vector files, such as .ai or .pdf, into a raster or bitmap format that printing devices understand. Even though digital applications are constantly changing their methods for separating colors from their primary components and getting the ink on the paper, understanding the background and the physical aspect of commercial printing is important.

We will discuss Acrobat tools that assist in resolving issues in that physical environment. What's the difference between dpi and ppi, which is the most common error occurring in manuals and help files? What is color separation? Why can there be issues with fonts? What is Preflight? We will tackle these topics next.

Understanding resolution

The term *resolution* is used in the context of a digital image, a monitor, and a printing device. A digital image's width and height are expressed in pixels. Unlike monitor pixels, image pixels have no physical size, and when viewed on a monitor, they are squares with specific color values arranged in columns and rows. *Actual size* viewing in Adobe applications refers to the magnification level when one image pixel corresponds to one monitor pixel. When the image is further enlarged, or you zoom in, you begin to see how individual pixels are arranged to create a photo, as shown in *Figure 11.1*:

Figure 11.1 – Pixels that create a bitmap image

In photo editing software, an image's width and height are measured in pixels, not inches or centimeters. Take the following example:

- A photo with 3,872 by 2,592 pixels (you can multiply the numbers to get the pixel count) printed on paper at 300 ppi measures 12.9" in width and 8.6" in height.

- The same photo resized to 25.8" width and 17.2" height will be printed at 150 ppi. High-quality publications require 225-300 ppi or close to that. Thus, **ppi** stands for image **pixel per inch** count *when printed*, also referred to as the effective resolution.

What is dpi? It stands for **dots per inch**, and it refers strictly to the ink-on-paper resolution of a printing device. Early desktop printers produced 300 dpi output, with later output improved to 600 dpi or 1,200 dpi. High-end printing presses produce a resolution of 2,400 dpi (dots of ink per inch of paper) or more for specialized projects. To produce crisp images, it takes multiple dots of ink to reproduce one image pixel. Similarly, tiny dots of ink in a high-resolution print produce fine lines in small fonts and strokes. Dpi and ppi are two types of resolution that are related, yet each term refers to a different property.

Another important aspect of output is consistent color in a publication that includes photos, charts, and backgrounds coming from many sources. We will review color issues next.

Understanding color

The most common technology to create color on paper is using four standard inks, also known as process inks: **Cyan, Magenta, Yellow, and Black (CMYK)**. When CMYK (**K** signifies black, but stands for **Key**) inks drop on paper in tiny dots, our eyes perceive an even area of color. Each ink is printed separately, and dots of ink must be aligned very precisely. The smaller the dots, the better the perception. High-resolution commercial presses use the CMYK color model for printing. Some publications are printed with additional inks added, such as a specific color spot ink, for example, metallic or varnish.

Spot inks were the norm in the past. The term refers to inks that are pre-mixed before the printing process begins, a bit like paint in home improvement stores, identified by a number in a library of standards, such as the **Pantone Matching System** (**PMS**), and added to the CMYK process. Not so long ago, it was common to add spot inks to reproduce a specific color precisely. As the color fidelity in CMYK output improved, spot inks were no longer used as often due to the significant production expenses that they add.

Figure 11.2 illustrates the process of creating color on paper using inks. Each ink is placed on a plate that stamps the paper in sequence.

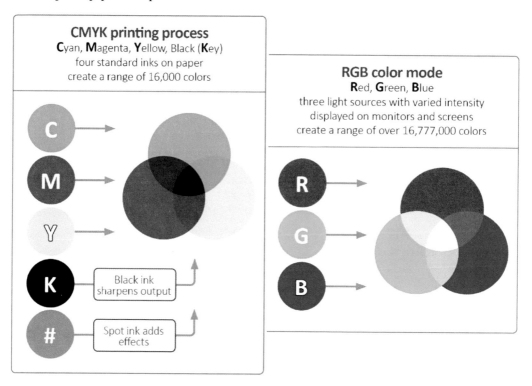

Figure 11.2 – CMYK and spot inks in commercial printing and RGB color on screen

Issues in color printing relate to how accurately and consistently the color is reproduced. A document layout includes images defined in RGB color mode; text and line art may be defined using CMYK color swatches and other combinations of colors. Additionally, each device and software may reproduce color in a unique way.

The next section will introduce some basic steps related to color management in printed publications.

Color management in Adobe applications

The **color management** options in Adobe applications help to manage all this color data to produce predictable and consistent color output throughout the entire creative and production process, which ends with printing.

When you work on a computer, you see RGB colors built with light. When you read a printed publication, you are seeing CMYK colors built by dots of ink on paper. Any device can capture or reproduce only a limited range of colors. A **color profile** describes the unique characteristics of a specific device. Color management maps the colors reproducible by one device to another. See the process illustrated in *Figure 11.3*:

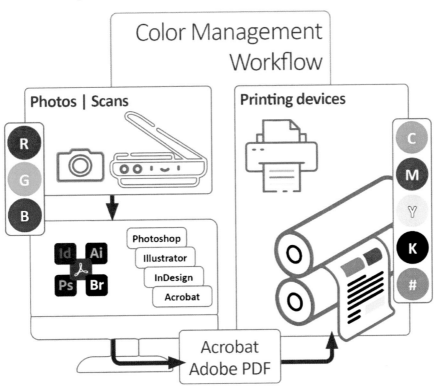

Figure 11.3 – Color conversion from RGB to CMYK

Adobe applications such as InDesign, Photoshop, Illustrator, and Acrobat share the **Adobe Color Engine** (ACE). The shared options allow you to synchronize the settings applied in each software. Don't expect this to be an entirely simple task. Setting up reliable color management in high-end publication production may require many checks, complex procedures involving additional hardware, and many conversations with printing company staff.

However, for designers working with Adobe applications, specifying the same color working space across the Creative Suite is a good start and takes only a few steps. Here they are:

1. In Acrobat, select **Edit | Preferences** (**Acrobat | Preferences** on macOS).

2. From **Settings**, select **North America Prepress 2** from the **Description** area at the bottom of the dialog box, which also explains why the setting should be used.

3. Click **OK** to close the **Preferences** dialog box.

4. The same settings should be selected in all applications of the Creative Suite (InDesign, Photoshop, and Illustrator).

Setting up and synchronizing the working space in your Adobe applications will display color consistently whether you edit an image in Photoshop or work with it in InDesign. It will also alert you if any additional setup is needed, such as handling color profiles.

Additional potential problems come from inks printed over existing inks on paper. We will next explore **Output Preview** to simulate color separations and ink coverage on paper to spot where problems may arise.

Working with Output Preview

The Output Preview tool simulates color separations on the screen, helping you to see areas of concern before the document is printed. Let's see how it works.

Open the **Print Production** tool, then select **Output Preview**. See the following screenshot:

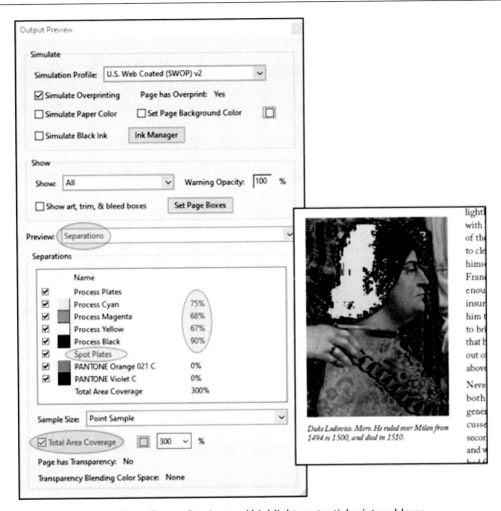

Figure 11.4 – Output Preview tool highlights potential print problems

Take a closer look at the list of inks in the example publication. You can see that in addition to standard CMYK inks, two spot inks appear in the list. Checking or unchecking a color in the **Separations** window will simulate what happens on paper when ink is not printed. Even if you've never visited a printing facility, you've likely seen a similar effect when your color desktop printer runs out of ink or toner.

Spot inks appear here as a result of errors in creating color swatches, and you can locate the areas and objects in the document pages where they are used. Here are the steps:

1. Check the checkbox on the left of **Process Plates** to hide coverage by CMYK colors. Only content using **Spot Plates** will remain visible on the pages. When you scroll to the opening page, you will see an orange box at the top of the page. Clearly, this color needs to be converted to be processed.

2. Check the checkbox to show **Process Plates** again.

When you show only one plate, it is displayed in gray. Gray conveys where the plate will transfer the selected ink on paper.

In press printing, inks often overlap or are laid on top of each other on paper. Scenarios in which this occurs could be when addressing **trapping**, a method to prevent white paper areas peeking out between color elements, when a designer uses registration color in error instead of black for objects on the page, or when text is printed over a background color area, which is referred to as overprinting. Very dark areas of photos may also have too much ink. Depending on the paper stock, the type of printing press, or the speed at which it runs, the amount of ink that exceeds **Maximum Total Ink Coverage** will result in muddy or smeared areas on paper.

Output Preview will highlight those regions so you can see them long before printing:

1. Click to check the **Total Area Coverage** checkbox and confirm that the field value is 300%. The default color of the highlight is green, but it can be changed.

2. Green patches will appear on page areas that meet or exceed the **Total Area Coverage** value, as shown in the photo on the right in *Figure 11.4*:

3. With your mouse, hover over the highlighted area and the rest of the photo to see how the actual **Total Area Coverage** value displayed inside the **Separations** window changes.

This quick check tells you that the photo is very dark and will cause a lot of ink coverage.

We have spotted two potentially expensive problems: spot color instead of the process used in the document and very dark areas in a photo that could smear. Expensive printing problems were avoided!

Color is only one of many issues you will need to deal with when working with commercially printed projects. We also need to understand how fonts need to be considered as a component of any publication. We will discuss that next.

Understanding fonts

Fonts used in a document are files external to the publication. Different applications access fonts in a shared folder to format text in a document. When a .pdf file is created, it is important to know how it will be used. PDF documents for online distribution need to have a small file size. To avoid large .pdf file sizes, publication text may be formatted using only commonly used system fonts, meaning those that most computers use. This may simplify the document design but will avoid the need to embed custom fonts. Reports, contracts, and books may be examples where formatting text using common fonts is sufficient.

A creative document design, on the other hand, may include a lot of different fonts that are not commonly used. To prevent an unexpected result due to replacements, fonts used during authoring should be embedded in the `.pdf` file. In commercial printing embedding, all fonts in `.pdf` are a requirement. Embedding fonts are avoided in publications distributed online as this could increase the file size.

Not everyone has adopted *OpenType* fonts and many older font types may still be in use, causing unexpected results. Even though PostScript fonts have reached the end of life in design applications, embedded *PostScript Type 1* fonts will print; just do not attempt to edit them.

Processing instructions on how to deal with fonts and other components, when a `.pdf` file is created, are stored in `.joboptions` files and edited in **Acrobat Distiller**. The selected settings are saved as **presets** and can be chosen when a specific `.pdf` output is needed. We will discuss the Distiller options in the next section and how the quality of PDFs is affected.

Customizing PDF output quality using Distiller settings

Acrobat Distiller uses settings to produce the visual components of `.pdf` files. These settings are selected and used by applications when exporting to a PDF. They are grouped into categories where image resolution, fonts, color, printing device processing, and compliance standards are defined. We will explore these settings next.

> **Important note**
>
> It is worth mentioning that an outdated method of creating `.pdf` files using Acrobat Distiller involved printing a document to a `.ps` file and then processing it in Distiller. *No such suggestion is made in this book.*
>
> The process of exporting to `.pdf` for both interactivity and press printing has been extensively covered in other chapters. The topics discussed here provide information on how to edit or create presets and save them as a `.joboptions` file, which is done using Distiller.

Open Acrobat Distiller on Windows by choosing **All Programs | Adobe Acrobat Distiller**. It opens as a small window with menus. Here is a screenshot:

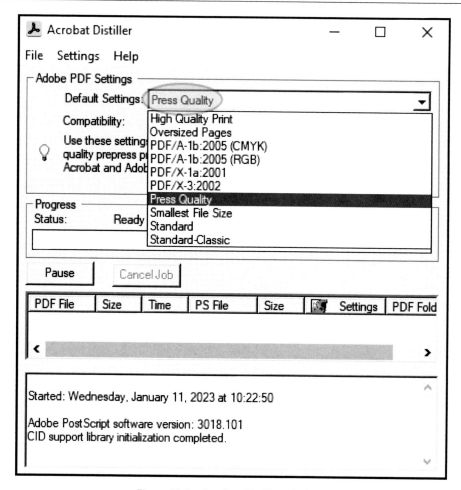

Figure 11.5 – Acrobat Distiller window

Distiller presets are labeled and can be selected from the dropdown. They contain many options, which produce certain outputs. All system applications have access to these options. They are selectable in MS Office PDFMaker, the **Print to PDF** dialog box, and all Adobe applications' **Export to PDF** options.

Here is a brief overview of what each preset is meant for:

- **High Quality Print** is defined for quality printing on desktop printers. Color and grayscale images are downsampled to 300 ppi and monochrome images to 1,200 ppi. All fonts are embedded, the color remains unchanged, and transparency is not flattened.

- **Oversized Pages** is to create PDFs for printing and viewing engineering drawings larger than 200 x 200 inches (508 x 508 cm).

- **PDF/A1b:2005 (CMYK** and **RGB)** standards are meant for the long-term preservation of electronic documents. PDF/A1b allows you to convert all colors in to CMYK or RGB, depending on which standard you have selected.

- **PDF/X1a (2001 and 2003)** is for files with all fonts embedded. The creation of a PDF from documents with fonts with license restrictions will fail. The PDF bounding boxes must be specified, and the color defined as CMYK, spot colors, or both. Transparency is flattened. The files must also describe the printing output intent.

- **PDF/X-3:2002** is for files with some restrictions. RGB-, LAB-, or ICC-based color spaces are also allowed if a color management workflow is defined and used. The files cannot contain music, movies of annotations that cannot be printed, form fields, or JavaScript and encryption. The ICC color profile, the color space of CMYK, and the output intent must be defined. The PDF bounding boxes must be specified.

- **Press Quality** is for high-quality print production, such as digital printing imagesetter or plate color separations. The quality of the content output is the most important. The file size is not a concern but preserving all the information that a commercial printer needs to print the document correctly is. Colors are converted in to CMYK, color and grayscale images are downsampled to 300 ppi, while monochrome images are downscaled to 1,200 ppi. All fonts must be embedded and transparency can be preserved.

> **Important note**
>
> Before sending a .pdf file to a commercial printer, find out what settings are recommended. The best option is to ask for a .joboptions file that will contain all the required settings. In some cases, you may need to create a custom .joboptions file with settings for a particular provider or project.

- **Rich Content PDF** is for interactive PDFs that include tags, hyperlinks, bookmarks, interactive elements, and layers. All fonts are embedded and the file is optimized. This preset was formerly labeled **eBook**.

- **Smallest File Size** is for files to display on the internet, or to distribute through email. PDFs are compressed and images are downsampled to a low resolution. All colors are converted to sRGB, and fonts are not embedded. Files are optimized.

- **Standard** is for desktop printing or digital copiers, as well as for publishing proofs to send to a client. Files are compressed and images are downsampled to low resolutions (the default is 72 ppi). Allowed fonts are embedded, but not the Windows font subset. All colors are converted in to sRGB, and the printing resolution is set to 600 dpi.

- **Standard-Classic** is for viewing and printing general business documents. Files are compressed and images are downsampled to low resolutions (the default is 150 ppi). All colors are converted in to sRGB, and the printing resolution is also set to 600 dpi.

We will now learn more about the available Distiller options by examining the settings in one of the presets just listed – **Press Quality**:

1. Select **Press Quality** from the dropdown, then from the top menu, select **Settings** | **Edit Adobe PDF Settings…** to open the full content of the dialog box options for the selected preset: **Press Quality**.

2. Since the **Press Quality** settings are defined for a high-resolution printing press, you will see corresponding values in place. In the **General** tab, **Resolution** is set to 2400 dpi.

3. Click **Images** in the left window to see the settings for images. Color, grayscale, and monochrome images have separate settings. The **Downsample** value defines the resolution range for images that may have been scaled down to fit a specific size in the layout. This means that if a photo has 3,000 by 3,000 pixel dimensions printed at 300 ppi, its dimensions will be 10" by 10". If the printed size needs to be 2.5" by 2.5", scaling down will create an image at 1,200 ppi. Downsampling eliminates extra pixels considered insignificant in favor of a smaller file size for transfer and storage to the printer. Downsampling optimizes the file for print processing, but due to removed pixel data, image quality is lost if scaled up after exporting to .pdf.

   Monochrome images refer to black and white shapes, often line art that, due to its high contrast, needs more pixels to look smooth. That is why the default value is 1,200 ppi.

4. Click the **Fonts** group of options in the left window. The policy for handling fonts is set here. Since the destination of our .pdf file is for commercial press printing, all fonts used in document production must be embedded, thus check **Embed all fonts**. Embedding prevents unexpected problems when fonts are missing, especially if .pdf text needs to be edited. **Subset embedded fonts when percent of characters used is less than: 100%** means all fonts are subsets, storing only the characters in use. This makes a unique font ID but creates a problem with editing the font. See the screenshot here:

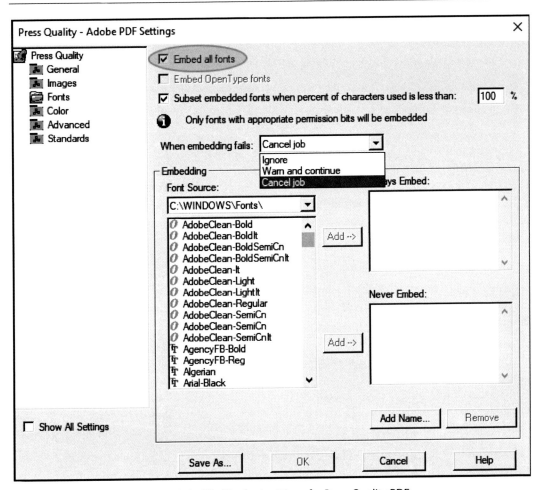

Figure 11.6 – Distiller font settings for Press Quality PDF

Notice that the **When embedding fails** option is set to **Cancel job**, meaning if you use fonts that cannot be embedded, this file cannot be sent to print on a press.

5. Click on **Color** to manage color in Distiller. Leaving **Adobe Color Settings | Settings File** set to **None** allows you to choose **Color Management Policies** from the dropdown and define appropriate settings in the **Working Spaces** options.

   If you choose a preset in **Adobe Color Settings | Settings File**, it takes over and all color management options in the dialog box are turned off.

6. The **Advanced** settings control processing a PostScript file into a .pdf file with details, useful when the document is printed on the press. The selection of these options will vary depending on the printing environment.

7. The **Standards** options help to ensure that the resulting `.pdf` file meets specific criteria. For example, **PDF/X** meets high-resolution print production requirements, while **PDF/A** meets standards for archiving. More details on this were listed earlier.

    Selecting **Compliance Standard** creates a report on file compliance and lists errors if there are any.

    When not compliant sets a policy for how Distiller should proceed: continue or cancel the job.

8. We have not made any changes to the settings, only reviewed them. If you make any selections and want to use them, save the new preset. Clicking the **Save As...** button will take you to a specific folder, `\AppData\Roaming\Adobe\Adobe PDF\Settings`, where `.joboptions` files are found by Acrobat and other applications for future use (**Library** | **Application Support** | **Adobe** | **Adobe PDF** | **Settings** on macOS).

9. Type a name in the dialog box, then click the **Save** button to close the dialog box and the **OK** button to close the Distiller settings dialog box.

Understanding the issues that we have discussed will allow you to create a `.pdf` file according to the specified requirements. However, in some cases, the files created do not meet the required criteria and need to be fixed. We will next explore methods for fixing issues related to ink and colors that we identified earlier in Output Preview.

Converting colors and working with Ink Manager

In a perfect world, things happen exactly according to plan. Well, I have not experienced a perfect world yet. And the publishing world is full of surprises. This is where Acrobat comes to the rescue and provides tools to spot potential issues before they become expensive printing problems.

Distiller provides settings before a file is converted in to `.pdf`. Once a `.pdf` file is created, potential fixes may need to be applied in Acrobat. One of the most common issues is when a document destined for printing uses RGB color space and swatches are defined as RGB instead of CMYK. I also often run into swatches built in error as spot inks when they clearly should be CMYK.

We will use the **Convert Colors** feature in Acrobat, where you can permanently convert the color definition in the document. Changes will be applied to the entire document. Here are the steps:

1. Select **Tools** | **Print Production** | **Convert Colors** to open a dialog box. See the following screenshot:

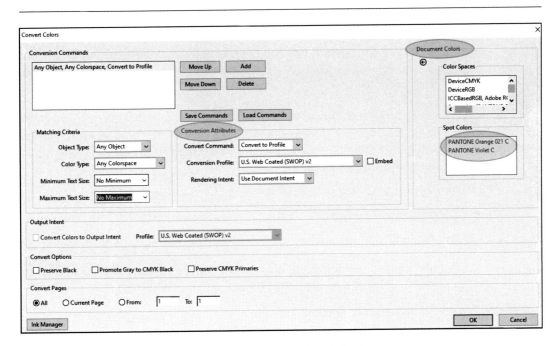

Figure 11.7 – Convert Colors dialog box

In this dialog box, you can define destination color spaces and for how long these changes should apply.

You can selectively choose what type of objects or color you want to convert in to a chosen profile. The following steps show you how to fix a document that uses two spot colors instead of CMYK.

2. Look at the **Document Colors** area, highlighted in the top-right corner of *Figure 11.7*. In the field below it, two spot colors are listed: **PANTONE Orange 021 C** and **PANTONE Violet C**. This document should not include these colors. All colors need to be defined as CMYK.

3. In the **Matching Criteria** group, select **Spot Color** for **Color Type** and notice that the updated **Conversion Commands** field at the top left of the window reflects the selection.

4. In the **Conversion Attributes** group, **Conversion Profile** is set to **U.S. Web Coated (SWOP) v2**. This will be the color space for the document and all spot colors will be converted. Keep in mind that CMYK is device specific, so confirm with your printing company first which profile should be used.

5. Click the **OK** button, then click **Yes** to acknowledge that the operation cannot be undone.

6. A progress bar will appear at the bottom right of the screen, and when done, your file will have been converted. You can test it by opening the **Convert Colors** dialog box again and you will see that the spot colors are gone. Be sure to save the file to keep the changes.

You may not want to change the color space of the entire document but need to fix spot colors. In a scenario where there are three similar swatches using slightly different definitions erroneously, you can specify that all three inks should be processed as one. To accomplish that, use **Ink Manager**. Here are the steps:

1. In the **Tools** panel, click **Print Production | Convert Colors | Ink Manager** or go directly to **Print Production| Ink Manager**. The same dialog box can be opened by using the top menu's **File | Print | Advanced | Output** options (listed in a window on the left edge of the dialog box) and then clicking the **Ink Manager** button.

2. Click a spot color in the list and then select **Ink Alias** from the dropdown.

   If a spot color needs to be printed as CMYK, check the checkbox on the left of the color name.

3. Click **OK** and proceed with either printing the document or converting the colors.

We've just fixed a .pdf file and avoided phone calls from a printing company asking whether we want to pay for adding two spot colors to the publication!

In the next section, we will explore the Preflight tool, which helps printing companies to fix any potential problems. Of course, if you suspect any issues with your final .pdf file before it goes to the printer, these tools are also for you!

Working with Preflight

PDF as a digital page is very complex. What we see on the screen does not reveal the range of settings contained in the file that are used for processing by various devices at the time of printing. To help analyze the content of a PDF and possibly fix problems, we will work with the Preflight tool.

Here are the steps:

1. In the **Print Production** tool, select **Preflight**. A feature-rich dialog box opens that stays open as long as you need it. Here is a screenshot:

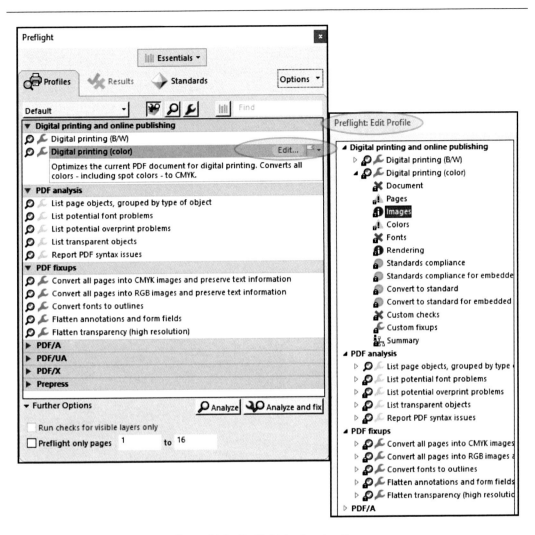

Figure 11.8 – Preflight tool and options

Preflight lists different types of profiles that come with an Acrobat installation. Custom profiles may be added, and existing ones may be edited. Profiles can be shared with others; they can be exported and imported. Some are provided for PDF analysis only and some provide both analysis and a fix. You can identify fixups by the wrench symbol.

The user defines specific values for the profiles after clicking the **Edit…** button on the right of a specific profile (highlighted). When a dialog box opens, you can see options that are part of the profile listed on the right of the Preflight panel (*Figure 11.8* shows only a part of a larger dialog box) that a .pdf file is compared to. Checking the document settings and comparing them against the Preflight values reveals errors. Errors are flagged and can be fixed using fixups. You can recognize which profile contains fixes due to the wrench symbol.

The right area of *Figure 11.8* shows a set of options that the **Digital printing and online publishing** profile contains. Take time to look at the settings and values in the dialog box. Click on each option and the large area on the right will reveal additional options with the values set or expected. There may be many values set that you want to change, which you can do by unlocking the settings. They come locked by default.

When you are done exploring, close the profile details by clicking the **OK** button. Let's test our profile:

1. Select the **Digital printing and online publishing** profile.

2. Click **Analyze** to get a report on any errors in your .pdf file. Only the checks of the profile will be executed for now and the PDF file will not be modified.

3. A detailed report appears listing everything that the profile included as a desired check. Here is a screenshot:

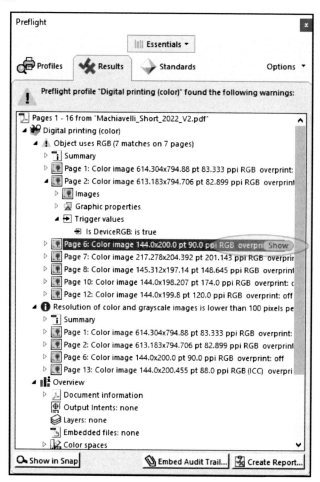

Figure 11.9 – Preflight analysis results report

4. Click on any item in the report, then on the **Show** button on the right to go to the image in the layout. It could be any triggered object, not just an image. The **Show in Snap** button will open a separate window where only the triggered object is displayed. You can now decide how to deal with the flagged item. In my example file, the main reason for flagging images was the resolution was too low.

5. To create a `.pdf` version of the report, click the **Create Report...** button. It can be shared with others if the source file needs extensive edits. Images with a low resolution would be a reason to reject printing. The report shows exactly which ones are the problem.

6. If the file errors can be fixed in Acrobat, you can click the **Analyze and fix** button. A different report will appear listing what was fixed. In my example file, the spot inks were converted in to CMYK, and compression was applied. Resolution cannot be fixed in this process.

We have had a look at advanced features used by print professionals to evaluate and, if possible, fix `.pdf` files before they are printed. It's quite a task just to read through all the options and settings in Preflight. The good news is that once you know them, you can use them over and over again.

Summary

In this chapter, we explored the tools needed in professional publishing. We learned about color models for paper printing and screen display. The Output Preview tool found potential problems related to ink use and coverage. We then converted color using Ink Manager. Reviewing Acrobat Distiller gave us a deeper look into the content and settings of a `.pdf` file before it is sent for commercial printing. Finally, we learned about the Preflight tool, which alerts us about any potential issues and offers us the possibility to correct some of those issues before printing.

The next chapter will introduce us to redacting options to preserve the privacy of documents that may need to be publicly available, and Bates numbering options. We will explore features that support a law office.

12

Privacy, Bates Numbering, and Other Specialized Features for A Law Office

In a world dominated by social media, cameras, and countless technologies in place recognizing our voice, faces, and locations, discussing privacy is somewhat contradictory. As we post personal photos and our living rooms are exposed to the public in video conference meetings or on the news, we still expect our taxes, resumes, medical records, and more to be inaccessible to the general public.

Even public figures expect that no one will use their credit card or social security number illegally. Since most office communication is done online, and the receipts or contracts are preserved as `.pdf` files, it is important to understand how to prepare these documents before they are distributed so that personal privacy is protected.

We discussed document security from the perspective of preventing unauthorized changes. In this chapter, we will discuss the security of personal information contained within a document. This may include personal names, ID numbers, and credit card information but also information not immediately visible but traceable, such as metadata, links, hidden text, or JavaScripts.

We will learn how to depersonalize a document so that it does not expose private information and work with tools to ensure that `.pdf` publications are acceptable in a law or medical office. Legal standards can be applied to redacting sensitive content, removing hidden data, and applying Bates numbering. Here are the main topics in our discussion:

- Redacting sensitive content and adjusting redaction marks
- Removing hidden content and sanitizing a PDF document
- Working with Bates numbering and options

We will start by learning how to find and remove information from a `.pdf` document.

Redacting sensitive content

Redacting means making sure that sensitive content is not visible or recognizable. In the physical world, it is usually done using permanent black markers. In the world of PDFs, it is possible to delete or obscure text or images using the **Acrobat Edit PDF** tool. Redacting, however, requires a specific mark resembling a black marker so that it is obvious that text or images have been deliberately obscured. In addition, any identifying information contained within the document code needs to be also removed.

Since redacting removes content permanently, we will visit **Acrobat Preferences** first to ensure that we don't damage original documents by accidentally overwriting the file. Oh yes, I have done that, and it was not pretty. Here are the steps:

1. Select the **Edit | Preferences** (on Mac, **Acrobat | Preferences**) options.

2. Select **Documents** from the options list in the left window.

3. In the **Redaction** group of settings, ensure that **Adjust filename when saving applied redaction marks** is **checked**. Here is a screenshot of the dialog box area with these settings:

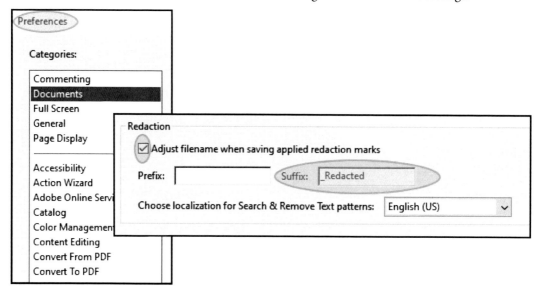

Figure 12.1 – Preferences for saving a redacted document.

We will work with a tax filing confirmation .pdf file that needs to be posted online as an instructional example. The information that we will redact includes the agency logo and instances of personal name, address, email, and phone number. Here are the steps:

1. From **Tools**, select the **Redact** tool and add it to the column on the right.

2. Click **Redact Text & Images** in the top toolbar that opens.

> **Important note**
> There are two steps to the redaction process for .pdf: marking text and/or images and then applying it. Always save changes as a separate file since redacted content cannot be restored. Be sure to preserve original document files as a backup.

3. Click-drag over an image to create an area for redaction. It will be applied later after all the content is marked. You will see a rectangle with red borders. Hovering over the markup will temporarily reveal the appearance of applied redaction.

4. Locate all instances of the personal name then click-drag with the same tool still active. Again, a red rectangle appears over marked areas.

5. Click-drag over all the remaining personal data: phone number, addresses, tax account ID number, bank routing number, bank account number, and more.

   If you peek at the **Comments** panel, you will see all markup appearing there too. Our marks are done. Return to the **Redact** tool.

In the next section we will learn how to customize redaction marks that readers will see in place of removed content.

Adjusting redaction marks

You can control what readers see as a replacement for original content. The redaction marks' appearance may be specified in **Redaction Tool Properties**. This is what we will do next. Here is a screenshot of the toolbar where you will find access to these settings:

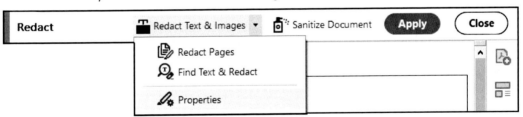

Figure 12.2 – Redact toolbar options

1. From the top toolbar, select the **Redact Text & Images | Properties** option. Here is a screenshot of the dialog box that opens, where you can choose new settings to replace the default black fill:

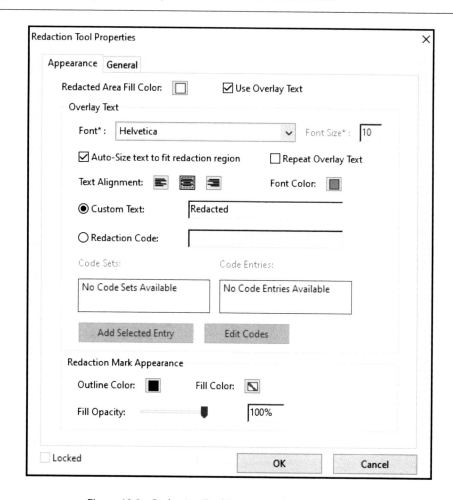

Figure 12.3 – Redaction Tool Properties dialog box options

2. I made these selections:

    •   **Redacted Area Fill Color:** White

    •   **Text Alignment:** Center

    •   **Custom Text:** Redacted

    Redaction Code maybe also selected if used by your organization.

3. Click **OK** to accept changes. You have prepared your document to finalize the process.

4. Click the **Apply** button in the top toolbar. Accept the **Apply redactions** alert and click **Continue**.

5. Save the file with the new name using the _Redacted suffix that we specified earlier in **Preferences**.

Pages in the document now display the word **Redacted** rather than the original content, which has been removed. All underlying code was removed also, so you cannot use panes or any alternate means to recreate what was redacted. That's a good thing.

In long documents, you can automate the process of finding text that needs to be redacted. Let's explore this feature next.

Finding content for redaction

An efficient method for redacting text is working with the **Find Text & Redact** feature. It is especially useful in long documents, such as contracts where text needs to be found and marked on many pages.

1. From the toolbar dropdown, select **Find Text & Redact** and accept the alert if it appears.

2. In the **Search** panel, type the text that you want to redact. In addition to literal text phrases, you can search for patterns to find credit card numbers, phones, and so on, as seen in the screenshot:

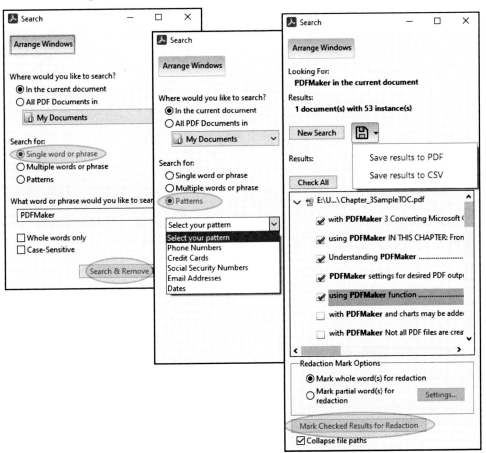

Figure 12.4 – The Find Text and Redact Search options and results

3. Once you have typed the text or made a selection, click the **Search & Remove** button.

4. The **Search** panel is now populated with instances where the phrase appears, but you still need to check each item to confirm the location and context of the phrase marked for redaction. If you know that all instances need to be removed, click the **Check All** button.

5. Click **Mark Checked Results for Redaction**. This means that instead of manual click-dragging to mark text, Acrobat will mark all the found phrases. Rectangles appear over the marked text. As with any automatic function, it is a good idea to review each page in the document before saving. Just in case.

    We marked the text for redaction and now we will apply it.

> **Important note**
> If you find areas that should not be marked, you can select the markup in the **Comment** panel and delete it.

6. Click the **Apply** button in the top toolbar, in the **Apply redactions** alert, turn off **Sanitize and remove hidden information**, and then click **Continue**.

7. Save the file with the _Redacted suffix. With that, you have completed the redaction of text content again.

We have learned how to find and permanently remove content on the pages of a document. In the next section, we will explore additional privacy protections by removing hidden code or data that may trace the publication to a person, location, or organization.

Removing hidden content and sanitizing a PDF document

Hidden data and metadata give away a lot of information about a document. The author, date of creation, the application that created the .pdf, digital signatures, form fields, scripts, and more. You can remove all this information in one step or choose selectively what should remain in the document.

We will use the **Sanitize Document** feature found on the **Redact** toolbar. It is also a default option appearing in the **Apply Redactions** alert box that we turned off before. Here are the steps:

1. Click **Sanitize Document** on the top toolbar and then click the **Selectively remove** option. The **Hidden Information** pane appears on the left of the screen. The dropdown options allow you to show all items that Acrobat is looking to remove or just those that are found in the document. Here is a screenshot:

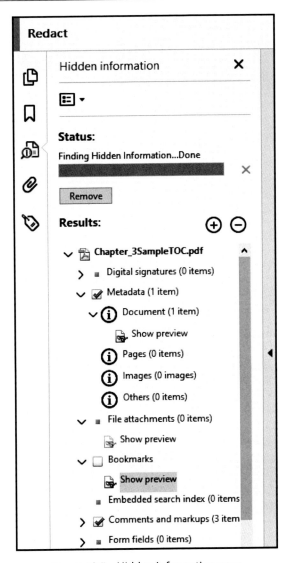

Figure 12.5 – Hidden Information pane

2. Select **Expand all** from the panel dropdown.

3. I unchecked **Bookmarks** since they are needed for navigation. The remaining data may be removed safely.

4. Click the **Remove** button on the pane. You will see confirmation that **Acrobat has removed all selected items...** at the bottom of the pane. You will need to save the file to keep the changes.

5. Save the file including the _Redacted suffix in the filename.

> **Important note**
>
> If you click **Sanitize Document** on the top toolbar, then in the **Sanitize document** alert, the **Remove all** selections for removal will be ignored. Every item in the pane will be removed and the document will be rasterized. You will be prompted to save a copy of the file.

The sensitive information in the `.pdf` document has been now removed. This method of processing files is clearly only appropriate for specific uses. Legal, medical, and other business professionals can be assured that private data will not be accessed by unauthorized parties.

In the next section, we will explore a very specific way that law offices prepare documentation for quick search and identification using Bates numbering.

Working with Bates numbering and options

Bates numbering, also referred to as **Bates stamping**, is a unique system of numbering pages that includes a reference or a code number, a branding image, such as a logo, company name, date, and more, in addition to the sequence of page numbers. It is used in legal and medical professions to quickly identify business receipts, images, documents used in trials, and so on. The original system was invented and patented by Edwin G. Bates in the late 1800s, thus the label for the system. It was a manual stamp with four digits 0000 to 9999 that advanced a rotating wheel each time it was pressed down. The resulting page numbers would be presented in four digits. Page 25, for example, would have had a 0025 stamp.

This invention and the system were adopted by law offices and courts. At that time, it was a great method to organize and identify information. As `.pdf` files have become the standard digital paper, we depend on a system that supports the electronic preservation and identification of evidence. Acrobat tools incorporate Bates numbering into a set of options in the **Edit PDF** tool. The numbers are placed on pages as headers or footers displaying up to 15 digits, a much higher number than the four available in the original stamp.

Acrobat creates copies of original files with a footer or header containing the Bates numbering sequence on each page. Files may be placed in a different folder from the original and get a new name but the sequence of unique numbering unifies them. The process is illustrated in *Figure 12.6's* chart:

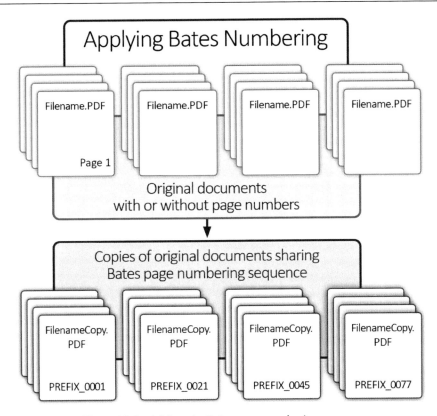

Figure 12.6 – Adding the Bates page numbering process

We will learn how to apply the Bates numbers next:

1. Open a `.pdf` document with at least 10 pages or more.

2. Open the **Edit PDF** toolbar and from the **More** dropdown, select the **Bates Numbering |
    Add…** option.

    A large dialog box opens where you can add and arrange all `.pdf` files included in the numbering
    sequence in the desired order using the **Move Up** and **Move Down** buttons. Here is a screenshot:

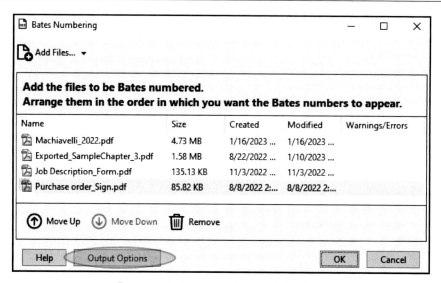

Figure 12.7 – Bates numbering dialog box

3. Once the files are arranged in the required order, click the **Output Options** button so you can specify the output file location and naming preference for the new files with pages numbered using a specific Bates number series. The original files are not affected. Here is a screenshot of this dialog box:

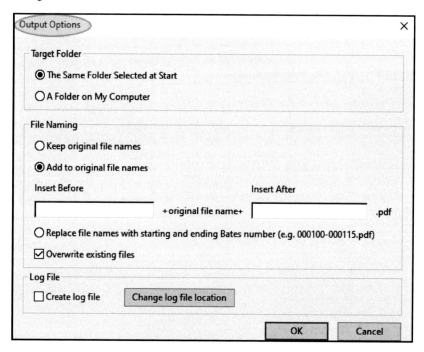

Figure 12.8 – Bates page numbered files output settings

The options available here are self-explanatory. Both fields allow you to enter either codes or phrases used to identify new documents. Click **OK** to accept changes.

Important note

Protected or encrypted files cannot be used for Bates numbering.

Only unsecured .pdf files can be included in the Bates numbering process in Acrobat. Non-PDF documents in a folder that was added will be excluded from the sequence.

4. A large dialog box named **Add Header and Footer** opens, but unlike a regular header/footer dialog box, this one has a unique option available for adding Bates numbering.

5. Place your insertion point in the **Center Footer Text** field.

6. Click the **Insert Bates Number...** button. Here is a dialog box and the content of button options:

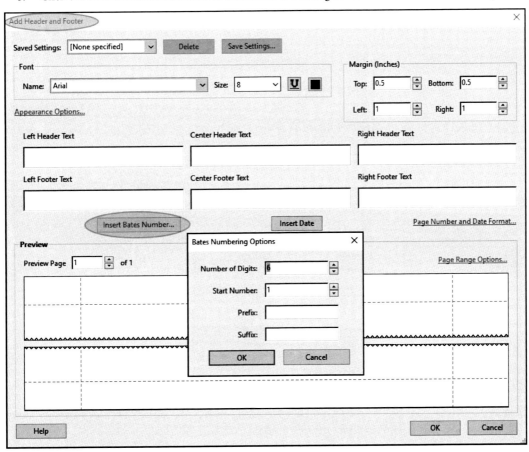

Figure 12.9 – Bates numbered header/footer dialog box.

7. You can type `Prefix` or `Suffix`. This is the unique reference identifier value that appears on the page. Click **OK** to accept changes.

8. The field now contains the entire set of characters as a variable instructing Acrobat how to create the page number sequence. The footer displays an example of the full number. You can only preview it on one page.

    You can format the footer by selecting the font, font size, and color and adjusting its position on the page using margin values at the top right area of the dialog box. When satisfied click **OK** to accept the settings.

9. Acrobat now processes all the files included in the sequence. When finished an alert appears with the message: **Bates Numbering has been successfully applied to X of X PDF files**. Click **OK** to accept.

10. Open the file browser and locate new files with the names you specified in the output options in *Figure 12.8*. All files in the series, although independent documents, display a footer with a numbering sequence for easy search and identification.

Isn't this great? You have successfully identified pages using the Bates numbering system:

-   If you need to change the sequence, you should remove the numbering and create a new one. Use the **Edit PDF** toolbar and select the **More | Bates Numbering | Remove...** options to start again.

-   If you need to add more documents to the series follow the same method, but when you click the **Insert Bates Number..** button, enter the next number in sequence in **Start Number:** (see *Figure 12.9*) and use exactly the same **Prefix:** or **Suffix:** value.

-   To search for all PDFs that use the same Bates sequence, select **Edit | Advanced Search**, then select the **All PDF Documents in | Browse for Location...** options and specify the folder, then enter the unique prefix or suffix, and click the **Search** button. Acrobat will list all files included in the series. Clicking any of them will open the file in Acrobat.

This is where we complete the overview of what Bates numbering is and how to apply it when needed. Hopefully, you will quickly recognize pages with this method of identification in place.

Summary

In this chapter, we explored the options and features that make `.pdf` documents acceptable in legal, medical, and other professions where privacy matters. We removed sensitive information, optimized documents using the **Sanitize** option, and unified different documents using Bates numbering.

The next and final chapter brings us to a final overview of techniques, shortcuts, user support groups, and other resources to help you expand your understanding of Acrobat.

13

Acrobat Pro Tools, Shortcuts, References, and Mac Notes

Congratulations! You have completed reading a book that contains many advanced technical topics. If you have read all the chapters, you have built a solid foundation of understanding Adobe Acrobat Pro and how to use it best in your projects. This chapter will provide you with shortcuts and references to many sources of user support and additional information that could not be easily included in each chapter.

The information presented in the following chapter includes the following:

- Converting MS Office files in to `.pdf` in macOS
- A complete list of Acrobat tools
- Acrobat keyboard key shortcuts
- Accessibility guidelines and a list of tags with an explanation of their meanings
- A comparison of features in different Acrobat versions
- Online references and user support options

This book was written using examples and methods in the MS Windows operating system environment. Although almost all functions work the same on macOS, some fundamental differences should be mentioned here.

The next section will discuss the specific methods that Mac users need to follow to create `.pdf` files when working with MS Office applications.

Converting MS Office files to PDF on macOS

Apple macOS has been a wonderful environment for creative professionals. From the very beginning, they embraced the **Graphical User Interface (GUI)**, rather than a code- and data-oriented world or personal computers at a time when standards were evolving and changing very quickly. We are now way beyond basic issues such as fonts, application availability, or software functions. Almost all features in Acrobat are the same as on Windows systems. Still, there are some major differences, which we will discuss here.

Beyond different keyboards, which can be addressed by providing both operating systems' keyboard key labels, creating, saving, and printing `.pdf` files require a different approach on Macs.

This book's focus and screenshots are centered on MS Windows and MS Office applications, mainly for the following reasons:

- Statistics from the past 10 years suggest that the actual usage rates (not the sales rates) of users around the world are close to 79% on Windows and close to 20% on macOS. Other platforms represent the remaining 1% of usage. These numbers shift, but Windows is the dominant platform for business operations. Macs dominate creative industries.

- Mac users do not depend on MS Office applications to the same extent as PC users.

- PDFMaker, while a powerful tool for creating interactive and accessible `.pdf` documents, is no longer supported on macOS.

- A number of applications used to publish technical documents are not supported on macOS. One of them is **Adobe FrameMaker**.

The next segment has been added to address the unique way that Mac users export publications to `.pdf`. Here, we will take an entirely macOS approach in creating `.pdf` in MS Office applications, where task steps are too different from Windows OSs for inclusion in the previous chapters.

In *Chapter 3, Converting Microsoft Office Files to Adobe PDF Using PDFMaker*, we discussed the details of text formatting options used when authoring a publication, and the impact these have on a final `.pdf` file. MS Office documents can be created and edited on either platform. Layout, fonts, images, and so on are fully supported in the same way. Thus, everything that a document needs applies when working both with Windows and Mac versions of the authoring software. In this section, we will explore only the last step affecting features within a document that are converted during the process of exporting to `.pdf`.

Mac users of MS Office applications have the option to create `.pdf` files either using the **Save As...** or **File** | **Print** | **PDF** functions. Interactive features built into MS Word documents, such as bookmarks, hyperlinks, and accessibility tags, are preserved or lost depending on the choice of process. We will explore both methods and compare the outcomes next.

Saving a Word document as a PDF

To preserve interactive elements when exporting a Word file to `.pdf`, follow these steps:

1. Select the **File** | **Save As...** options.

2. In the dialog box that opens, select the **File Format:** | **Export Formats** | **PDF** option.

3. Select the **Best for electronic distribution and accessibility (uses Microsoft online service)** option and click **Export**, as shown in the following screenshot:

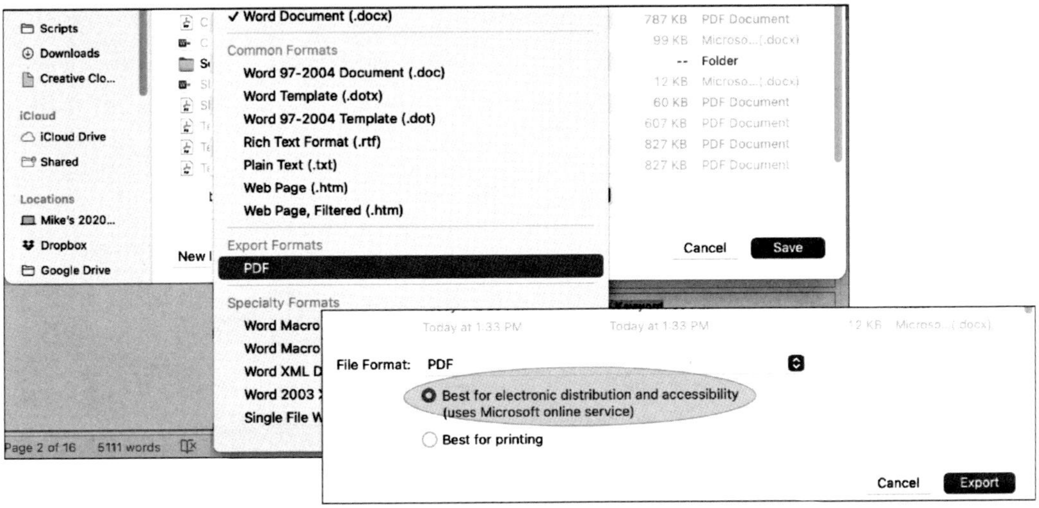

Figure 13.1 – Exporting to .pdf from MS Word on a macOS, preserving document interactivity

A document properly formatted in Word and exported to `.pdf` using this method contains bookmarks, accessibility tags, and links. Checking the **File | Properties… | General** tab will show that the document was created by Microsoft Word.

Metadata field content is also preserved from the source files in the **File | Properties…** dialog box's **Summary** tab, where the document title, subject, author, and other metadata are entered.

This method does not give a lot of control to a user; in fact, it requires processing the document using a Microsoft online service. However, it does preserve interactivity in the document and important structures for accessibility.

Another method to create a `.pdf` file is to print a Word document to an Adobe PDF virtual printer, as discussed in the next section.

Printing a Word document to Adobe PDF

The classic method of creating `.pdf` files in the MS Office suite of applications is to print them to a virtual printer, labeled Adobe PDF. Here are the steps:

1. Select **File | Print…** from the top menu to open the print options dialog box.

2. Select **Save as Adobe PDF**, as shown in this screenshot:

Figure 13.2 – Printing to Adobe PDF from MS Word on macOS

You will have two options to choose from:

- **Adobe PDF Settings** as saved in **.joboptions** (the Acrobat Distiller options were discussed in *Chapter 11, Using Acrobat for Professional Publishing*). On macOS, Acrobat Distiller is opened in the **Applications | Adobe Acrobat Pro** group of apps.

- The **After PDF Creation** dropdown allows you to launch **Adobe Acrobat** or select **Launch nothing**. Click **Continue**.

3. Type a filename in the **Save As:** field, select the location, and then click the **Save** button.

The resulting .pdf file does not have bookmarks, accessibility tags, or any other interactive content, as expected. It is suitable for print on paper, as defined in the Distiller settings. Metadata fields are filled with information about the owner of the application and the Word filename, rather than fields saved in MS Word metadata of the source document.

MS Excel and MS PowerPoint do not preserve any interactivity when creating a .pdf file, using either method. There are some third-party applications or online services that support the conversion of MS Office for Mac documents in to .pdf files, or vice versa.

Hopefully, this section brings us closer to the details of the most recent (2023) process of creating a .pdf in MS Word in a macOS environment. Stay tuned for updates. Surely, they will come.

The next section will give you a list of all the tools available in Acrobat, with some notes from the author.

A complete list of Acrobat tools

Looking at the **Tools** screen in Acrobat Pro gives you an idea of what all of them do. However, I always find it hard to remember which tool has the options that I am looking for, especially those obscure ones that I use only once in a while. Here is the complete list of tools and some notes to help you find options that are hidden:

Tool	Notes
Create & Edit group	
Create PDF	Options include creating a PDF from any format: Single File, Multiple Files, Scanner, Web Page, Clipboard, Blank Page
Combine Files	Creates a single file from many PDFs or creates a Portfolio. Tools: **Add Files...** and **Add custom page** (cover page for macOS).
Organize Pages	Displays page thumbnails for rearranging as needed. Options: **Extract, Insert...**, **Add custom/cover page**, **Replace**, and more. Tools to remember: the **Add custom/cover page** app and **Split** to divide a long document into smaller parts.
Edit PDF	Tools: **Edit, Add Text, Add Image, Link, CropPages, Header & Footer, Watermark**, and more with **Bates numbering** and **Background color** change options
Export PDF	Options: Export your PDF to any format: MS Word, Spreadsheet, MS PowerPoint, Image, HTML Web Page, and more. The **Export all images** checkbox extracts **individual** images from a .pdf document, rather than exporting each full page as an image.
Scan & OCR	Options: **Insert, Enhance, Recognize Text, Bates numbering**, and a **Crop** tool
Rich Media	Tools: **Add 3D, Add Button, Add Sound, Add Video**, and the **Select Object** tool, the same as in **Prepare Form** toolbar. The **Prepare Form** tool automatically adds interactive form fields if a document has none. In documents with action buttons, the **Rich Media** tool allows you to edit or remove them without adding form fields.
Add custom page (cover page on macOS)	A new tool on its own that launches online Adobe Express templates and page layout functions
Forms & Signatures	
Request Signatures opens the Fill & Sign toolbar	The **Fill & Sign** toolbar repeats **Request E-Signatures** as a function (*I am still wondering who designed these tools this way...ha-ha!*)
Prepare Form	Options to start: **Single File, Scanner**, and **Create New**. All tools to create and edit interactive forms and functions including JavaScript editor and locator.

Certificates	Toolbar tools: **Digitally Sign, Time Stamp, Validate All Signatures, Certify (Visible Signature)**, and **Certify (Invisible Signature)** to sign or certify a document when the digital signature area is not defined as a field
Share & Review	
Share	Opens the **Share with Others** dialog box, the same as the top-right corner of the screen. No toolbar is associated with this tool
Send for Comments	Same as the previous point
Comment	A complete set of text review and page markup tools, including the **Stamp** tool options.
Stamp	The **Stamp** tool, Stamps Palette, Custom Stamps, and **Bates numbering** is here too
Compare Files	Options: Old File versus New File. Very useful review tool for tracking and saving a report on document changes.
Measure	Tools: Measuring, Object Data, Geospatial Location used for architectural plans, engineering drawings, maps, and so on, helping to measure distances and dimensions directly in .pdf
Protect & Standardize	
Protect	The **Protect Using Password** and **Remove Hidden Information** functions are accessed from the toolbar. The advanced options dropdown expands the document protections.
Redact	Toolbar options: Redact and **Sanitize Document**, which rasterizes the content, including text fonts
PDF Standards	Options: Save as PDF/A, PDF/X, or PDF/E. The **Preflight** panel with profiles is also here.
Optimize PDF	Options: Reduce File Size, Advanced Optimization, Optimize Scanned Pages, and Preflight. **Advanced Optimization** opens a dialog box with detailed settings to control the optimization process, including **Audit space usage…**, which gives a report in bytes and percentages on what elements contribute to a file size total. The **Preflight** panel is here too.

Print Production	**Output Preview** simulates CMYK print process plates among other print simulations.
	Convert Colors addresses color issues.
	Flattener Preview identifies and displays print areas, with potential issues in documents with transparencies.
	Set Page Boxes, **Add Printer Marks**, **Fix Hairlines**, **Ink Manager**, and **Trap Presets** are specialized tools to get files ready for press printing.
Accessibility	Tools for testing and adding accessibility
Customize	
Create Custom Tool	Allows you to create a custom-named toolset with functions that you need most often. Displays in the **Tools** column panel on the right.
Action Wizard	The toolbar gives access to existing actions, streamlining repetitive tasks that can also be used as checklists. You can create your own actions.
Index	A compact method for searching long PDF documents. This approach to searching PDF content is being deprecated.
JavaScript	A toolbar with access to options to create and test custom scripts
And that's all the Acrobat tools, folks!	

Table 13.1 – A list of Acrobat Pro tools

It is a good idea to take time to test all the tools. This will help you to decide which method you prefer when performing functions, since most of them can also be accessed through panes and menus.

In the following section, we'll see a table with keyboard shortcuts listed so that you can work more efficiently than if you depended on menus or toolbars alone.

Acrobat keyboard key shortcuts

Acrobat presents all its options in menus and toolbars. To use them, you must click a mouse, often multiple times. When you multiply that by instances of the functions accessed throughout the workday, you can see why using shortcuts is good for your body or at least your hands. Many tools in Acrobat can be selected by a tap on a keyboard key, rather than clicking a toolbar.

To enable that, you need to open the **Edit** | **Preferences** | **General** option (**Acrobat** | **Preferences** on macOS), and in the **Basic Tools** group, check the **Use single-key accelerators** checkbox. Without this step, tapping the keyboard will not give you any tools.

To get a tool, tap a keyboard key; to perform a function that involves more than one key, hold down keyboard key combinations all at the same time.

Here is a by-no-means-complete list of some useful function shortcuts and tool keys:

Function	Windows	macOS	Function	Windows	macOS
FILE MENU			**VIEW MENU**		
Open	*Ctrl+O*	*Cmd+O*	**Rotate View ↻ or ↺**	*Shift+Ctrl+ +or –*	*Shift+Cmd+ +or –*
Create PDF from File	*Ctrl+N*	*Cmd+N*	**First/Last Page**	*Home* or *End*	*Home* or *End*
Create PDF from Web Page	*Shift+Ctrl+O*	*Shift+Cmd+O*	**Previous/Next Page**	↻ or ↺	↻ or ↺
Save	*Ctrl+S*	*Cmd+S*	**Go to Page**	*Shift+Ctrl+N*	*Shift+Cmd+N*
Save As	*Shift+Ctrl+S*	*Shift+Cmd+S*	**Previous/Next View**	*Alt+↻ or ↺*	*Cmd+↻ or ↺*
Close	*Ctrl+W*	*Cmd+W*	**Automatically Scroll**	*Shift+Ctrl+H*	*Shift+Cmd+H*
Close All	*Alt+Ctrl+W*	*Option+Cmd+W*	**Zoom To**	*Ctrl+Y*	*Cmd+Y*
Properties	*Ctrl+D*	*Cmd+D*	**Actual Size**	*Ctrl+1*	*Cmd+1*
Print	*Ctrl+P*	*Cmd+P*	**Zoom to Page Level**	*Ctrl+0*	*Cmd+0*
Exit	*Ctrl+Q*	*Cmd+Q*	**Fit Width**	*Ctrl+2*	*Cmd+2*
EDIT MENU			**Fit Visible**	*Ctrl+3*	*Cmd+3*
Undo	*Ctrl+Z*	*Cmd+Z*	**Reflow**	*Ctrl+4*	*Cmd+4*
Redo	*Shift+Ctrl+Z*	*Shift+Cmd+Z*	**Navigation Pane**	*F4*	
Cut, Copy, and Paste	*Ctrl+X, C, V*	*Cmd+X, C, V*	**Properties Bar**	*Ctrl+E*	*Cmd+E*
Select All	*Ctrl+A*	*Cmd+A*	**Toolbars**	*F8*	*Fn+F8*
Deselect All	*Shift+Ctrl+A*	*Shift+Cmd+A*	**Menu Bar**	*F9*	*Shift+Cmd+M*
Check Spelling	*F7*	*F7*	**Grid**	*Ctrl+U*	*Cmd+U*
Find	*Ctrl+F*	*Cmd+F*	**Reading Order**	*Shift+Ctrl+U*	*Shift+Cmd+U*
Advanced Search	*Shift+Ctrl+F*	Shift+Cmd+F	**Rulers**	*Ctrl+R*	*Cmd+R*
Preferences	*Ctrl+ K*	Cmd+K	**Line Weight**	*Ctrl+5*	*Cmd+5*
TOOLS			**Read Mode**	*Ctrl+H*	*Ctrl+Cmd+H*
Edit PDF	*T*	*T*	**Full-Screen Mode**	*Ctrl+L*	*Cmd+L*
Link	*L*	*L*	**Activate Read Out Loud**	*Shift+Ctrl+Y*	*Shift+Cmd+Y*
Hand	*H*	*H*	**Read This Page Only**	*Shift+Ctrl+V*	*Shift+Cmd+V*

Marquee Zoom	Z	Z	Stop (Reading)	Shift+Ctrl+E	Shift+Cmd+E
Select	V	V	WINDOW MENU		
Return to Hand or Select tool	Esc	Esc	Cascade	Shift+Ctrl+J	Shift+Cmd+J
Redaction	Shift+Y	Shift+Y	Tile Horizontally	Shift+Ctrl+K	Shift+Cmd+K
Cycle Stamp, Attach File	Shift+J	Shift+J	Tile Vertically	Shift+Ctrl+L	Shift+Cmd+L
Edit Forms	Shift+Ctrl+7	Shift+Cmd+7	COMMENTS		
NAVIGATION PANELS			Add Sticky Note	Ctrl+6	Cmd+6
Insert Pages from File	Shift+Ctrl+I	Shift+Cmd+I	Highlight Text	U	U
Insert Blank Pages	Shift+Ctrl+T	Shift+Cmd+T	Add Stamp	J	J
Delete Pages	Shift+Ctrl+D	Shift+Cmd+D	Next Comment	Tab	Tab
Crop Pages	Shift+Ctrl+T	Shift+Cmd+T	Previous Comment	Shift+Tab	Shift+Tab
Rotate Pages	Shift+Ctrl+R	Shift+Cmd+R	EFFICIENT ZOOM & PAN		
New Bookmark	Ctrl+B	Cmd+B	Drag Mouse to Zoom	Ctrl+Spacebar	Cmd+Spacebar
Output Preview	~	~	Pan the View	Spacebar	Spacebar
Preflight	Shift+Ctrl+X	Shift+Cmd+X	Zoom In/Out	Ctrl + +or –	Cmd + +or –
Expand Child Tags	Ctrl+click tag	Cmd+click tag	Next task pane	Ctrl+Tab	Option +Tab

Table 13.2 – A list of Acrobat Pro keyboard shortcuts

Test the keys listed here; you may find more in the Acrobat help files. I have found that some functions or tools have multiple shortcuts. There are lots of options to choose from. All of them make you more efficient.

The next section completes the discussion on accessibility covered in *Chapter 5, Remediation for Accessibility in PDF Publications*, by providing references to guidelines and a complete list of accessibility tags.

Accessibility guidelines and list of tags

Accessibility is a global issue, with countries adopting different methods to address it. Here is a brief list of references to laws and guidelines in some regions.

Laws and guidelines by country

A source for international guidelines on the accessibility of information distributed in an electronic format is the **Web Accessibility Initiative (WAI)**, an organization that operates under the umbrella of the **World Wide Web Consortium (W3C)**. Documents compliant with standards developed by the WAI generally meet the laws of most countries. However, to ensure legal compliance, it is necessary to review the laws of each country or region.

A difference between guidelines and laws is that failing to follow guidelines does not bring legal penalties. On the other hand, failure to comply with laws may result in legal or financial penalties, often significant. The following table lists only some English-speaking regions:

Country or region	Law or guideline	Reference website
Global	*Web Content Accessibility Guidelines (WCAG)*	`https://www.w3.org/WAI/`
Global	*ISO 14289 (PDF/UA) standard*	`https://www.pdfa.org/resource/iso-14289-pdfua/`
Australia	*Disability Discrimination Act 1992*	`https://www.australia.gov.au/accessibility`
Canada	*Standard on Web Accessibility*	`https://www.tbs-sct.canada.ca/pol/doc-eng.aspx?id=23601`
European Union	*Web Accessibility Directive – Directive (EU) 2016/2102 of the European Parliament and of the Council of 26 October 2016 on the accessibility of the websites and mobile applications of public sector bodies*	`https://eur-lex.europa.eu/eli/dir/2016/2102/oj`
New Zealand	*Web Standards, effective from July 2019*	`https://www.digital.govt.nz/standards-and-guidance/nz-government-web-standards/new-web-standards-for-july-2019/`
United Kingdom	*Equality Act 2010 guidance – understanding accessibility requirements for public sector bodies*	`https://www.gov.uk/guidance/accessibility-requirements-for-public-sector-websites-and-apps`
United States of America	*Americans with Disabilities Act (ADA)*	`https://www.ada.gov/2010ADAstandards_index.htm`
United States of America	*Section 508 of the Rehabilitation Act of 1973*	`https://www.section508.gov`

Table 13.3 – A list of references for accessibility guidelines globally (English-speaking countries only)

As you review the guidelines, observe how different organizations comply with them in your region.

In the next section, you will find a list of accessibility tags and the meaning of each one. Most tags are applied automatically by the software that converts a publication in to `.pdf`, but some content may need manual tagging to expressly describe it. That can be done in Acrobat. Use the following table as a reference:

Adobe Acrobat predefined PDF accessibility tags

Full name	Tag	Meaning
Article	`<Art>`	A continuous body of text such as an article
Annotation	`<Annot>`	An inline element for annotations such as comments and videos that are not a link
Bibliography Entry	`<BibEntry>`	A description of the source of information, which may also include a label as a child element
Block Quote	`<BlockQuote>`	A text quote, attributed to someone other than the author of the document
Caption	`<Caption>`	Text describing the content of a table or a figure.
Code	`<Code>`	An inline element for computer program text embedded within a document
Division	`<Div>`	A basic block-level element or group of block-level elements
Document	`<Document>`	The root element of a document's tag tree
Figure	`<Figure>`	An image providing information related to document text
Form	`<Form>`	A PDF form element, and a parent of interactive form fields in a document structure
Formula	`<Formula>`	A math formula element
Heading	`<H>`	Phased out or deprecated
Heading Level 1	`<H1>`	A heading element should appear as the first child of any higher-level division. Six levels of headings (`<H1>`–`<H6>`) are available to nest document sections.
Heading Level 2	`<H2>`	
Heading Level 3	`<H3>`	
Heading Level 4	`<H4>`	
Heading Level 5	`<H5>`	
Heading Level 6	`<H6>`	
Index	`<Index>`	A list of entries with identifying text and reference elements, linking each entry with the content in the main body text
Label	`<LBL>`	A label for a bullet, name, or number that identifies it as a unique group of paragraphs within a document's body text

Link	`<Link>`	An inline element for a hypertext link that takes a reader to a specific destination within the same document or an external one, such as a web page
List	`<L>`	A list or a sequence of paragraphs with similar meanings where each item is identified by a label. It is also a parent element to list items.
List Item	`<LI>`	Any one child of a list. Child elements in a list element should be list item elements. Each list item element can include a label element and must include a required label body element as a child.
List Item Body	`<LBody>`	The descriptive content of a list item
Note	`<Note>`	An inline element for explanatory text, such as a footnote or endnote, that is referred to in the main body of text
Paragraph	`<P>`	A block-level element with generic body text
Part	`<Part>`	A part element that splits a large document into smaller chunks and can group smaller parts together, such as articles, divisions, or section elements
Quote	`<Quote>`	An inline text attributed to someone other than the author of the main text. It is different from text within a blockquote element, which tags one or more paragraphs.
Reference	`<Reference>`	A citation to text or data found elsewhere in a document – an inline element
Section	`<Sect>`	A general container element type, similar to a division (`DIV Class="Sect"`) in HTML, and usually a component of a part element or an article element
Span	`<Span>`	Any inline segment of text. A common use of a span entry element is to delimit text associated with a given set of styling properties.
Table	`<Table>`	A table is a two-dimensional arrangement of data or text cells that contains table row elements as children and can have a caption element as its first or last child element
Table Data Cell	`<TD>`	A table cell that contains non-header data
Table Header Cell	`<TH>`	A cell within a table containing header text, or a label for one or more rows or columns in a table
Table of Contents	`<TOC>`	An element containing a structured list of items and labels for those items. A table of contents element has its own hierarchy.

Table of Contents Item	`<TOCI>`	A child element of a table of contents element
Table Row	`<TR>`	One row of headings or data in a table. A table row element may contain table header cell elements and table data cell elements.

Table 13.4 – PDF accessibility tags and their meanings

Describing content using accessibility tags refines how context is understood by visually impaired readers. Although it will take more time and effort, it adds value to any publication. Use these tags well.

Applications change, but this reference will give you an overall view of what you can do using each version. For a detailed discussion, refer to *Chapter 1, Understanding Different Adobe Acrobat Versions and Services.*

Feature comparison of different Acrobat versions

As you look for specific features, keep in mind that they do change. For the latest list, refer to the Adobe website: `https://www.adobe.com/acrobat/pricing`.

In the next section, we will explore available support for Acrobat users.

Sources for troubleshooting PDFs, updates, and fixes

There is no book that will cover all topics, especially when the subject is very dynamic and constantly changes. Acrobat is such a subject. As a globally used software running on different operating systems, new components are added, some are removed, features are supported or deprecated, and so on. In this environment, you will probably go online and get up-to-date information to resolve any issues. To help you search for information, here are some links to resources for training and references:

- Adobe Inc.'s main website with the latest software subscription plans and other general Adobe and Acrobat information: `https://www.adobe.com`

- Acrobat help and user guide home page: `https://helpx.adobe.com/support/acrobat.html`

- JetSet Communications, Inc. a training and consulting company with unique learning resources for most Adobe desktop applications: `https://jetsetcom.net`

- Acrobat users' forums where questions are answered directly by other users: `https://acrobatusers.com/forums` and `https://community.adobe.com`

Stay tuned for more news and changes.

Summary

This brings us to the conclusion of exploring Adobe Acrobat Pro tools and features. You have completed the entire book. By no means was this an exhaustive guide, but I hope it has built a foundation and given you the confidence to explore more in-depth features that matter to you personally. Do enjoy using Acrobat in so many different contexts.

Congratulations! I also want to thank you for taking the time to read this book. I hope our paths cross someday.

Index

Packtpub.com

Subscribe to our online digital library for full access to over 7,000 books and videos, as well as industry leading tools to help you plan your personal development and advance your career. For more information, please visit our website.

Why subscribe?

- Spend less time learning and more time coding with practical eBooks and Videos from over 4,000 industry professionals

- Improve your learning with Skill Plans built especially for you

- Get a free eBook or video every month

- Fully searchable for easy access to vital information

- Copy and paste, print, and bookmark content

Did you know that Packt offers eBook versions of every book published, with PDF and ePub files available? You can upgrade to the eBook version at packtpub.com and as a print book customer, you are entitled to a discount on the eBook copy. Get in touch with us at customercare@packtpub.com for more details.

At www.packtpub.com, you can also read a collection of free technical articles, sign up for a range of free newsletters, and receive exclusive discounts and offers on Packt books and eBooks.

Other Books You May Enjoy

If you enjoyed this book, you may be interested in these other books by Packt:

Adobe Illustrator for Creative Professionals

Clint Balsar

ISBN: 9781800569256

- Master a wide variety of methods for developing objects
- Control files using layers and groups
- Enhance content using data-supported infographics
- Use multiple artboards for better efficiency and asset management
- Understand the use of layers and objects in Illustrator
- Build professional systems for final presentation to clients

Mastering Adobe Photoshop Elements 2023 - Fifth Edition

Robin Nichols

ISBN: 9781803248455

- How to retouch images professionally, replace backgrounds, remove people, and resize your images
- Animate parts of your photos to create memes to wow your social media fans
- Showcase your photos and videos with all-new collage and slideshow templates
- Use image overlays to create unique depth of field effects
- Discover advanced layer techniques designed to create immersive and powerful illustrations
- Take your selection skills to the next level for the ultimate in image control
- Develop your illustration skills using the power of Elements' huge range of graphics tools and features
- Easily create wonderful effects using Adobe's awesome AI technology

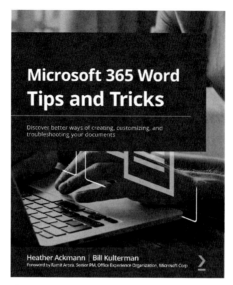

Microsoft 365 Word Tips and Tricks

Heather Ackmann, Bill Kulterman

ISBN: 9781800565432

- Track a document's changes as well as comment on and review changes by others, both locally and remotely

- Use Word's navigation and view features to improve productivity

- Generate more consistently formatted documents with Styles

- Perform common tasks through simple formatting techniques, Quick Parts, customizing AutoCorrect/AutoFormat, and memorizing keyboard shortcuts

- Troubleshoot the most frustrating formatting problems experienced by Word users

- Create more universally accessible documents by adding Alt Text using the accessibility checker and other Word features

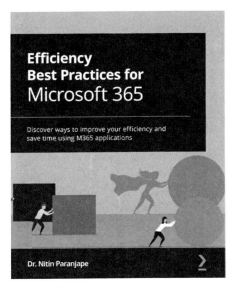

Efficiency Best Practices for Microsoft 365

Dr. Nitin Paranjape

ISBN: 9781801072267

- Understand how different MS 365 tools, such as Office desktop, Teams, Power BI, Lists, and OneDrive, can increase work efficiency
- Identify time-consuming processes and understand how to work through them more efficiently
- Create professional documents quickly with minimal effort
- Work across multiple teams, meetings, and projects without email overload
- Automate mundane, repetitive, and time-consuming manual work
- Manage work, delegation, execution, and project management

Packt is searching for authors like you

If you're interested in becoming an author for Packt, please visit `authors.packtpub.com` and apply today. We have worked with thousands of developers and tech professionals, just like you, to help them share their insight with the global tech community. You can make a general application, apply for a specific hot topic that we are recruiting an author for, or submit your own idea.

Share Your Thoughts

Now you've finished *Adobe Acrobat Ninja*, we'd love to hear your thoughts! Scan the QR code below to go straight to the Amazon review page for this book and share your feedback or leave a review on the site that you purchased it from.

`https://packt.link/r/1-803-24817-3`

Your review is important to us and the tech community and will help us make sure we're delivering excellent quality content.

Download a free PDF copy of this book

Thanks for purchasing this book!

Do you like to read on the go but are unable to carry your print books everywhere?

Is your eBook purchase not compatible with the device of your choice?

Don't worry, now with every Packt book you get a DRM-free PDF version of that book at no cost.

Read anywhere, any place, on any device. Search, copy, and paste code from your favorite technical books directly into your application.

The perks don't stop there, you can get exclusive access to discounts, newsletters, and great free content in your inbox daily

Follow these simple steps to get the benefits:

1. Scan the QR code or visit the link below

https://packt.link/free-ebook/9781803248172

2. Submit your proof of purchase
3. That's it! We'll send your free PDF and other benefits to your email directly

Made in the USA
Middletown, DE
15 February 2024

49858698R00195